Praise for *The Pyrotechnic Insanitarium*

"*The Pyrotechnic Insanitarium* is both highly entertaining and deeply disturbing in a way that Mark Dery has made his own. The ever-growing pathologies of millennial America show up clearly on the X-ray screen of his penetrating analysis. Racily written, and filled with shrewd insights, this guidebook to the madhouse of the modern world is essential reading."—J. G. Ballard, author of *Crash*

"Dery . . . mines Julia Kristeva and *Entertainment Weekly* with equal verve. . . . A provocative work of cultural criticism."—Scott Stossel, *The Atlantic Monthly*

"With clarity and force Mark Dery has captured the tone of our times, taking us on a dizzying roller-coaster ride through the chaos of the modern world. A choice contribution to the study of American culture."—Stuart Ewen, author of *All Consuming Images*

"Dery proves a provocative and cuttingly humorous guide . . . [with] a particular brilliance for collecting cultural detritus and bringing unseen connections to light."—Tom Vanderbilt, *Wired*

"Dery . . . marshals a vast pop vocabulary with easy wit."—James Poniewozik, *The New York Times Book Review*

"A hoot of a read, an eye-opener that pokes fun at both stuffed-shirt postmodern intellectualism and capitalist excess with equal glee."—E. Burns, *The San Francisco Bay Guardian*

"Mark Dery is a sane guide to some very insane times. He has a good eye for the most bizarre and grotesque elements of contemporary American culture. . . . But whatever the subject, Dery deftly places it in the larger context of massive social and economic change. *The Pyrotechnic Insanitarium* is neither celebration nor invective, but something rarer and much more valuable; a master clinician's diagnosis of the symptoms of postmodernity." —Steven Shaviro, author of *Doom Patrols: A Theoretical Fiction about Postmodernism*

"At the center of Dery's high-speed chase through the information landscape is a firm sense of moral gravity. Trust him when the world gets scary."—Andrew Ross, author of *Real Love: In Pursuit of Culture Justice*

"Dery is one of those rare writers with a deep enough insight into the American soul, with an eloquence in all its stuttering dialects, to look America in its dark and gazeless eye, and not blink."—McKenzie Wark, *Higher Education* (Australia)

"A series of essays that has the fin-de-millennium on the analyst's couch . . . Dery's observation of today's pathological public sphere is both horrific and hilarious."—David Hurst, *Chico News & Review*

"Wildly entertaining."—Robert David Sullivan, *The Boston Phoenix Literary Supplement*

"Dazzling . . . Armed with a vast and varied vocabulary of cultural references, [Dery's] contextual aperture adjusts with amazing swiftness. . . . Indispensable millennial reading . . . In his confident and searingly intelligent essays, Dery proves himself fit for the task of hyper-linking the disparate components of our culture together."—Michael Depp, *Gambit Weekly*

"Mark Dery pokes his finger directly into the soft spots in the millennial American mind. *The Pyrotechnic Insanitarium* manages to get serious and make for fun reading at the same time."—Howard Rheingold, author of *Virtual Communities*

"Well-read, intellectually agile, and blessed with seemingly total pop-culture recall."—Elaine Showalter, *The Village Voice Literary Supplement*

"So brilliant it blinds . . . There is pleasure in such writing, the pleasure of the spooky theme park with its dazzling lights and its hilarious rides that whirl you senseless."—Celia Storey, *The Arkansas Democrat-Gazette*

"Required reading for all persons entering or living in the USA . . . A veritable road map of sideshow American culture on the highway to hell . . . Entertaining and informative, disturbing and delightful."—www.disobey.com

THE
PYROTECHNIC
INSANITARIUM

American Culture on the Brink

MARK DERY

GROVE PRESS
New York

Published simultaneously in Canada
Printed in the United States of America
FIRST PAPERBACK EDITION

The following essays first appeared in far shorter, substantively different form in the following publications: "Have An Angst Day": "Shameless Dread," *Suck* (www.suck.com), January 20, 1998. "Cotton Candy Autopsy": "Jokers Wild," *World Art,* issue #3, 1995. "Return to Abnormalcy": "The New Freak Chic," *The Village Voice Literary Supplement,* April/May 1998. "Anus Horribilis": "Dump and Dumper," *The Village Voice,* June 18, 1996. "Mad Cows and Englishmen": "Damien Hirst," *World Art,* issue #4, 1996. "Mysteries of the Organism": "All That Is Solid Melts Into Air," *Suck,* September 12, 1997. "Nature Morte": "Lost in the Funhouse," *World Art,* #2, 1995. "Past Perfect": "Past Perfect," *21.C,* issue #24, 1997. "Trendspotting": "Trendspotting," *21.C,* issue #24, 1997. "Grim Fairy Tales": "Grim Fairy Tales," *World Art,* issue #18, 1998. "The Unheimlich Maneuver": "The Unheimlich Maneuver," *Suck,* March 28, 1997. "Empathy Bellies": "Empathy Bellies," *Feed* (www.feedmag.com), April 24, 1998. "Wild Nature, Wired Nature": "Wild Nature," *21.C,* #4, 1996. "Space Oddities": "The Cult of the Mind," *The New York Times Magazine,* September 28, 1997.

"Laughing Boy" by Randy Newman © 1968 (Renewed) by Unichappel Music Inc. All Rights Reserved. Used by permission of Warner Bros. Publications U.S. Inc.

Library of Congress Cataloging-in-Publication Data

Dery, Mark, 1959–
The pyrotechnic insanitarium : American culture on the brink
/ Mark Dery.
p.   cm.
Includes bibliographical references.
ISBN 0-8021-3670-2 (pbk.)
1. Popular culture—United States.   2. United States—
Civilization—1970–   I. Title.
NX180.S6D48   1999
306'.0973—dc21   98-40837
                                                     CIP

Grove Press
841 Broadway
New York, NY 10003

00 01 02 03   10 9 8 7 6 5 4 3 2 1

CONTENTS

ACKNOWLEDGMENTS

All but two of these essays (the Introduction and the Conclusion) first appeared, in far shorter form, in magazines and webzines, where they profited from the sharp wits and savage pencils of various editors. Jeff Salamon at *The Village Voice;* Ana Marie Cox and Joey Anuff at *Suck;* Lenora Todaro at *The Village Voice Literary Supplement;* Kyle Crichton at *The New York Times Magazine;* Steven Johnson at *Feed;* Sarah Bayliss at *World Art;* and Ray Edgar at the late, lamented *21.C* guarded against stylistic excess and grammatical offense. But to Ashley Crawford, publisher of *World Art* and *21.C,* goes the editorial Croix de Guerre for grace under fire, barstool bonhomie, and the courage—increasingly rare in the magazine world—to encourage my Imp of the Perverse. My essays on evil clowns ("Cotton Candy Autopsy") and formaldehyde photography ("Nature Morte") would have remained evil gleams in my eye without his impassioned advocacy, not to mention financial support.

I'm grateful, as well, to the participants in the WELL discussion topic "Clowns Suck"; "Cotton Candy Autopsy" was much improved by their posts and private e-mail. And Phil Snyder's obsessive screeds in his 'zine, *Eyewash,* shed a darkly funny light on clownaphobia.

The inimitable Gretchen Worden, the Mutter Muscum's greatest treasure, provided information and inspiration in equal measure for "Nature Morte." To me, she will always be the keeper of the keys to the Pathological Sublime. And I count myself fortunate for having met Allan Ludwig, whose incomparable photos of Mutter exhibits (created in collaboration with Gwen Akin) lend a ghastly beauty to "Nature Morte." I was buoyed by his antic wit, and spurred on by his gleeful exhortations to shine a light into the darkest corners of our cultural cabinet of curiosities.

I'm indebted to David J. Skal for his inexhaustible study, *The Monster Show: A Cultural History of Horror*. His thoughts on *Frankenstein* as a story about "scientific man's desire to abandon womankind and find a new method of procreation that does not involve the female principle" planted the seed that grew into "Empathy Bellies."

Andrew Ross's *The Chicago Gangster Theory of Life: Nature's Debt to Society* proved an invaluable intellectual lockpick, essential in cracking the deeper meanings of the Unabomber in "Wild Nature, Wired Nature." More generally, I'm deeply appreciative of Andrew's continued support of my perilous tap dance in the minefield between pop intellectualism and academic criticism.

McKenzie Wark's pithy, peppery broadsides, in person and on-line, challenged me to broader, deeper thinking about the country that he views with that characteristically antipodean mix of humor, horror, and what his fellow Australians call "cultural cringe."

In Orlando, Michael Hoover and Lisa Stokes were hilariously disaffected tour guides through the overdetermined landscape of "Dislando" and Celebration. Their wry critique of Disney's dream of "a place that takes you back to that time of innocence" informs "Past Perfect."

In the time-honored tradition of Grub Street hacks, I've depended heavily on the kindness of strangers in procuring illustrations for this book. I'm beholden to the photographers, artists, galleries, collectors, and companies who provided the unforgettable images, at little or no cost, that saved my readers from drowning in a sea of unrelieved type.

Although we never made it to the altar, I'm thankful to Verso editors Mike Davis and Michael Sprinker for their courtship and early words of encouragement.

Anton Mueller, my long-suffering editor at Grove Press, maintained an admirable aplomb in the face of the protracted agony of this book's delivery, from CMOS snafus to malfunctioning motherboards.

Naturally, *The Pyrotechnic Insanitarium* would never have seen the light of day without the tireless efforts of my agent, Laurie Fox, and everyone else at the Linda Chester Literary Agency, where hopes of an Oprah Winfrey benediction for one of my books spring eternal.

But I owe my greatest debt of gratitude, as always, to my wife, Margot Mifflin: intellectual foil, fellow scribbler, inseparable other—the only one who truly understands all the unspoken, unspeakable things.

INTRODUCTION:
THE PYROTECHNIC
INSANITARIUM

A scenic postcard from the City of Fire: Luna Park, Coney Island, 1906. Museum of the City of New York, Gottscho-Schleisner Collection.

Dreamland's Burning

With the electric light as a sorcerer's apprentice, Coney Island's three great amusement parks—Steeplechase, Luna Park, and Dreamland—conjured up a "city of fire," its eerie aurora visible 30 miles out to sea. It dazzled all who saw it at the turn of the century. One writer described Luna as a "cemetery of fire" whose "tombs and turrets and towers [were] illuminated in mortuary shafts of flame."[1] Even the saturnine Maxim Gorky was swept up in a transport of rapture at the sight of Luna at night, its spires, domes, and minarets ablaze with a quarter of a million lights. "Golden gossamer threads tremble in the air," he wrote. "They intertwine in transparent, flaming patterns, which flutter and melt away, in love with their own beauty mirrored in the waters. Fabulous beyond conceiving, ineffably beautiful, is this fiery scintillation."[2] Another writer called Coney a "pyrotechnic insanitarium," a phrase straight out of a carny barker's pitch that perfectly captures the island's signature blend of infernal fun and mass madness, technology and pathology.[3]

On the day that Dreamland burned, the island became a pyrotechnic insanitarium in ghastly fact. In the small hours of the morning on May 27, 1911, a fire broke out in Hell Gate, a boat ride into the bottomless pit. The inferno tore through Dreamland's lathe-and-plaster buildings, the "uncontrolled flames leaping higher than any of Coney's towers, animals screaming from within cages where they were trapped to burn to death, and crazed lions . . . running with burning manes through the streets"—a scene worthy of Salvador Dali at his most delirious.[4] In three hours, the wedding-cake fantasia of virgin-white palaces, columns, and statuary was reduced to acres of smoldering ruins, never to be rebuilt.

Now, as we stand at the fin-de-millennium, Dreamland is burning again.

It's a commonplace that something is "out of kilter" in America, as Senator John Kerry put it in the aftermath of the Oklahoma bombing; that "everything that's tied down is coming loose," as Bill Moyers has observed; that "the world has gone crazy," as the Unabomber declared, in his official capacity as Op-Ed essayist and mad bomber.[5]

The Unabomber is a man with his finger on the nation's pulse—or is it a detonator? These are the days of "burn-and-blow," in bomb-squad lingo, from the mass destruction in Oklahoma City and the World Trade Center to the explosion at the Atlanta Olympic Park. The live grenade found in a newspaper-vending box in Albuquerque is just one more statistic in the growing number of bombings, up to 1,880 in 1993 from 442 a decade earlier.[6]

There's a growing belief that mere anarchy is loosed upon the world, as Yeats foretold; that the best lack all conviction, while the worst—terrorists like the Unabomber and Timothy McVeigh, cult leaders like David Koresh of the Branch Davidians and Marshall Applewhite of Heaven's Gate fame—are full of passionate intensity. The cultural critic James Gardner believes that we live in "an age of extremism," a time of "infinite fracturing and polarizing," when extremism "has become the first rather than the last resort."[7]

In Don DeLillo's *Underworld,* a character laments the end of the Cold War: "Many things that were anchored to the balance of power and the balance of terror seem to be undone, unstuck. Things have no limits, now. . . . Violence is easier now, it's uprooted, out of control, it has no measure anymore, it has no level of values."[8] A headline in *The New York Times* says it all: A WHOLE NEW WORLD OF ARMS RACES TO CONTAIN.[9] The Bomb, which used to be the measure of a superpower's John Wayne manhood, seems a little less impressive in a world where technology and the post–Cold War arms market have outfitted many Third World countries with nukes of their own, ballistic missiles armed with poison gas, or deadly germs.

And for truly cash-strapped nations, there's always the devastatingly effective car bomb—"the poor man's substitute for an air force," in the words of one counterinsurgency expert.[10]

Worse yet, we live at a moment when a lone wacko, like the mad scientist in Richard Preston's 1997 novel *The Cobra Event,* could tinker together the biological equivalent of a suitcase nuke. President Clinton, whom aides have described as "fixated" on the threat of germ warfare, was so unnerved by Preston's tale of a sociopath who terrorizes New York City with a genetically engineered "brainpox" that he ordered intelligence experts to evaluate its credibility.[11] The book apparently played a catalytic role in Clinton's decision to initiate a hastily conceived multi-million-dollar project to stockpile vaccines at strategic points around the country.

Even nature seems to be committing random acts of senseless violence, from airborne plagues like the Ebola virus to the chaos wrought by El Niño. Sometimes, of course, nature has a little help from our highly industrialized society, which has introduced us to the delights of food-related illnesses like mad-cow disease and postmodern maladies like multiple chemical sensitivity, poetically known as "twentieth-century disease."

Between 1980 and 1990, the number of fungal infections in hospitals doubled, many of them attributable to virulent new supergerms that eat antibiotics for breakfast.[12] Sales of antibacterial soaps, a voodoo charm against the unseen menaces of staph and strep and worse, are up. So, too, is the consumption of bottled water—a "purified" alternative to the supposed toxic soup of lead, chlorine, *E. coli,* and cryptosporidium that slithers out of our taps. The Brita filter is our fallout shelter, the existential personal flotation device of the nervous nineties.

But, all this gloom and doom notwithstanding, there's a darkly farcical, Coneyesque quality to the nineties, a decade captivated by celebrity nonentities like Joey Buttafuoco and Tonya Harding and Lorena Bobbitt and Heidi Fleiss and, as this is written, the cast of "zippergate," starring Monica Lewinsky. The increasingly black comedy of American society is writ small in the information flotsam that drifts with the media current—back-page stories like the one about the Long Island men accused of conspiring to kill local politicians, whom they believed were concealing evidence of a flying saucer crash, by lacing the officials' toothpaste with radioactive metal.

The postmodern theorist Arthur Kroker believes that millennial culture is manic-depressive, mood-swinging between "ecstasy and fear, between delirium and anxiety."[13] For Kroker, the "postmodern scene" is a panic, in the sense of the "panic terror" that some historians believe swept through Europe at the turn of the last millennium, when omens of apocalypse supposedly inspired public flagellation and private suicides. But, he implies, it's also a panic in the somewhat dated sense of something that's hysterically funny (with the emphasis on *hysterical*). Fin-de-millennium America is an infernal carnival—a pyrotechnic insanitarium, like Coney Island at the fin-de-siècle.

The Electric Id: Coney Island's Infernal Carnival

Our historical moment parallels Coney's in its heyday: In the late nineteenth and early twentieth centuries, America was poised between the Victorian era and the Machine Age; similarly, we're in transition from industrial modernity to the Digital Age. Like Americans at the last fin-de-siècle, we have a weakness for those paeans to the machine that Leo Marx called "the rhetoric of the technological sublime." Nicholas Negroponte, the director of MIT's Media Lab and the author of the gadget-happy technology tract, *Being Digital,* believes that digital technologies are a "force of nature, decentralizing, globalizing, harmonizing, and empowering."[14] Fellow traveler John Perry Barlow, a breathless cyberbooster, proclaims a millennial gospel that borrows equally from the Jesuit philosopher Teilhard de Chardin, Marshall McLuhan, and Deadhead flashbacks to the sixties notion that we're all connected by a cosmic web of psychic Oobleck. In the media and on the lecture circuit, Barlow heralds the imminent "physical wiring of collective human consciousness" into a "collective organism of mind," perhaps even divine mind.[15]

In the middle of the last century, writers similarly intoxicated by the invention of wireless telegraphy had equally giddy visions. "It is impossible that old prejudices and hostilities should longer exist, while such an instrument has been created for an exchange of thought between all the nations of the earth," Charles Briggs and Augustus Maverick wrote of the telegram in 1858.[16] In 1899, a pop science magazine informed its readers that "the nerves of the whole world" were "being bound together" by Marconi's marvel; world peace and the Brotherhood of Man were at hand.[17]

Our dizzy technophilia would have been right at home in Coney, where revelers thrilled to Luna's Trip to the Moon, Dreamland's Leap-Frog Railway (which enabled one train to glide safely over another on the same track), and the world's greatest displays of that still-novel technology, the electric light. Dreamland's powerhouse was a temple of electricity with a façade designed to look like a dynamo; inside, a white-gloved engineer ministered to the machines and lectured awed visitors on the wonders of electrical power.

But the what-me-worry futurism of cyberprophets like Barlow shares cultural airspace, as did Coney's visions of technological promise in their day, with the pervasive feeling that American society is out of control. Politicians and pundits bemoan the death of community and the dearth of civility, the social pathologies caused by the withering of economic opportunity for blue-collar workers or the breakdown of the family or the decline of public education or the acid rain of media violence or all of the above.

Coney's Jules Verne daydreams of high-tech tomorrows took place against a backdrop of profound social change and moral disequilibrium. Turn-of-the-century America was accelerating away from the starched manners and corseted mores of the Victorian age, toward a popular culture shaped by mass production, mass media, and the emerging ethos of conspicuous consumption. Coney's parks were agents of social transformation, briefly repealing the hidebound proprieties of the Victorian world and helping to weave heterogeneous social, ethnic, and economic groups into a mass consumer society.

America was moving from what the economist and social theorist Simon Patten, writing at the peak of Coney's popularity, called a "pain economy" of scarcity and subsistence to a "pleasure economy" that held out at least the promise of abundance.[18] Steeplechase's trademark "funny face"— a leering clown with an ear-to-ear, sharklike grin—personified the infantile psychology of the new consumer culture, with its emphasis on immediate gratification and sensual indulgence. Coney was a social safety valve for an ever more industrialized, urbanized America, appropriating the machines of industry in the service of the unconscious. (Fittingly, Sigmund Freud had just opened a Dreamland of his own in *The Interpretation of Dreams,* a book published in 1899 but shrewdly imprinted with the momentous date of 1900 by Freud's savvy publisher).

At once a parody of industrial modernity and an initiation into it, Coney was a carnival of chaos, a madcap celebration of emotional abandon and exposed flesh, speed and sensory overload, natural disasters and machines gone haywire.[19] Rides like Steeplechase's Barrel of Love and Human Roulette Wheel hurtled young men and women into deliciously indecent proximity, and hidden blow holes whipped skirts skyward, exposing the scandalous sight of bare legs. (This at a time when, according to the historian John F. Kasson, "the middle-class ideal as described in etiquette books of the period placed severe restraints on the circumstances under which a man might presume even to tip his hat to a woman in public.")[20]

The Russian critic and literary theorist Mikhail Bakhtin coined the term "carnivalesque" to describe the high-spirited subversion, in medieval carnivals, of social codes and cultural hierarchies. Similarly, Steeplechase, Luna, and Dreamland turned the Victorian world upside down in an eruption of what might be called the "electric carnivalesque." According to Kasson, Coney "declared a moral holiday for all who entered its gates. Against the values of thrift, sobriety, industry, and ambition, it encouraged extravagance, gaiety, abandon, revelry. Coney Island signaled the rise of a new mass culture no longer deferential to genteel tastes and values, which demanded a democratic resort of its own. It served as a Feast of Fools for an urban-industrial society."[21]

But to much of what we would now call the cultural elite, Coney looked less like a Dionysian feast than like the grotesque banquet in Tod Browning's *Freaks*. As a "gigantic laboratory of human nature . . . cut loose from repressions and restrictions," in the words of the son of Steeplechase's founder, amusement parks offered a precognitive glimpse of the emerging mass culture of the Machine Age.[22] The cultural critic James Huneker, for one, had seen the future, and was duly appalled. "What a sight the poor make in the moonlight!" he shuddered.[23] Where modernist painters like Joseph Stella delighted in the "carnal frenzy" of Coney's "surging crowd," Huneker recoiled in horror from the raucous masses. No fan of Freud's "return of the repressed," he pronounced Luna Park a house of bedlam in a frighteningly literal sense. "After the species of straitjacket that we wear everyday is removed at such Saturnalia as Coney Island," he wrote, "the human animal emerges in a not precisely winning guise. . . . Once en masse, humanity sheds its civilization and becomes half child, half savage. . . . It will lynch an innocent man or glorify a scamp politician with equal facility.

Hence the monstrous debauch of the fancy at Coney Island, where New York chases its chimera of pleasure."[24]

Huneker gave voice to middle-class anxieties about the revolt of the masses, their simmering sense of social injustice brought to a boil by urban squalor and industrial exploitation. At the same time, he bore witness to the growing influence of ideas imported from social psychology, such as the notion that surrendering to one's unconscious impulses could invite actual lunacy, or the theory that the crowd, as a psychological entity, was irrational and immoral—a fertile agar for the culturing of "popular delusions" and mob violence.[25]

Coney materialized the waking nightmares of a middle class haunted by the specters of working-class unrest and the "mongrelization" of Anglo-Saxon America by recent waves of swarthy immigrants from southern and eastern Europe. To Huneker and his constituency, Coney's "Saturnalia" marked the passing of the Enlightenment vision of the public as an informed, literate body, responsive to reasoned argument and objective fact. In its place, Coney ushered in the crowd psyche of mass consumer culture—lowbrow rather than highbrow, reactive rather than reflective, postliterate rather than literate, susceptible to the manipulation of images rather than the articulation of ideas.

The primacy of images in the new mass culture, a sea change that inverted the traditional hegemony of reality over representation, was especially disconcerting. In his hugely influential 1895 book, *The Crowd: A Study of the Popular Mind,* the French social psychologist Gustave Le Bon argued that the crowd "thinks in images," confusing "with the real event what the deforming action of its imagination has imposed thereon. A crowd scarcely distinguishes between the subjective and the objective. It accepts as real the images evoked in its mind."[26] Coney represented the apotheosis of the fake, and critics like Huneker were unsettled by its perverse mockery of palpable fact and visual truth, from its impossibly opulent "marble" facades (a mixture of cement, plaster, and jute fibers) to the larger-than-life spectacles of its staged disasters and simulated adventures. Confronted with the "jumbled nightmares" of Luna's architecture—a proto-postmodern mélange of baroque grotesques and *Arabian Nights*—Huneker observed, "Unreality is as greedily craved by the mob as alcohol by the dipsomaniac."[27]

Coney is as good a symbol as any of the historical process William Irwin Thompson calls "the American replacement of nature." The phenom-

enon gathered speed in Coney's heyday with the fateful conjunction of technologies of reproduction such as chromolithography (1840s) and motion
pictures (1895) and the rise of a consumer culture mesmerized by the images of desire made possible by such technologies. The trend had begun in
the 1830s with photography, whose ability to skin the visual image inspired
Oliver Wendell Holmes to declare that "form is henceforth divorced from
matter."[28] Its runaway acceleration continues in our wired world, where
Barlow proposes that the inhabitants of the Internet should secede from
reality, since cyberspace isn't bound by the legal or social codes of the
embodied world, which are "based on matter" and "there is no matter
here."[29] In the Luna Park we now inhabit, the permeable membrane between fact and fiction, actual and virtual, is in danger of dissolving altogether.

Dreamland's fiery demise marked the end of an age. "It took people
awhile to realize that they hadn't just lost a park, that something had changed,"
notes *American Heritage* editor Richard Snow.[30] By the 1920s, Coney was a
victim of its own success. It still glowed as brightly as ever, attracting crowds
of a million on a good day where once it drew a few hundred thousand, but
now it was merely a peeling pasteboard temple of cheap thrills and popular
pleasures, not the electric apparition of a coming age. "The authority of the
older genteel order that the amusement capital had challenged was now crumbling rapidly, and opportunities for mass entertainment were more abundant
than ever," writes Kasson. "A harbinger of the new mass culture, Coney Island
lost its distinctiveness by the very triumph of its values."[31]

On September 20, 1964, the lights at Coney's last surviving park,
Steeplechase, went out forever, one at a time, as a bell tolled once for each
of the 67 years the park had been open and a band played "Auld Lang Syne."
But Coney's disappearance into history only conceals the fact that all of
America has become a pyrotechnic insanitarium.

Trust No One: Conspiracy Theory in the Age of True Lies

Keepers of the Enlightenment flame like Huneker worried about the reign
of unreality and unreason at Luna Park, but reassured themselves that the
sleep of reason ended at its gates. By contrast, contemporary rationalists
see themselves as embattled guardians of the guttering candle of reason in
a new dark age.

None dare call it conspiracy: A portent of doom from Craig Baldwin's tongue-in-cheek exercise in metaconspiracy theory, *Tribulation 99*. Photo: Craig Baldwin.

In *The Demon-Haunted World: Science as a Candle in the Dark,* Carl Sagan worries that "as the millennium edges nearer, pseudoscience and superstition will seem year by year more tempting, the siren song of un-reason more sonorous and attractive."[32] *The Skeptical Inquirer,* the house organ of the Committee for the Scientific Investigation of Claims of the Paranormal, resounds with nervous talk of growing scientific illiteracy and the "rebellion against science at the end of the twentieth century" by a popu-lace weary and increasingly wary of the human and environmental costs of military-industrial abuses of science. A recent issue announced "an unprec-edented $20 million drive for the future of science and reason," grimly noting, "Human beings have never understood the material universe as thoroughly as they do today. Yet never has the popular hunger for super-stition, pseudoscience, and the paranormal been so acute."[33]

Ironically, millennial America is also gnawed by that all *too* ratio-nal rage for order known as conspiracy theory—the belief that nothing is meaningless, that all of history's seemingly loose ends are interwoven in a cosmic cat's cradle of dark import. The grand design of this tangled world-wide web is known only to the unseen schemers who secretly weave our reality—and to those few of us who TRUST NO ONE, but who know that THE TRUTH IS OUT THERE, as *The X-Files* has it. Fox "Spooky" Mulder, the *X-Files* agent obsessed with unraveling the conspiracy's Gordian knot, is our Everyman, a quintessentially nineties blend of smirking cynic (about official institutions) and true believer (in seemingly everything else, from shape-shifting Indians to telekinetic fire starters to reincarnated serial killers to garden-variety E.T.s).

Conspiracy theory is at once a symptom of millennial angst and a home remedy for it. An ectoplasmic manifestation of our loss of faith in authorities of every sort, it confirms our worst fears that the official reality, from Watergate to Waco, is merely a cover story for moral horrors that would make the portrait of Dorian Gray look like a Norman Rockwell.

But conspiracy beliefs are also a source of cold comfort. At the end of the century that gave us the Theory of Relativity, the Uncertainty Principle, and the Incompleteness Theorem, conspiracy theory returns us to a comfortingly clockwork universe, before the materialist bedrock of our worldview turned to quicksand. Conspiracy theory is a magic spell against the Information Age, an incantation that wards off information madness by organizing every scrap of the free-floating data assaulting us into an impossibly ordered scheme. Unified field theories for a hopelessly complex, chaotic world, conspiracy beliefs are curiously reassuring in their "proof" that *someone, somewhere* is in charge.

Conspiracy theory is the theology of the paranoid, what Marx might have called the opiate of the fringes if he'd lived to read *The New World Order* by Pat Robertson. It "replaces religion as a means of mapping the world without disenchanting it, robbing it of its mystery," writes the literary critic John A. McClure. It "explains the world, as religion does, without elucidating it, by positing the existence of hidden forces which permeate and transcend the realm of ordinary life."[34]

Like fundamentalist Christianity, conspiracy theory accepts on faith the presumption that social issues can be reduced to a Manichean struggle between good and evil. Like the New Age, it embraces a faith in the interconnectedness of all things, a cosmic holism not unrelated to the "holographic universes," "morphogenetic fields," and "nonlocal connectedness"

of quantum mysticism. The one-world government of conspiratorial nightmares offers a paranoid analogue to the coming "planetary consciousness"
of New Age prophecies.

Conversely, the New Age has its own Smiley-face take on conspiracy theory in Marilyn Ferguson's *Aquarian Conspiracy,* in which she holds
that undercover agents of cosmic consciousness have infiltrated secular
culture like some transcendental fifth column. Then, too, there's the gag-
gingly cute New Age concept of "pronoia"—the sneaking suspicion that
everyone is conspiring to help you.

Conspiracy theory is an explanatory myth for those who have lost
their faith in official versions of everything, including reality. "When men
stop believing in God, it isn't that they then believe in nothing: they believe in everything," says a character in Umberto Eco's darkly funny send-
up of conspiracy theory, *Foucault's Pendulum.*[35] "I want to believe," the phrase
on a UFO poster in Fox Mulder's office, is one of *The X-Files'* shibboleths.

But even for those of us who don't want to believe (or won't admit
that we do), conspiracy theory has become the horoscope of the late nineties, a kitschy charm against chaos, a novelty song to whistle in the gathering millennial gloom. It's a manifestation of the postmodern zeitgeist, whose
knowing sensibility is neatly summed up in the computer hacker's expression "ha-ha-only-serious."

By no coincidence, tongue-in-cheek conspiracy theories are classic examples of the ha-ha-only-serious sensibility. Thomas Pynchon's *The
Crying of Lot 49* is a precursor, but the ur-text is undeniably the *Illuminatus!*
trilogy, by Robert Shea and Robert Anton Wilson, a sprawling chronicle
of the millennia-long power struggle between the anarcho-surrealist, chaos-
worshipping Discordians and the evil, autocratic secret society known as
the Illuminati. The Church of the SubGenius, an acid (in both senses) satire
of fundamentalist Christianity and right-wing paranoia, is also a touchstone
of ha-ha-only-seriousness. According to the church's "lunatic prophecies
for the coming weird times," the SubGenii are the frontline in an apocalyptic battle against a global conspiracy of "Mediocretins, Assouls, Glorps,
Conformers, Nuzis, Barbies, and Kens—FALSE PROPHETS and PINK
BOYS who have made NORMALITY the NORM!"[36]

Movies like *Men in Black* and *Conspiracy Theory* let us have our paranoia and mock it, too, as do books like *The 60 Greatest Conspiracies of All Time*
(Jonathan Vankin and John Whalen), the *Big Book of Conspiracies* (Doug

Schwa: Red alert for the alien invasion, hyperironic spoof of the millennial
zeitgeist, artful GenX-ploitation—or all of the above? Copyright ©1996
Schwa Inc., all rights reserved; www.theschwacorporation.com.

Moench), and *It's a Conspiracy: The Shocking Truth About America's Favorite
Conspiracy Theories* (The National Insecurity Council).

The Schwa phenomenon plays to the postmodern mood as well. A
brainchild of the graphic artist Bill Barker, Schwa is a somewhat inscrutable
conceptual art project about "control, conspiracy, absurdity and despair,"
disguised as a cottage-industry venture into GenX tchotchkes.[37] (Or is it
the other way around? Trust no one!) Schwa's black-and-white "alien defense products"—buttons, stickers, comic books, Alien Repellent Patches,
Lost Time Detectors, and glow-in-the-dark T-shirts, most of them emblazoned with the archetypal almond-eyed alien head—use the paranoid folklore of alien invasion to lampoon millennial anxiety. "From alien detection
to alien survival, there is now, for the first time, a complete line of actual
objects you can own that will end your doubts about the unknown, right
now, *forever*!" promises one Schwa pamphlet.

At the same time, Schwa's red-alert warnings about the alien conspiracy, whose "subliminal coercion" and "bipolar marketing techniques"
are washing the brains of those unknowing dupes the "Stickpeople," is a
cartoon critique of our ad-addled, TV-o.d.'d culture. "Media manipulation
campaigns are crucial to the success of any Schwa world operation," informs
the *Schwa World Operations Manual,* a handbook for humans who'd like to
try *their* hands at world domination. "Past experiences have helped us come
up with a number of robust slogans which, if properly used as campaign
kernels, will achieve the maximum amount of psychological pliability. . . .
'Export Television Slavery' and 'TVs Are Needles' are perfect illustrations
of this approach."[38] Ironically, the *Manual* cites the early Schwa phenomenon itself (a "modest, small-scale and cryptic" effort involving "the heavy
use of keychains and stickers") as a textbook example of the covert penetration of the public mind. You may already be a Stickperson.

Craig Baldwin's underground masterpiece, *Tribulation 99: Alien
Anomalies Under America* (1991), also improvises on the intertwined themes
of conspiracy theory and alien invasion in the ha-ha-only serious mode,
though to a more pointedly political end. Baldwin's film is a barrage of jump-
cut imagery, snipped from Atom Age rocket operas and creature features
and glued together with tense, hoarsely whispered narration. In a clench-
jawed, Deep Throat voice, the narrator weaves virtually every major article of paranoid faith into the mother of all conspiracy theories.

Tribulation 99 is a tangled tale of alien invaders, Marxist revolu-
tionaries, cattle mutilation, the Watergate break-in, and, of course, the
assassination of JFK. True to the ha-ha-only serious spirit, Baldwin's deadpan mockumentary crosses paranoid delusions with suppressed history,
interweaving snippets of *War of the Worlds* and news footage of the American invasion of Grenada, the cracked belief in a hollow Earth and the cold
facts of U.S. covert operations in Latin America.

"What came to a head [in *Tribulation 99*] was the whole Iran-Contra
affair, Oliver North's trial," says Baldwin. "I wanted to make a statement
that was critical of the CIA and our meddling in foreign countries, and it
seemed to be a new [way to use] this creative material, these paranoiac
rants." He was struck by the unnerving way in which certain ideas hovered
"between the official, political history and the very unofficial paranoiac
version of things. There were often these weird alignments. Sometimes it
was easier to believe the UFO stuff than it was to believe the CIA story that

Alien mind control: Blueprint for psychic dictatorship from the
Schwa World Operations Manual. Copyright © 1996 Schwa Inc., all
rights reserved; www.theschwacorporation.com.

story that was used to justify our intervention in some country. So I lined
them up, superimposed them. . . . I took real, political material and retro-
fitted it with the fantastic, wacko literature."[39]

Like *Tribulation 99, The X-Files* explores the borderland between
suppressed fact and wacko fancy, between national nightmares and the bad
dreams of solitary weirdos, be they lone gunmen or mutant contortionists
who subsist on human livers. And like Baldwin's movie, the series cloaks a
deepening distrust of government in the pulp mythology of an alien conspiracy. *The X-Files* is about two lone-wolf FBI agents, Mulder and his
female partner Dana Scully, who investigate cases involving paranormal phenomena, classified as "X" files: giant flukeworms, gender-morphing aliens,
Satan-worshiping substitute teachers. It's a thankless task, one that often

earns the duo their boss's ire, not to mention the wrath of the quintessential old boys' network, the conspiratorial Syndicate—Well-Manicured Man,
Fat Man, and Cigarette-Smoking Man, a.k.a. Cancer Man (who, it can now
be revealed, was behind the assassinations of both Kennedys and Martin
Luther King, Jr.). For these gray eminences, genetically engineering human-
alien hybrids using techniques perfected by Nazi eugenicists and orches-
trating a government cover-up of the whole nasty business is all in a few
decade's work.

The antigovernment sentiment that hangs menacingly over *The
X-Files* first appeared on our mental horizons during Watergate (though it
took Ronald Reagan's covert policy of benign neglect toward a government
he openly regarded as "not the solution but the problem" to whip this free-
floating contempt into the angry thunderhead it is today). *The X-Files* is
haunted by the restless ghosts of Watergate and Vietnam, with Richard
Nixon, the patron saint of conspiratorial realpolitik and bunker paranoia,
at their head. The Machiavellian stratagems of the Syndicate recall the ruthless maneuverings of the shifty-eyed president who forged an enduring link
in the American mind between the White House and dark deeds: break-
ins, buggings, shoe boxes filled with money, and shady deals with Howard
Hughes. The evil old white guys even *look* like Tricky Dick: As one writer
noted, Syndicate members "all have a faintly jowly, Nixonian cast to them."[40]
Deep Throat, the trench-coated Virgil who guides Mulder into the netherworld of alien cover-up, takes his name from the mysterious Watergate
informant. Even the show's Nazi themes have Nixonian echoes in the thinly
veiled Naziphilia of G. Gordon Liddy, the Watergate burglar who named
his dirty-tricks brigade ODESSA, after the underground association of
former SS members, and who titled his memoirs *Will* (as in *Triumph of the*).

Chris Carter, the *X-Files'* creator, speaks for a generation when he
says, "I'm 40. My moral universe was being shaped when Watergate happened. It blew my world out of the water. It infused my whole thinking."[41]

At the same time, the show strikes a sympathetic chord with its
huge following (20 million and counting) because it plays on our millennial
fears. The Syndicate's ongoing attempt to create a human-alien master race,
and episodes like "The Erlenmeyer Flask," about a plot to spread an extraterrestrial virus via gene therapy, hint at uneasiness over genetic engineering at a time when eugenics is sexy again, rehabilitated by a new wave of
genetic determinists after decades of disrepute. The conspirators' use of

alien implants to track their human guinea pigs, and the homicidal psychosis triggered by ATMs and cell phones in the episode "Blood," give shape to the future shock that shadows the cyberhype of the nineties. That no one ever *really* dies on the show, that everyone is reincarnated or reanimated, is a symptom of the graying Baby Boom's anxious premonitions of mortality. As well, episodes that have grim fun with forty-something hysteria about teenage anomie ("D.P.O.," "Syzygy") make light of the Boomers' worst fear: that they've become their parents.

The *X-Files* tells electronic campfire stories about social upheaval, moral vertigo, and the breakneck pace of technological change at the end of the century. "I really think the world is spinning out of control," says Carter. "There's no work ethic anymore and no real moral code. I'm trying to find images to dramatize that."[42]

Sometimes, of course, we prefer our paranoia lite, as in *The Truman Show* (1998), a movie in which the New Age dream of pronoia comes nightmarishly true. Unbeknownst to Truman Burbank, his life is a TV show, a global obsession with its own line of merchandise and theme bars. His fishbowl world is surveilled by 5,000 miniature cameras and sealed inside a giant biodome. Everyone in his postcard-perfect, litter-free town of Seahaven, including his doting Stepfordian wife and his beer-swilling good buddy, is a paid actor. From a control booth concealed in the fake moon, the show's godlike producer can cue the sun or cause a little rain to fall into Truman's life.

In time, however, Truman begins to suspect that he's at the heart of a benign conspiracy. Ultimately, he strikes, like Ahab, at the pasteboard mask of his fabricated reality (though with happier results). "How can the prisoner reach outside except by thrusting through the wall?" says Ahab.[43] In unwitting fulfillment, Truman rams the nose of his boat through the painted wall of the biodome. Trying to dissuade him from leaving the Disneyesque utopia of a world where every smiling cast member is conspiring to help him, the omniscient producer offers an inside-out version of *X-Files* wisdom: "There's no more truth out there than there is in the world I created for you."

We cheer Truman on in his jailbreak from a place where he can Trust No One, into the Truth Out There—until we remember, with a slightly sinking feeling, that Out There is right here. What will become of the sweet naïf, the boy in the TV bubble, in a world where it isn't always morning in America and the corner newsie doesn't greet him cheerily by name? For those who've seen their quality of life fray around the edges, unraveled by the slashing of public services and fears of violent crime, the notion of a benevolent conspiracy dedicated to ensuring that we always have a nice day holds a bittersweet appeal. The Disney executives who dreamed up the eerily Seahavenlike planned community of Celebration, in Orlando, Florida, know this well.

There's a techno-logic to the popularity of paranoia in fin-de-millennium America. "This is the age of conspiracy," says a character in Don DeLillo's *Running Dog*, the age of "connections, links, secret relationships."[44] Like conspiracy theory, the Information Age is about hermetic languages, powerful cabals, maddeningly complex interconnections: software code, encrypted data, media mergers, global networks, neural nets.

In fact, conspiracy theory and the Information Age are joined at the hip: both sprang from the brow of the Enlightenment, whose unshakable faith in rationalism and materialism made technological modernity possible. The sleep of reason may breed monsters, but so does an excess of rationality: conspiracy theory's fetishization of information and its Newtonian faith in a universe of clockwork causality are diseases of the Age of Reason.

In one of history's more delicious ironies, those true sons of the Enlightenment, the Illuminati, are also the unwitting fathers of modern conspiracy theory. The Illuminati were a Masonic secret society formed in eighteenth-century Bavaria to further the Enlightenment goal of a rational, humanist society, freed from centuries of domination by crown and church. The group only lasted from 1776 until 1785, but by 1797, when the eminent Scottish scientist John Robison published *Proofs of a Conspiracy Against All the Religions and Governments of Europe, carried on in the Secret Meetings of Free Masons, Illuminati, and Reading Societies,* the Illuminati were fast becoming posthumous stars of paranoid fantasy. Two centuries later, they're still close contenders, after international Jewry and the U.N., for the role of the dark architects of global domination—the secret schemers behind the French and Russian revolutions, the elders of Zion, *and* the rise of Hitler (!).

In their *Dialectic of Enlightenment,* Theodor Adorno and Max Horkheimer argue that Enlightenment reason degenerated into the "instrumental reason" of the modern age, which uses technology to control people and nature in the name of capitalist profit. Following Adorno and Horkheimer's

logic, Enlightenment rationalism, taken to extremes, becomes the command-
and-control mind-set of military-industrial technocracy, which in turn gives
rise to the techno-paranoia of conspiracy theory: fears of surveillance via
microchip implants, Satanic domination through universal product codes,
U.N. invaders guided by stickers on highway signs. (Ironically, the wild-
fire spread of conspiracy theories and antigovernment networking would
be impossible without Information Age innovations such as computer bulletin boards, desktop publishing, and shortwave radio broadcasting.)

Simultaneously, the computer interfaces whose metaphors are
beginning to structure our worldview—the World Wide Web, Microsoft's
Windows—seem to confirm the paranoid assumption that everything is
connected, that everything is a symbol, fraught with hidden meanings.
Clicking through Windows' infinite regress of menus and submenus or leaping from hyperlink to hyperlink across the Web, we enter the mind of
Casaubon, one of the lunatic editors (who just might be CIA operatives) in
Foucault's Pendulum. "I was prepared to see symbols in every object I came
upon," he says. "Our brains grew accustomed to connecting, connecting,
connecting everything with everything else."[45]

Also, there's a weird parallelism between conspiracy theory and
the academic vogues of the past few decades. Semiotics, which sees everything from Ted Koppel's hair to superheroes as part of a cultural code to
be cracked, is no stranger to the paranoid style. The pop semiotician Wilson Bryan Key made a career of conjuring up the specter of Madison Avenue mind control. His contribution to what McLuhan called "the folklore
of industrial man," the notion that "subliminal seductions" are lurking in
every ad, lives on in the mind of every teenager who has ever performed
the parlor trick of revealing, to amazed and amused friends, the word SEX
written on the surface of a Ritz cracker, the naked woman hidden in the
liquor-ad ice cubes, the man with the hard-on concealed in the foreleg of
the camel on the front of a pack of regular, unfiltered Camels.

Along with semiotics, other conspiratorial academic trends include
deconstruction, which teaches that meaning is a mercurial thing, impossible to pin down, and New Historicism, which argues that the notion of
"objective" history, free from cultural biases, is a naïve fiction, and that every
historical account can therefore be read and dissected as literature. All three
schools of critical thought conceive of the cultural landscape as a literary
text, replete with hidden meanings. And all three veer perilously close to

conspiracy theory when they willfully stretch or shave the text to fit Pro-crustean ideologies. At such moments, they meet their demented doppel-gänger, conspiracy theory, coming from the opposite direction.

Conversely, the best conspiracy theorists are unhinged scholars, virtuosos of overinterpretation and amok "intertextuality" (the lit-crit notion that every work is inextricably intertangled in a web of allusions to other texts). In his classic study, *The Paranoid Style in American Politics,* Richard Hofstadter argues that the paranoid mentality "believes that it is up against an enemy who is as infallibly rational as he is totally evil, and it seeks to match his imputed total competence with its own, leaving nothing un-explained and comprehending all of reality in one overreaching, consis-tent theory. It is nothing if not 'scholarly' in technique. [Senator Joseph] McCarthy's 96-page pamphlet *McCarthyism* contains no less than 313 foot-note references, and [Robert H. Welch, Jr.'s] fantastic assault on Eisen-hower, *The Politician,* is weighed down by a hundred pages of bibliography and notes."[46]

Thus it is that Ron Rosenbaum, a connoisseur of crackpot herme-neutics, calls the obsessives who mine the Warren Commission Report for buried truths "the first deconstructionists."[47] He thrills to the flights of interpretive fancy of Kennedy assassination buffs like Penn Jones, conspiracy theorists "whose luxuriant and flourishing imaginations have produced a dark, phantasmagoric body of work that bears . . . resemblance to a Latin American novel (Penn is the Gabriel Garcia Lorca of Dealey Plaza, if you will)."[48]

The 26-volume Warren Commission Report is the *Finnegans Wake* of paranoid America. Indeed, Don DeLillo, who traces our "deeply unsettled feeling about our grip on reality," our disquieting sense of the "randomness and ambiguity and chaos" of things to "that one moment in Dallas," has called the Warren Report the novel that James Joyce might have written if he had moved to Iowa City and lived to be a hundred.[49] It is the Mount Everest of outsider exegesis, challenging virtuosos of conspiracy theory to ever greater heights of interpretive excess. The acknowledged masters of this under-ground art, like the reclusive octogenarian James Shelby Downard, have used the historical facts of the Kennedy assassination (such as they are) as a springboard for breathtaking leaps of logic and intertextual acrobatics.

A self-styled student of "the science of symbolism," Downard beck-ons us to follow him through a maze of synchronicities that leads, by twists and turns, to a mind-warping conclusion: that official history is a blind for a monstrous conspiracy of Masonic alchemists hell-bent on the conquest of the collective id—the "control of the dreaming mind" of America. The Masons' master plan involves three alchemical rites, one of which, an ancient fertility rite known as the killing of the king, was reenacted in the assassination of JFK.

In his essay "King-Kill/33: Masonic Symbolism in the Assassination of John F. Kennedy," Downard plumbs the dark depths of Eros and Thanatos in the murder of JFK—"a veritable nightmare of symbol-complexes having to do with violence, perversion, conspiracy, death and degradation."[50] In a tour-de-force of surrealist explication, he dredges up connections between Jack Ruby, who was born Jacob Rubinstein, and a "jack ruby," pawnbroker's slang for a fake ruby, which somehow leads to the Ruby Slippers in The Wizard of Oz, the "immense power of 'ruby light,' otherwise known as the laser," and the ruby's symbolic associations with blood, suffering, and death.

Downard's discursive, free-associated style defies synopsis, but a brief excerpt from his essay offers a taste of his inimitable voice:

> Dealey Plaza breaks down symbolically in this manner: "Dea" means "goddess" in Latin and "Ley" can pertain to the law or rule in Spanish, or lines of preternatural geographical significance in the pre-Christian nature religions of the English. For many years, Dealey Plaza was underwater at different seasons, having been flooded by the Trinity River until the introduction of a flood-control system. To this trident-Neptune site came the "Queen of Love and Beauty" [Jackie Kennedy] and her spouse, the scapegoat in the Killing of the King rite, the "Ceannaideach" (Gaelic word for Kennedy meaning "ugly head" or "wounded head").[51]

For Downard, it all adds up: "Masonry does not believe in murdering a man in just any old way and in the JFK assassination it went to incredible lengths and took great risks in order to make this heinous act . . . correspond to the ancient fertility oblation of the Killing of the King." Despite Downard's dead seriousness about his subject, his writing betrays a Casaubonlike delight in spinning out far-flung connections, in pushing the interpretive envelope beyond the physical realities of entry wounds and bullet trajectories, into the metaphysical.

But conspiracy theory is more than lunatic hermeneutics, Information Age psychosis, a paranoid theology for a nation losing its religion, or a posttraumatic reaction to Watergate and Waco. It's also a panic-attack reaction to everyday life in the age of *Totally Hidden Video,* where a little paranoia is admittedly in order. Again, DeLillo in *Running Dog:*

> We're all a little wary. . . . Go into a bank, you're filmed. . . . Go into a department store, you're filmed. Increasingly, we see this. Try on a dress in the changing room, someone's watching you through a one-way glass. Not only customers, mind you. Employees are watched too, spied on with hidden cameras. Drive your car anywhere. Radar, computer traffic scans. They're looking into the uterus, taking pictures. Everywhere. What circles the earth constantly? Spy satellites, weather balloons, U-2 aircraft. What are they doing? Taking pictures. Putting the whole world on film.[52]

These days, surveillance cameras seem to peer, as in *The Truman Show,* from every nook and cranny in our public spaces, especially the high-tech workplace. Software monitors the keystroke speed, error rate, bathroom trips, and lunch breaks of data-entry clerks, telemarketers, and other postindustrial workers, enabling an Orwellian degree of oversight that would have gladdened the heart of Frederick Winslow Taylor, father of the "scientific management" of the modern workforce.

Computer networks have opened our credit histories and medical records to the prying eyes of employers, insurers, and direct-mail marketers. An e-mail ad for "Net Detective" software asks, "Did you know that with the Internet you can discover EVERYTHING you ever wanted to know about your EMPLOYEES, FRIENDS, RELATIVES, SPOUSE, NEIGHBORS, even your own BOSS!" On-line snoopers who pony up $22 will be able to "look up 'unlisted' phone numbers," "check out your daughter's new boyfriend!" and "find out how much alimony your neighbor is paying!"

Increasingly, though, we're embracing our paranoia and learning to love the cam: "Spy shops" like New York City's Spy World and Counter Spy Shop are proliferating in response to consumer demand for devices like the teddy bear with a tiny video camera concealed in one eye, just the thing for nervous parents who want to spy on their nannies.

Less laughably, a December 1997 report delivered to the European Commission confirmed the long-suspected existence of the ECHELON system, a global electronic surveillance network operated by the U.S.'s shadowy National Security Agency that "routinely and indiscriminately" eavesdrops on e-mail, fax, and even phone communications around the world, using artificial-intelligence programs to search for key words of interest.[53] And while the government may not be secretly implanting micro-chip tracking devices in our buttocks, as Timothy McVeigh believed, tough-on-crime types like Senator Dianne Feinstein are clamoring for a mandatory national I.D. card with an electronic fingerprint or voiceprint. *Privacy Journal* publisher Robert Ellis Smith thinks biometric federal I.D. cards would be a grave threat to civil liberties, a step down the slippery slope to the government implants of McVeigh's fever dreams.[54] Not that there isn't ample cause for concern right now: In recent years, the FBI has reportedly spent $2 billion annually to assemble a databank of genetic information about American citizens.[55]

The revelation that the government is reading our e-mail, eaves-dropping on our conversations, spying on us from earth orbit, and archiving our genetic data casts a somewhat charitable light on conspiracy theory. So does the by now universal realization that the government does, in fact, flagrantly flout the will of the people, trample the law, and attempt to cover up its skullduggery. From COINTELPRO to Iran-*contra,* the bizarre capers of the postwar decades are stranger than paranoid fiction: Who could make up CIA operations like MK-ULTRA, a covert $25 million–dollar mind-control experiment in which unwitting human guinea pigs (one of whom later committed suicide) were dosed with LSD? Or the agency's $21 million–dollar program to harness the surveillance powers of "remote view-ing," the supposed psychic ability to see distant or hidden objects with the mind's eye?[56]

At least the millions in tax dollars the CIA flushed down the toilet for its Keystone Kops-meet-the-Psychic Friends Hotline scheme buy a few pained guffaws. But the laughter curdles when grimmer truths come to light, like the U.S. Energy Department's Cold War experiments in which 16,000 people, including infants and pregnant women, were exposed to radiation, or the 1950 germ warfare experiment in which a Navy minesweeper sprayed

San Francisco with rare *Serratia* bacteria, sending 11 unknowing victims to the hospital and one to the cemetery.[57]

As we numbly skim the list of atrocities our government has perpetrated on its own citizens, often with corporate America as a cozy co-conspirator, Sven Birkerts's defense of paranoia comes to mind: "Paranoia is a logical response to a true understanding of power and its diverse pathologies."[58] A literary critic who came of age in the sixties, Birkerts defines paranoia as "what happened when the illusions of the counterculture collapsed and the true extent of the political web became apparent."[59] To him, the "paranoid" worldview is the political equivalent of X-ray specs, revealing what passes for public discourse in our infotainment age to be mere "distraction, spectacle, and the bromides of public relations." It rips away the tabloid sideshow banners of our TV culture to expose the stark reality of a democracy in crisis, "the deeper exchanges of our body politic controlled by the machinations of an elite."[60]

Birkerts is fond of the countercultural maxim that paranoia is just "a heightened state of awareness." Indeed, the worst thing about some of the late-night paranoid musings known as conspiracy theories is that they're true. America really *does* use its imperial power to prop up repressive regimes that are sympathetic to U.S. foreign policy and business interests, and to subvert democratically elected governments that aren't. According to David Burnham, a reporter who specializes in law-enforcement issues, the FBI ("the most powerful and secretive agency in the United States today") really *is* an Orwellian spook house whose routine conduct—indulging its surveillance fetish with databases of information about millions of law-abiding citizens while turning a blind eye on civil rights abuses and corporate crime—is incompatible "with the principles or practices of representative democracy."[61] And, as Birkerts suspects, the corporate newsmedia really *are* instruments of social control, galvanizing public opinion in support of elite agendas.

Of course, in the been-there, done-that, media-savvy nineties, none dare call it conspiracy; better, perhaps, to borrow the fashionable lingo of chaos theory. For example, the media's propagandistic function might be described as an "emergent phenomenon," a pattern that comes into being not as a result of deep-laid plans by a nefarious cabal but through the complex interaction of elements in a turbulent system. These elements include the increasingly concentrated ownership and bottom-line orientation of the dominant media outlets; the censorship exercised by the mass media's primary income source, their advertisers; and the media's reliance on pre-spun information provided by government and business sources and prefab "experts" selected and supported by vested interests. As Edward S. Herman and Noam Chomsky argue in *Manufacturing Consent: The Political Economy of the Mass Media,* these factors "interact with and reinforce one another," filtering out *systemic* critiques of free-market economics, multinational capitalism, and American foreign policy and leaving only the news that's "fit to print."[62]

Herman and Chomsky aren't lone gunmen. Media critics like Ben Bagdikian and Herbert Schiller and organizations like Fairness and Accuracy In Reporting and Project Censored have excavated mountains of evidence of the corporate newsmedia's instrumental role in mustering mass support for "the economic, social, and political agenda of privileged groups that dominate the domestic society and the state," as Herman and Chomsky put it.[63] For those who dismiss such charges as Chicken Little leftism, consider the following:

> • In 1985, the public-television station WNET lost its corporate funding from Gulf + Western after it showed the documentary *Hungry for Profit,* which critiqued multinational corporate activities in the Third World. Despite one source's flabbergasting claim that station officials did all they could to "get the program sanitized," Gulf + Western was much vexed, and withdrew its funding. One of the company's chief executives complained to the station that the show was "virulently anti-business if not anti-American." The *Economist* drily noted, "Most people believe that WNET would not make the same mistake again."[64]

> • In 1989, a federal investigation revealed that as many as 60 percent of the bolts American manufacturers used in airplanes, bridges, and nuclear missile silos might be defective. A report scheduled to be aired on NBC's *Today* show noted that "General Electric engineers discovered they had a big problem. One out of three bolts from one of their major suppliers was bad. Even more alarming, GE accepted the bad bolts without any certification of compliance for eight years." The unflattering reference to GE was removed from the story before it aired. By curious coincidence, GE also happens to own NBC.[65]

• In 1990, images of an overwrought young Kuwaiti woman tes-
tifying before the Congressional Human Rights Caucus mesmerized American TV viewers. Identified as an anonymous "hospital
volunteer" (her identity had to be kept secret to ensure her safety,
we were told), the girl tearfully recounted a shocking tale of
premature babies torn from their incubators and left to die on
the cold hospital floor by soldiers in the Iraqi forces that invaded
Kuwait. Her testimony was instrumental in mobilizing public
support for Operation Desert Storm. After the war was over,
the girl was revealed to be the daughter of the Kuwaiti ambassador. Her whereabouts during the purported events have never
been verified, and her horror story remains unsubstantiated to
this day. What is certain, however, is that the Caucus meeting
was orchestrated by the elite public-relations firm Hill and
Knowlton, which helpfully provided the witnesses who testi-
fied. The Kuwaiti family in exile had hired Hill and Knowlton to
muster public support for U.S. military intervention.[66]

Institutional critiques buttressed by examples of deep, *systemic* flaws
such as these stand in stark contrast to the morality plays favored by mainstream commentators, in which "bad apples" like Richard Nixon or Michael
Milken or Mark Fuhrman are scapegoated while the system that produced
them goes unchallenged—an analysis that actually serves to *reaffirm* the
essential soundness of the status quo. Herman and Chomsky anticipate the
knee-jerk response to such indictments. "Institutional critiques," they write,

> are commonly dismissed by establishment commentators as
> 'conspiracy theories,' but this is merely an evasion. . . . In fact,
> our treatment is much closer to a 'free market' analysis, with
> the results largely an outcome of the workings of market forces.
> Most biased choices in the media arise from the preselection of
> right-thinking people, internalized preconceptions, and the
> adaptation of personnel to the constraints of ownership, organi-
> zation, market, and political power.[67]

In other words, no one's in charge; in the late twentieth century, the real
conspiracies have many tentacles but no heads.

Thus, as evidence mounts of covert government operations, corporate surveillance, and the propagandistic function of the media, it's becoming increasingly clear that some conspiracy theories are true lies.

On the other hand, sometimes a paranoiac is only a paranoiac. Judging from recent events, a startling number of Americans have crossed over, into the paranoid parallel world of *The X-Files*. They "know" that the rumor-shrouded suicide of the White House deputy counsel Vince Foster was actually the murder of a Man Who Knew Too Much, authorized at the highest level. They "know" that TWA Flight 800 was accidentally blown out of the sky by "friendly fire" from a U.S. Navy cruiser (if it wasn't zapped by unfriendly aliens, that is). They "know" that Area 51, an ultrasecret military base hidden away in the Nevada desert, is more than a proving ground for black-budget spycraft like the delta-shaped Aurora, the diamond-shaped "Pumpkin Seed," and the usual complement of Nightstalkers, Goatsuckers, and Grim Reapers (more prosaically known as stealth fighters). According to the true believers in David Darlington's *Area 51,* it's also the birthplace of the AIDS virus, the resting place of the Roswell aliens, and the final destination of all those missing kids on milk cartons, who end up as the subjects of unspeakable experiments conducted in the base's underground labs. Rumors abound, writes Darling, that Area 51 is overseen "not by such earthbound lackeys as Congress or the President or even the Air Force, but by the Bilderbergs/Council on Foreign Relations/Trilateral Commission/One World Government/New World Order—different names for the clandestine cabal operating within/outside the military-industrial complex. These renegade powermongers [will] stop at nothing to achieve their aim, which [is] no less sinister or ambitious a goal than worldwide domination."[68]

To the worldly-wise, such beliefs have a campy appeal; they sound like the political equivalent of the B-movie classic, *The Incredibly Strange Creatures Who Stopped Living and Became Mixed-Up Zombies.* But the joke sours when we realize that what Hofstadter famously called "the paranoid style in American politics"—the Manichean belief that a sinister yet subtle conspiracy is waging covert war on the American Way of Life—is back with a bang, and its devotees are deadly serious.

Unmarked black helicopters, ominous portents of the U.N.'s imminent invasion of the American heartland, darken the mental skies of the estimated 10,000 to 40,000 Americans in the right-wing antigovernment militia movement. Their sympathizers may number in the hundreds of thousands. The hate-group expert Kenneth S. Stern calls the militia movement the "fastest-growing grassroots mass movement" in recent memory.[69]

In these times, a man like Timothy McVeigh—"a very normal, good American serving his country," in the words of his Army roommate—can morph into a paranoid antigovernment extremist who believes the Army has implanted a microchip in his buttocks to track his whereabouts.[70] In the eerie night-vision world of *The Spotlight, Patriot Report,* and the other far-right periodicals that McVeigh devoured, Mongolian hordes are massing in the mountains; members of the infamous Crips and Bloods gangs are being trained as shock troops for the invasion; Russian forces are waiting for zero hour in salt mines under Detroit; and the Amtrak repair yards in Indianapolis are slated for conversion into an enormous crematorium, the final solution for all who resist the New World Order. Some even claim that the conspiracy is hiding its plan for dividing up the land of the (formerly) free in plain sight, in a map on the back of a kid's cereal box.[71]

McVeigh's pillow books included *Operation Vampire Killer 2000* by the former Phoenix police sergeant Jack McLamb, a call to arms to police and military personnel to mobilize against the "elitist covert operation" whose stated goal is a "'utopian' Socialist society" and "the termination of the American way of life" by—when else?—the year 2000.[72] According to McLamb, the shadowy wire pullers behind the coming one-world government include international bankers, the Illuminati, the "Rothschild Dynasty," Communists, the IRS, CBS News (!), the Yale secret society Skull and Bones, "humanist wackos," space aliens, and, of course, the U.N.[73]

McVeigh's conspiracy theories read like an *X-Files* script written by Thomas Pynchon. They would be comic relief if they hadn't ended in apocalypse: the explosion of a truck filled with 4,000 pounds of ammonium nitrate fertilizer near the Alfred P. Murrah Federal Building in Oklahoma City, on April 19, 1995, killing 168 innocent people. "Today, the far right is more active than ever, with subversive attacks being planned all across the country," writes the militia watcher James Ridgeway.[74] A correspondent for the far-right magazine *The Spotlight* claims to have received a spooky, unsigned postcard postmarked Oklahoma City, April 17. Blank on the back, its only message is the image on front, an ominous, Depression-era photo of a twister churning across the Dustbowl. The caption reads, "Dust storm approaching at 60 mi. per hr." Kerry Noble, an antigovernment extremist convicted in a 1983 plot to blow up the Murrah building as a "declaration of war" against the U.S. government, speculates that the postcard's cryptic message might be that "things were set in motion" by the Oklahoma bombing. "There's another dust storm coming across," he says.[75]

Twenty Oh-Oh: Panic Attack in the Year 2000

McVeigh was a disaffected loner (aren't they all?), a Lee Harvey Oswald for the nineties. He was a man who lived his life in small rooms, to use DeLillo's haunting phrase for Oswald, in his novel *Libra;* a man who tried to cheer himself after his discharge from the Army by sleeping in children's sheets embellished with images of Garfield the Cat. But he's hardly alone. From alien abductions to encounters with angels, recovered memories to multiple personalities, Satanic ritual abuse to serial-killer fandom, "cutting" as abject fashion statement to S&M as mainstream lifestyle option, our media landscape seems to be dominated by solitary obsessions and subcultural crazes, "extraordinary popular delusions and the madness of crowds," as Charles Mackay put it in his classic book of the same name.

Are we on the eve of a new age of unrest and unreason? Or are the visions of excess and premonitions of doom haunting millennial America mere numerology—the same mass manias that have bedeviled the Western world every thousand years? Is there "some sinister hysteria in the air out here tonight, some hint of the monstrous perversion to which any human idea can come," as Joan Didion wondered in *Slouching Towards Bethlehem?*[76] Or is it just the smell of Chaos, the new scent from Donna Karan?

Either/or questions for both/and times. In *Century's End,* his history of the fin-de-siècle as a cultural phenomenon, Hillel Schwartz maintains that "certain cultural constellations come to the fore at the ends of centuries, time and again." One turn-of-the-century theme, he notes, is "dichotomy or doubling," what he calls "janiformity," after the two-faced Roman god Janus, whose twin visages faced in opposite directions.[77] Thus, the answer to the millennial question that echoes through this book—Has the world gone crazy?—is fittingly fin-de-siècle: yes and no. The received opinion that American society is out of control is at once an apocalyptic myth *and* a social reality, a media fiction *and* a fact of everyday life.

As Schwartz points out, the heavy tread of rough beasts slouching toward Bethlehem is heard right about now every hundred years, as are the annunciatory trumpets of the Christian millennium (and, these days, the New Age). "At century's end," he reminds us, "we are inevitably host to an oxymoronic time: the best and the worst, the most desperate and the most exultant; the most constrained and the most chaotic."[78] So far, he notes, "each century's end has been a comedy: we have always made it through, and we have regularly been surprised at just how we did it. Bombast of the 'New Age' on one side, bomb blasts of desperation on the other, the century's end has typically made fools of us even as we have made terrible fools of ourselves."[79] The belief that we are history's witnesses to extremes of social fragmentation and moral malaise, that we stand at critical junctures and teeter on the brink of momentous decisions, is part and parcel of the fin-de-siècle; the fin-de-millennium simply turns up the cultural volume tenfold. The madness and mayhem of the nineties looms larger in our minds because of the numerological juju of the approaching moment when our digital clocks will click up triple zeros (a bit of calendrical hocus-pocus, we should remember, whose deep, dark significance will be lost on the millions who reckon religious time by non-Christian calendars). A wag at *The New Yorker* once suggested we pronounce the first year of the third millennium "twenty oh-oh"—"a nervous name for what is sure to be a nervous year."[80]

At the same time, even the most dedicated debunkers concede that our fin-de-siècle chaos seems more extreme, somehow, than America at the turn of the last century or Europe in the year 1000. "Talk at century's end is always of critical moments and irrevocable decisions," writes Schwartz, "but in these times the choices are etched most starkly as good will or holocaust, ecology or extinction, higher consciousness or the end of (Western) civilization. The millennial pivots seem more razor-edged than ever."[81]

Of course, as he notes elsewhere, the paradises lost and doomsdays deferred of each successive fin-de-siècle have been postponed till the next century's end. Consequently, the accumulated weight of centuries' worth of great expectations bears down on the year 2000. "That we have been preparing for the end of our century further in advance than people in any other century means that those Manichean tensions common to the fin-de-siecle experience will be exaggerated in the 1990s," Schwartz writes. Comparing the end of the twentieth century to a black hole, he asserts, "The millennial year 2000 has gravitational tides of maximal reach. Its entire preceding hundred years, our century, has come to be felt as a final epoch, a time of grotesque extremity, beginning perhaps with the deaths of one hundred thousand horses during the Boer War. By 1945, if not much earlier, the century had become an apocalyptic century."[82]

New World Disorder

Ours *has* been an age of extremes, a turbulent century wracked by two global wars that consumed millions of lives. In those apocalyptic struggles, and in the scattered conflicts, systematic genocides, and ethnic cleansings that have followed, an estimated 187 million people have been killed or allowed to die by human decision, making ours the most murderous century on record.[83] The Second World War was followed by a period of economic growth and social transformation that the historian Eric Hobsbawm believes "probably changed human society more profoundly than any other period of comparable brevity."[84] This golden age came to an end in 1973, when "the world lost its bearings and slid into instability and crisis."[85] We live, he claims, in the "crisis decades": the years from 1973 up to and including the present moment, when the plate-tectonic shifts of globalization and the transition from industrial production to information manipulation have shaken the economic, political, and social structures of the nation-states to their very foundations. This awesome transformation, he contends, is "the greatest, most rapid and most fundamental in recorded history."[86]

The cultural chaos all around us is more than a millennial attack of panic disorder. It's symptomatic of a universal crisis made possible by the postwar emergence, for the first time in history, of a single, increasingly integrated global economy that flows over, under, and around the borders, laws, and ideologies of nation-states. "The tensions of troubled economies have undermined the political systems of liberal democracy, parliamentary or presidential," as well as the political systems of Third World countries, writes Hobsbawm.[87] In a world where everything's connected, economic spasms ripple around the globe with electroshock speed.

The titanic forces of the transnational economy are by their very nature pulling the nation-state apart, while a social and moral crisis, reflecting postwar upheavals in societal structures, is eroding the rationalist and humanist foundations of modern society. And it gets worse, Hobsbawm assures us. Adopting the past tense of a future already upon us, he notes that the philosophical framework that came unglued in the late twentieth century

> was not only one of the assumptions of modern civilization, but also one of the historic structures of human relations which modern society inherited from a pre-industrial and pre-capitalist past, and which, as we can now see, enabled it to function. It was not a crisis of one form of organizing societies, but of all forms.[88]

In fact, then, American culture on the brink of the millennium *is* far from equilibrium. The nation's sense of balance, its belief (however fanciful) in common dreams and a collective destiny, has been thrown permanently out of kilter by the vertigo of global capitalism's New World Order.

Gone are the expectations of lifetime employment with a single employer and a steadily rising standard of living that were the birthright of every American (or at least every white male American) during the postwar Golden Age. Corporate earnings are up, but for many, the American Dream has been permanently downsized. Working Americans have watched real wages fall by 19 percent between 1972 and 1994, and manufacturing jobs migrate to nations where pay is low and labor unions happily nonexistent.[89] Fired white-collar workers are being rehired as "contingent workers" or "permatemps" by the very companies that jettisoned them. They're returning from the dead as contract workers for temp agencies, the health insurance and pension plans of their previous working lives a bitter memory.[90]

For the low-skilled, our burgeoning service sector has jobs to spare in the cubicle purgatory of customer relations, catalogue sales, and telemarketing. And in the lowermost circles of minimum-wage hell, one finds the clerk and cashier positions known as "McJobs" in the underground 'zine of the same name, which defines them as any "low-pay, low-prestige, low-benefit, no-future job in the service sector. Frequently considered a satisfying career choice by people who have never held one."[91] Of course, there are worse fates than jerking java at the local Starbucks: Despite seven years of virtually uninterrupted economic growth, approximately 50 million

Americans, 19 percent of the population, live below the national poverty line, in the Hobbesian state of nature brought to you by free-market economics, where Aid to Families with Dependent Children is a fading memory and health insurance a rich man's fancy.[92]

Meanwhile, happy days are here again for the economic elite who have been well rewarded by the "boom economy" ballyhooed in business magazines. The CEOs at the nation's biggest companies earn an average of $8.7 million a year, and investment income is making the 1 percent of the population who control 38 percent of the nation's assets wealthier than most of us can even imagine.[93] Manufacturers are targeting the status-hungry nouveaux riches with snob-appeal consumer goods: Ford has just doubled production of its upscale sport utility vehicle, the Ford Expedition, while discontinuing four cheaper cars aimed at the less affluent.[94]

The Organization for Economic Cooperation and Development recently reported that "by any measure, the United States has the most unequal distribution of income of any advanced industrialized country."[95] The ever-widening income inequality between the economic elite and the downsized masses—greater, as of 1995, than at any time since the Great Depression—is tearing the fabric of American society to shreds.[96] The former secretary of labor Robert B. Reich has warned of the societal cost of what he terms the "secession of the successful," the withdrawal from public life of an Information Age elite "linked by jet, modem, fax, satellite and fiber-optic cable to the great commercial and recreational centers of the world, but . . . not particularly connected to the rest of the nation."[97] Nor is all secession figurative: Growing numbers of wealthy or solidly middle-class Americans are joining what Edward J. Blakely and Mary Gail Snyder claim, in *Fortress America: Gated Communities in the United States,* are the 8.4 million of their fellow citizens who have walled themselves off in gated communities—gulags for the affluent, with their own private security forces, street maintenance, recreation, and entertainment.

More ominously, the secession of the successful is mirrored by the secession of the disaffected. Wage labor, ill served by politicians who have pledged fealty to corporate contributors, has stayed away from the polls in growing numbers: Between 1960 and 1988, the number of blue-collar voters who turned out for presidential elections fell by a third.[98] On the radical right, "people with no past or future" like the Montana Freemen are retreating into secessionist utopias like the group's Justus Township or backwoods enclaves like the white-separatist community of Elohim City in the Ozarks.[99]

It would be vulgar Marxism to suggest that the wage gap is the sole cause of social atomization and anomie in postindustrial America. But it would be equally blinkered to deny the obvious relationship between the growing inequity of U.S. society and the subterranean river of disillusion and disaffection just beneath the surface of American life. Distrust of the federal government runs deep in the American grain, but it's surely no coincidence that the secessionist, survivalist, and militia movements have drawn their numbers from the downwardly mobile lower middle class, specifically the angry white men whose median wages have been falling for more than two decades. Undeniably, the black helicopters and blue-helmeted U.N. troops that trouble their restless sleep are night terrors brought on by a shifting social landscape, where women in the workplace and the nation's rapidly morphing racial complexion are challenging white male privilege on all fronts. But visions of unmarked helicopters and one-world governments are also specters of the *real* New World Order of global capitalism, where free-trade agreements like NAFTA and GATT have sown the seeds of rage in workers whose factories have closed and whose jobs have been shipped south of the border or overseas. "The American Dream has all but disappeared, substituted with people struggling just to buy next week's groceries," wrote an embittered reader of the Lockport, New York, *Union-Sun & Journal* in 1992. "Do we have to shed blood to reform the current system? I hope it doesn't come to that. But it might."[100] The writer's name was Timothy McVeigh.

The Atrocity Exhibition: Pathological Media, Media Pathologies

In the final analysis, the economic upheaval, social tensions, and moral vertigo of our moment *are* historically unique. The sweeping "economic and techno-scientific process of the development of capitalism, which has dominated the past two or three centuries," has brought us to "a point of historical crisis," writes Hobsbawm.[101]

In addition, the looming millennium makes the shadows of anxiety and unrest creeping across American society seem even darker. As well, our sense of cultural chaos is heightened by another societal condition unique to our times: the oozing insinuation of the mass media, bloblike, into every corner of the public arena and every crevice in the individual unconscious.

Increasingly, the media form the connective tissue of our lives. In the past, says J. G. Ballard, we assumed that the external world represented reality and that our mental worlds were the realm of fantasy. Now, he argues, these roles have been reversed: "We live in a world ruled by fictions of every kind—mass merchandising, advertising, politics conducted as a branch of advertising, . . . the increasing blurring and intermingling of identities within the realm of consumer goods, the preempting of any free or original imaginative response to experience by the television screen."[102] The media landscape we inhabit is a postmodern Coney Island where the real and the unreal, the sublime and the obscene, the horrific and the hilarious commingle freely—a mass-media Luna Park where "thermonuclear weapons systems and soft drink commercials coexist in an overlit realm ruled by advertising and pseudoevents, science and pornography," as Ballard puts it.[103] In *Serial Killers: Death and Life in America's Wound Culture,* Mark Seltzer argues that the media have created a "pathological public sphere" dominated by

> shock and trauma; states of injury and victim status; the wound, the disease, the virus, and epidemics of violence; disaster, accident, catastrophe, and mass death; the abnormal normality of paranoia and psychosis; the pornography of mass-mediated desires and other forms of addiction and artificial life.[104]

We're titillated and terrified by the feeding frenzy du jour and the evening's snuff news, distracted and deadened by the Hollywood hype of the week and the celebrity nonentity of the hour (whatever happened to the Kato Kaelin Global Fan Club?). Public discourse is drowned out by anchorclones maundering on about the incriminating stain on Monica Lewinsky's dress, the distinguishing characteristic on the presidential penis, the electronic canonization of Lady Di.

There's a fearful synergy at work these days, in which the tabloid pathologies produced by our manic media are sensationalized by those same media—amplified and echoed back at us in an ever-faster feedback loop. Copy-cat criminals, celebrity stalkers, O. J. Simpson trial addicts, and the hate-radio callers and afternoon talk-show audiences who abandon themselves to ritualized orgies of scapegoating remind us that we live more and more inside a mass-media echo chamber. Michael Macias, a Long Island high school football player, was run over and nearly cut in half by a car when he lay down in the middle of a busy highway in imitation of a scene in the movie *The Program*. After seeing *Natural Born Killers* six times, Nathan Martinez shaved his head and donned tinted shades in homage to one of the movie's serial killers. Arrested for blowing away his stepmother and half-sister, he reportedly observed, "It's nothing like the movies." On the other side of the looking-glass, reality-based fantasy becomes fantasy-based reality: pulp fiction made flesh.

Perhaps the ultimate media pathology is the on-camera suicide, an overlit nightmare that crosses Paddy Chayefsky's *Network* with *Faces of Death*. On the morning of July 15, 1974, Chris Chubak, the anchorwoman of a Sarasota, Florida, show called *Seacoast Digest,* greeted her viewers with an unscripted announcement. "In keeping with Channel 40's policy of bringing you the latest in blood and guts in living color," she said, "you're going to see another first—an attempt at suicide." Pulling out a gun, she put it to her head and blew her brains out on camera.[105]

It bears noting that those who lay the blame at the media's feet for the actions of the desperately despondent, the sociopathic, or the fatally stupid make common cause with moral crusaders like Bob Dole, William Bennett, and Michael Medved. The belief that the media should be made safe for the Michael Maciases and Nathan Martinezes of the world is no less ludicrous than the notion that the Internet should be child-proofed on behalf of Barney and his charges. Such arguments are founded on a Hunekerian vision of the masses as an impulsive, impressionable booboisie (tube-oisie?) in need of moral stewardship and intellectual guidance from its betters. More egregiously, the shoot-the-messenger argument shifts the burden of responsibility from the individual, his or her legal guardians, and the very social welfare agencies defunded by conservatives like Dole to that reliable straw man, the media.

That said, there's no denying that tabloid news and Hollywood slaughterfests thrive on social pathologies. Obviously, it's moral myopia of the first order to argue that the Fox network and Time Warner conjure such pathologies out of thin air, as if economic inequity and social injustice had no hand in their creation. But it's equally willful blindness to deny that splatter news and big-screen bloodbaths not only feed on but to some degree amplify social pathologies.

A 1994 issue of the *Media Culture Review,* a publication of the Institute for Alternative Journalism, notes that crime rates have been "essentially flat" for a decade, but that the number of crime-related stories on network newscasts in 1993 "more than doubled from the previous year, a level of coverage completely out of proportion with the crime rate. And the number of murder stories more than tripled."[106] In 1994, George Gerbner, dean emeritus at the University of Pennsylvania's Annenberg School for Communications, conducted a study of the social impact of TV violence. He concluded that "heavy viewers are more likely than comparable groups of light viewers to overestimate one's chances of involvement in violence; to believe that one's neighborhood is unsafe; to state that fear of crime is a very serious personal problem; and to assume that crime is rising, regardless of the facts of the case. . . . Other results show that heavy viewers are also more likely to have bought new locks, watchdogs, and guns for protection."[107]

"McLuhan predicted the global village," said J. G. Ballard, in 1989, "but what he didn't predict was this extreme volatility and nervousness." Ballard hazarded a prediction of his own. "I see the world of the nineties being swept by media blizzards of excitement and panic," he said. "The average individual will be unable to predict what's going to happen in the next ten minutes, which produces a retreat inward or a turning towards some of the less attractive defenses. You'll see people resorting to the extreme measure and the extreme metaphor much more quickly than they ever did in the past. *Blue Velvet* offers a much more accurate vision of the future than *Blade Runner:* You have this ordinary American suburb which is populated by people like the Dennis Hopper character, Frank, with motives of the most unpredictable and extreme kind shafting through people's lives."[108]

A decade later, Ballard's words seem premonitory, and the window display of a video store on Haight Street, in San Francisco, seems like a sign of the times. A veritable pantheon of alt.culture demigods, it features T-shirts silkscreened with the images of the affectless killers from *Reservoir Dogs;* Al Pacino as the blood-drunk mobster in *Scarface;* Marlon Brando as the unhinged Colonel Kurtz in *Apocalypse Now;* Jack Nicholson as the leering, mugging psycho-dad in *The Shining;* Henry, the shock-haired weirdo in *Eraserhead;* John Hurt as the hideously deformed *Elephant Man;* and, of course, Dennis Hopper as Frank, the charismatic sociopath in *Blue Velvet.* Late in the twentieth century, these are our household deities.

In many ways, ours is the America Coney foretold at the turn of the last century. Coney prefigured our pop-goes-the-psycho-killer appetite for violence and horror in morally uplifting horror shows like Hell Gate and simulated disasters such as The Fall of Pompeii and Fire and Flames, which featured the burning of a four-story building. Our current fixation with human oddities like the Elephant Man or self-made weirdos like Henry had its counterpart in Coney's Freak Street. Dreamland had Samuel Gumpertz's Congress of Curious People, an assembly of "living wonders" from all over the world; we have *The Weekly World News, The Jerry Springer Show,* and "Hank, the Angry Drunken Dwarf," a Howard Stern regular who garnered 208,000 votes, in an on-line poll, for one of *People* magazine's "50 Most Beautiful People."

More broadly, the mass consumer culture Coney celebrated, with its infantile psychology and its bourgeois anxieties, is still very much with us. Then, too, the fat raspberry that Steeplechase's "funny face" blew at Enlightenment reason heralded the twentieth century's embrace of chaos and nonlinearity in physics, the accidental and the irrational in avant-garde art. Luna's rejection of the pompous monumentality of Beaux Arts architecture for a zany eclecticism presaged the playful kleptomania of postmodernism: Arata Isozaki's Team Disney building and Michael Graves's Dolphin Hotel at Disney World owe an obvious debt to the "Free Renaissance" aesthetic of the Luna designer Frederic Thompson. On a deeper level, our head-first immersion in artificial worlds can be seen, in its embryonic state, in Coney's simulated sleigh rides through the Swiss Alps and submarine voyages to the bottom of the sea, and in the unabashed artificiality of the parks' dreamlike environments. The real-life grand guignol of local news and Fox Television shockumentaries like *When Animals Attack* has its inauspicious precedent in the much-publicized electrocution of an aging elephant named Topsy, a grotesque entertainment provided, at Coney, by Thomas Edison.

But it's the Coneyesque contrast between escapist simulation and social reality, democratic promise and corporate oligarchy that truly makes millennial America a pyrotechnic insanitarium. Turn-of-the-century commentators hailed Coney as a crucible of democratic egalitarianism, its carnivalesque spirit and seething crowds melting down differences of class, race, and nationality. One journalist lauded the "frank assumption of equality" at

Coney, where "bare human nature, naïve and unashamed, stands up . . . and cries out 'Brother.'"[109] But outside the island's dream world, where the robber barons ruled and the gross economic and social inequities of the Gilded Age were in full force, "bare human nature" wore a social Darwinian face.

Now, at the turn of another century, we're running the same program again: the Gilded Age, version 2.0. Once again, American society is profoundly imperiled by a yawning chasm between the obscenely wealthy and the chronically overdrawn, between sublime fantasy and sordid reality. In places like Medina, Washington, near Microsoft headquarters, and Woodside and Atherton in Silicon Valley, the prosperous few are building cybermansions in apparent homage to their robber-baron forebears.

Charles Simonyi, Microsoft's chief programmer, lives in the 20,500-square-foot, $10 million bachelor pad that he wished into existence on the shores of Lake Washington. It's a futuristic apparition plunked down amid natural beauty, with an enclosed swimming pool, a private computer lab, and a Jetsonian nervous system that turns off the lights, shuts down the fireplace, and adjusts the blinds when Simonyi turns in for the night. In contrast to Simonyi's techno-villa, Lawrence J. Ellison, the billionaire founder of the Oracle Corporation, is building a $40 million, 23-acre shrine to the archaic. His Japanese retreat in Woodside will feature a "moon house" for meditative moments, a hot tub nestled in a cast-bronze boulder, and a compound with hand-adzed beams and walls of Okabe clay, the better to soak up the house's "physical and spiritual energy," according to Ellison's designer-builder.[110] In Atherton, Intuit's cofounder Tom Proulx and his wife, Barbara, are expanding their English country house into a 10-acre estate with formal gardens and a golf course. They're also wiring it for "smart house" features like Simonyi's. At a house-wrecking party to tear down a fifties-style house that stood between them and their dreams of empire, the Proulxes donned hard hats and whacked golf balls through the picture windows, just for fun.

Simonyi, Ellison, the Proulxes, and the rest of the megarich geek elite are the Vanderbilts, Carnegies, and Morgans of our day. On the eve of the year 2000, their America is the land of the long boom. But for the cash-strapped many, the Shining City on a Hill looks more and more like a burning Dreamland.

In *Circus Americanus,* Ralph Rugoff's deliberation on what might be called the *virtualization* of reality in contemporary America, a Las Vegas casino owner waxes philosophical. "There's only so far you can go from reality before it becomes either a nightmare or a cartoon," he says.[111] But if you go a little further, you arrive at the pyrotechnic insanitarium of nineties America, a giddy whirl of euphoric horror where cartoon and nightmare melt into one.

A USER'S GUIDE TO *THE* PYROTECHNIC INSANITARIUM

The Pyrotechnic Insanitarium is a collection of essays. Each refracts the mega-trends and microshifts of American culture late in the twentieth century through the prism of a mass fad, a subcultural craze, a pop archetype, a work of art, a TV show, a corporate enterprise, a technological breakthrough, or the night-vision world-view of a mad bomber, a millennial cult, a conspiratorial underground.

Readers expecting point-by-point exposition and the methodical accumulation of evidence, building to a full-throated peroration in which every loose end is tied up and every hidden truth revealed, are advised to abandon hope before entering. An attempt to plot the nonlinear dynamics of millennial America, *The Pyrotechnic Insanitarium* is by necessity as perverse and polymorphous as its subject. Shapeshifting between antithetical positions and inconsistent styles, digressing wildly (and without apology), it's a product of its multitasking, channel-switching, Web-surfing times.

In a sense, *The Pyrotechnic Insanitarium* embodies the cultural logic of the fin-de-millennium, when postmodern critics talk the talk of post-Freudian, "anti-Oedipal" psychology, of "boundary dissolution" and "liquid subjectivity" and the "decentered" self. The philosopher Gilles Deleuze, *the* voguish thinker of the '90s, opined, "We are habits, nothing but habits. The habit of saying 'I.'"[1] For that matter, why accept the received truth that such a thing as language even exists? ask Deleuze and his collaborator Felix Guattari, in *A Thousand Plateaus*. There is no language per se, they contend, "only a throng of dialects, patois, slangs, and specialized languages."[2] The only thing holding the "essentially heterogeneous reality" of the mother tongue together is a collective act of will.

Likewise, the end of the twentieth century is a time when post-modernists like the novelist Robert Coover and the literary critic George P. Landow see in hypertext programs a means of dethroning the authority of the author and, by implication, the very notion of hierarchy. "Hypertext programs and the Net are webs of footnotes without central points, organizing principles, hierarchies," writes the feminist cyber-theorist Sadie Plant.[3] In Plant's mind, such technologies invert the traditional hierarchy of center over margins. Fatefully, the footnote and its close cousin the endnote *do* seem to be encroaching, kudzu-like, on the main narrative or argument. In recent books like *Mr. Wilson's Cabinet of Wonder* by Lawrence Weschler, a full fourth of which consists of whimsical, divagating endnotes, and David Foster Wallace's *Infinite Jest,* where even the endnotes have footnotes, the end matter threatens to overgrow the main body of the book entirely.

While that's hardly the case in this book, *The Pyrotechnic Insanitarium* is a Gutenbergian artifact that rewards nonlinear reading and welcomes readers at ease with mental hyper-links—far-flung, associative leaps of logic. It's tuned to the keynote assumption of our age of Nets and Webs and massively parallel Connection Machines—namely, that information exists not in discrete atoms of fact but in synergistic meshworks and unexpected juxtapositions. As Gregory Bateson famously observed, "Information consists of differences that make a difference."[4] In turn, noted Marshall McLuhan, "when information is brushed against information, the results are startling and effective."[5] *The Pyrotechnic Insanitarium* is an obsolete hunk of dead-tree hardware that went to sleep and dreamed it was a Web page.

Which, of course, it (and every other book) always was, as Foucault pointed out, years before hypertext or the Net. "The frontiers of a book," he wrote, "are never clear-cut: beyond the title, the first lines, and the last full stop, beyond its internal configuration and its autonomous form, it is caught up in a system of references to other books, other texts, other sentences: it is a node within network."[6]

1 / HAVE AN ANGST DAY: THE *SCREAM* MEME

I scream, you scream, we all scream for Munch's *Scream:* Inflatable angst in the Age of Irony.
On the Wall Productions, Inc./ Photo by Keeven Photography, St. Louis, MO.

A specter is haunting pop culture—a wild-eyed figure, hands clapped to his head, mouth contorted in a silent shriek of angst.

Amid the social fragmentation and moral free fall of the late twentieth century, Edvard Munch's fin-de-siècle painting *The Scream* (1893) seems suddenly relevant. In true nineties fashion, the tormented face of one man's despair and alienation has been resurrected and pressed into service, through pop culture pastiche and parody, as the poster child for self-mocking millennial dread. Once shorthand for the Age of Anxiety, Munch's Screamer has been updated for the age of terminal irony as a manic-depressive version of *Saturday Night Live*'s Mr. Bill. Generic-faced and gender-neutral, the Screamer is a ready-made sign of the times: a Smiley face with an ontological migraine.

As an ironic icon, Munch's tormented Screamer is the Smiley's dark double. (It's also a close cousin of that other ambassador of alien nation, the almond-eyed E.T. of Whitley Strieber fame. The National U.F.O. Museum in San Francisco displays a copy of *The Scream* in its window, accompanied by the caption "Norwegian Alien," and ufologist Phil Patton calls the ubiquitous Strieber alien "an echo of Munch's *Scream*—the very face of modern angst!")[1]

Like *The Scream,* the Smiley lends itself to cultural poaching. The glazed, goofy face originated as a lapel button for the feelin' groovy gang in the sixties (a veiled reference, perhaps, to electric Kool-Aid by way of its obvious resemblance to the cartoon face on the Kool-Aid pitcher?). In the early seventies, Middle America appropriated the symbol, which soon became an emblem of lobotomized good cheer. Around 1988, fans of acid house music resurrected and refunctioned it as in-crowd code for the pie-eyed bliss brought on by the drug Ecstasy, a meaning underscored by the bullet hole that often embellished Smiley's forehead. To ravers, the moon face with the knowing grin symbolized the liquefaction of the ego through drugs, nonstop dancing, and immersion in a seething cauldron of hot bod-ies—a heady mix of "carnal frenzy" and "surging crowds" similar in spirit to the Coney Island that overwhelmed Joseph Stella. In *Generation Ecstasy: Into the World of Techno and Rave Culture,* Simon Reynolds calls Ecstasy a "rem-edy for the alienation caused by an atomized society."[2]

If *The Scream* is our all-purpose symbol of alienation, the ravers' Smiley is the cartoon muse of a cure (if only a temporary, pharmaceuti-cal one) for the dislocation and disillusion of modern life. True to Hillel Schwartz's observation that end-of-the-century cultures abound in images of duality, the Screamer and the Smiley are yin-and-yang opposites and each in turn is Janus-faced, displaying its surface meaning or another, more ironic aspect, depending on the cultural context.

The anguished Munch-kin first caught the media eye in 1988, when a shirt emblazoned with *The Scream* and the spine-chilling phrase PRESIDENT QUAYLE" embodied liberals' worst nightmare. But it took Macaulay Culkin's are-we-having-fun-yet? impersonation of the Screamer in the ad blitz for the hugely successful *Home Alone* (1990) to implant the image in pop con-sciousness. Since then, the icon has proved to have legs, as the pundits say. Infesting coffee mugs, mousepads, keychains, wallpaper, switch plates, and the warning icons and "panic buttons" in computer programs, Munch's Screamer has attained the status of a cultural virus—what the evolutionary biologist Richard Dawkins calls a "meme."

About memes: The analogy between cultural and genetic transmis-sion was popularized by Dawkins, who coined the term "meme" for ideas that infect a culture by leaping from one host brain to another, in much the same way that viruses travel from body to body. A meme is a "unit of cul-tural transmission," he writes, in his 1989 book *The Selfish Gene.* "Examples of memes are tunes, ideas, catchphrases, clothes fashions, ways of making pots or of building arches."[3]

Since it's virtually the only word for the information viruses in-festing our media landscape, Dawkins's neat little piece of intellectual code has itself proved highly contagious. Unfortunately, it's badly in need of ideological debugging. By clothing social reality in biological metaphor, the meme transforms culture into nature. It's a tricky move, in light of the intellectual history of the twentieth century, which is littered with nasty ideas about gender, race, and class passing themselves off as laws of nature. Social Darwinism, the pseudo-evolutionary theory that undergirded the ruthless self-interest of Gilded Age capitalists like Carnegie and Rockefeller, is an infamous example of this sort of thinking.

A century later, genetic determinism is back with a vengeance, riding the coattails of genetics' emergence as *the* cutting-edge science and growth industry—of the coming millennium. The air is thick with talk of gene therapy and genetic screening, and biology-is-destiny arguments have crept back from the shadows to which they were banished by the stigma of Nazi eugenics. The 1994 best-seller lists included *The Bell Curve,* which promotes the noxious theory that the social and economic dominance of America's largely white "cognitive elite" over an overwhelmingly nonwhite, I.Q.-deficient criminal underclass is the product of superior genes, not social conditions. In such times, we're well advised to view sociobiological concepts like the meme with some wariness. I use the term throughout this book because it's virtually unavoidable, but I use it advisedly.

The *Scream* meme seems to be everywhere these days. "Hope your birthday's a SCREAM!" the Screamer shrieks on a birthday card. The marathon runner Andrea Bowman pledged allegiance to the no-pain, no-gain ethos of hard-core jockdom by having *The Scream* tattooed on her leg. The political cartoonist Rob Rogers put a face on the heartland horror of the Oklahoma bombing by transplanting *Scream* heads onto the dour farmers in Grant Wood's *American Gothic.* In one of its best-known incarnations, *The Scream* serves as a wacky conversation piece in homes and offices across America in the form of the inflatable *Scream* and *Scream* Jr. dolls sold by On the Wall Productions. (Covering every psychological base, the company even sells a talisman against millennial angst, a smiley-faced figurine named Little Happy Guy.) And, in the loftiest tribute a consumer society knows, Munch's angst-racked Everyman has even been transformed into a TV pitchman—a Ray-Banned swinger in a computer-animated spot for the Pontiac Sunfire, a car that "looks like a work of art" and "drives like a real scream." Most famously, of course, the painting inspired the Halloween mask worn by the teen-ocidal slasher in Wes Craven's *Scream:* a baleful skull whose elongated gape makes it look like a Munch head modeled in Silly Putty.

The Scream strikes a sympathetic chord because we, like Munch, are adrift at the end of a century, amid profound societal change and philosophical chaos, when all the old unsinkable certitudes seem to be going the way of the *Titanic*. But whereas Munch's existential gloom and doom were a psychological affair, deeply rooted in his mother's untimely death and the hellfire Christianity of his stern father, our millennial anxiety is more public than private, the toxic runoff of information overload: worries about contaminated food and sexually transmitted diseases and flesh-eating viruses, apocalyptic visions inspired by the millennium computer bug, mounting concerns over global warming, fear of domestic terrorism, paranoia about nightstalking pedophiles and teenage "superpredators," recovered memories of satanic ritual abuse and alien abduction, premonitions of black helicopters over America.

Even so, the Screamer does feel our private pain in one important regard: It incarnates the everyday uncertainties of the endangered middle class. The Screamer is an unsmiley face for the group that Robert Reich calls the "anxious class, most of whom hold jobs but are justifiably uneasy about their own standing and fearful for their children's futures."[4] In *Middle Class Dreams,* by Stanley Greenberg, poll respondents offer a guided tour of the social and economic ruins left behind by Reaganomics. The middle class, they believe, is being crushed by mounting debt, despite the fact that both parents are working long hours, "sacrificing family life, and putting children at risk, but only to pay for basics, not to really get ahead."[5] There's near consensus among those interviewed that their children will inherit a minimum-wage future in which owning a home and even obtaining a college education may be beyond their means. Thus, there's a cultural logic to the political cartoon portraying the Screamer as "John Q. Public," clutching a pink slip, and to the book review that uses *The Scream* to illustrate the point that the downsized, belt-tightening middle class hides its financial worries. "They don't clap palms against cheeks, in the Edvard Munch style, and scream bloody frightened murder," writes the reviewer.[6]

But while *The Scream* is a ready-made emblem of middle-class fears, it's all wrong for the multitasking, split-screen psychology of our wired world. *The Scream* personifies the introverted, alienated psychology of modernism, a psychology literalized in Munch's painting by the roughly circular movement of the viewer's eye, which makes the world literally revolve around the solipsistic Screamer. More accurately, the Screamer *is* its world. In *The Scream,* the subjective has swallowed the objective; the Screamer's emotions color everything we see, dying the landscape strange colors, twisting it into alien shapes. The swirling sky, the undulating hills, the shimmying, wraithlike body of the Screamer itself: Everything in *The Scream* vibrates with the psychic shriek of the hysterical Screamer.

By contrast, the postmodern self is thoroughly colonized by the media reality outside it. In Oliver Stone's *Natural Born Killers,* for example, the exteriorized subconscious of *The Scream* has been turned inside out. In Munch's proto-Expressionist painting, the Screamer's mental anguish engulfs the world around him; in Stone's movie, the white noise of the mass media rushes into the psychological vacuums inside the characters, drowning out their mental voices. Childhood memories are relived as an imaginary sitcom, complete with laugh track. Nature has been replaced by second nature: the world outside the characters' windows consists of flickering TV images. Celebrity is the only real life, reflection in the camera eye the only confirmation that the self truly exists.

Postmodern psychology is a product of the movement from McLuhan's Gutenberg Galaxy into the postliterate world of electronic media. McLuhan argued that the psyche as we know it—the sharply demarcated, inward-turning ego of the modern age—is a by-product of the print medium. The printing press "created the portable book, which men could read in privacy and in isolation from others." This, in turn, fostered "the new cult of individualism. The private, fixed point of view became possible and literacy conferred the power of detachment, non-involvement."[7]

Our transition from book culture to screen culture is marked by the collapse of the critical distance between the inner self and the interface, by our immersion—perhaps even dissolution—in the ever-accelerating maelstrom of the media spectacle. In *Postmodernism,* Fredric Jameson characterizes this shift as one in which "the alienation of the subject is displaced by the latter's fragmentation."[8] The book gave us the bounded, centered self; interactive, immersive media like hypertext, multi-user domains (MUDs), and virtual reality give us the unbounded, decentered selves postmodern theorists are always talking about. The psychology of the modern age—Munch's age—was centripetal; postmodern psychology is centrifugal.

Of course, deconstructing the "I" has been a popular philosophical pastime ever since David Hume declared the self "nothing but a bundle or collection of different perceptions, which succeed each other with inconceivable rapidity, and are in a perpetual flux and movement."[9] But now the self is subject to a data deluge beyond Hume's wildest imaginings, a media bombardment that is distracting and disorienting us with breaking news, weekend updates, talk-show banter, radio chatter, taglines, catchphrases, voice-mail, e-mail. Information overload is spinning the ego off its axis.

At the same time, our growing interaction with computers and our increasing interchanges with others through computers is blurring the boundaries between self and other, human and machine. Sherry Turkle, a clinical psychologist who has given much thought to our interaction with computers, believes that headfirst immersion in the simulated worlds inside computers is challenging the accepted definition of the self as a fixed, stable identity.

Postmodern Angst: The Screamer as Multiple Personality, by neo-surrealist Ron English. Copyright © 1999 Ron English / www.popaganda.com.

The on-line role-playing that takes place in MUDs is a textbook example. "When each player can create many characters in many games, the self is not only decentered but multiplied without limit," writes Turkle. She quotes a devoted MUDder named Doug:

> Doug talks about playing his characters in [Microsoft-type on-screen windows] and says that using windows has made it possible for him to "turn pieces of my mind on and off. I split my mind. . . . I can see myself as being two or three or more. And I just turn on one part of my mind and then another when I go from window to window. I'm in some kind of argument in one window and trying to come on to a girl in a MUD in another, and another window might be running a spreadsheet program or some other technical thing for school. . . . And then I'll get a real-time message that flashes on the screen as soon as it is sent from another system user, and I guess that's RL [real life]. RL is just one more window, and it's not usually my best one."[10]

Pulling a philosophical U-turn, Turkle offers the hope that our increasing immersion in virtual realities will integrate our egos rather than disintegrate them, helping us "achieve a vision of a multiple but integrated identity whose flexibility, resilience, and capacity for joy comes from having access to our many selves."[11]

Others are less sanguine about the longtime psychological effects of out-of-body experiences in virtual worlds. "I think people are going to feel an increased fragmentation of self," says the human resources consultant Philip Nicholson. "They won't be able to hold the pieces together. How do you keep a coherent space if you're going in and out of spaces that don't exist?" He analogizes the symptoms of information overload to posttraumatic stress syndrome: "Our whole environment has become so complex that we live our lives in splinters. For each splinter, someone reflects back to us, but it's difficult to find someone who reflects back the whole sense of who we are."[12]

Obviously, the postmodern self isn't immune to alienation. But while Munch's alienation sprang from the existential fear that he was a drifting speck in a godless cosmos (after all, his contemporary, Nietzsche, had just pronounced God dead), ours arises from a spreading sense of isolation in a world where "reaching out and touching someone" means, more often than not, talking to a message machine. As growing numbers join the more than 9 million Americans who telecommute to their corporate workplaces and the 14.2 million who work out of their homes, the loneliness of the long-distance worker is becoming legend.[13] Loneliness is a constant companion for telecommuters and the self-employed, whose lifeline to the world outside their electronic cottages is a fiber-optic cable. According to a national survey by the corporate consultants Link Resources, isolation was the worst of the five drawbacks to telecommuting cited by home-based workers who had opted to return to the office.[14]

A sense of disconnection haunts the wired life, despite the fact that "we're all connected," as a New York Telephone ad insisted. The photographer Steven Meisel plugged in to this feeling in his celebrated Calvin Klein ads, in which young, upscale white people stand around, exuding a fashionable lassitude, their blank gazes never meeting. Staring out at us with empty mannequin eyes, they seem to mock our own isolation and alienation, implicit in the ersatz togetherness fostered by "event movies" like *Titanic,* the desperate loneliness of that dorky AOL feature that asks if I'm wondering whether anyone from my "Buddy List" is on-line, the hollow promise that we can go home again via virtual communities on electronic bulletin boards.

Despite our blithe appropriation of *The Scream,* then, we're worlds apart, psychologically, from Munch's fin-de-siècle Screamer. Munch's was the age of anxiety, plagued by nineteenth-century maladies like hysteria, neurasthenia, melancholy, and morbidity. Ours is the age of irony, of Dennis Miller and Fox Muldur, *Talk Soup* and *Pop-Up Video, Scream* and *Seinfeld.* After viewing an exhibition of fin-de-siècle art, Munch's paintings among them, the postmodern theorist Arthur Kroker decided that what's missing from the fin-de-millennium is genuine melancholy. "The notion of melancholia as an authentic form of longing and remembrance" has been "eviscerated" by entertainment media, says Kroker.[15] In these deadpan, knowing times, we feel like telling Munch's black-clad hysteric to drop some Prozac and *shallow up,* already. The movie critic David Denby notes that the new generation of postliterate, media-savvy moviegoers

> go blank whenever their older friends, through some lapse of
> decorum, speak of the moral valence of a given piece of behav-
> ior in a movie. . . . Lighten *up,* they say. After all, these are

just images. . . . That [these same moviegoers] can sit through
the cartoon violence of *Replacement Killers* without annoyance
suggests not dissociation but a set of responses learned from
the media, at a safe remove, before they are learned from life.[16]

Denby's moviegoers are a lot like the characters in Wes Craven's
Scream, a movie about a Munch-masked psychopath with a Blockbuster
clerk's knowledge of slasher movies who puts it to twisted use, carving up
teenage girls in tight shirts. A self-consciously ironic slasher movie, *Scream*
walks the knife edge between deconstruction and disembowelment, manic
humor and gut-bucket horror. As the body count rises, the teenage characters banter facetiously about whether or not movie violence breeds real-
life evils. They ponder the existential brainteaser of the Quentin Tarantino
era: Are we living in a movie? In *Scream*'s media–fun house reality, there's
no question: The killer stages the movie's opening slaughterfest as a game
show from hell; later, one deranged character kills one of his teenage bud-
dies, then quips, "'We all go a little mad sometimes'—Anthony Perkins,
Psycho." In one giddily postmodern sequence, we watch a tabloid TV crew
watching a live, hidden-camera feed of the teenagers watching the slashers
genre classic, *Halloween*. This is the moment when the philosopher Jean
Baudrillard's portentous pronouncement that "the real is no longer real"
becomes a sight gag. The teens theorize the golden rules of the slasher genre,
whose transgression is inevitably met with messy retribution ("Never, ever,
ever, under any circumstances, say, 'I'll be right back!'"). Of course, they
break the rules and meet horribly gory ends, since life really *is* a movie.
Scream ends in an over-the-top denouement that is equal parts grand guignol
and Three Stooges routine (like the gore-soaked screwball comedy of Tarantino's *Reservoir Dogs*). The bogeyman is graphically dispatched and the in-
trepid ingenue lives to see a new day. True to the genre, however, an even
more unspeakable horror waits in the wings: Tori Spelling will play the girl
in the movie version of her living nightmare.

Denby worries that "a good part of the young audience wants the
euphoria of weightlessness, of not feeling a thing ('I *hate* drama,' a friend
of my 14-year-old son told me with some heat)."[17] This delight in the delivery from depth, from the dead weight of content, is quintessentially
postmodern. Behind it lurks the dream of liberation from any ties to embodied reality, into the Luna Parks and Dreamlands of the mind, be they

mainstream media or the virtual worlds of the Net. Ever since the invention of photography, images tethered to the material world have yearned
to float free of referentiality. In the prophetic words of Oliver Wendell
Holmes, photography rendered matter "of no great use any longer, except
as the mold on which form is shaped."[18] But Denby, a man of the book
despite his role as film critic, "cannot shake the naïve habit of reacting to
images as if they actually referred to something."[19] In contrast, the generation of moviegoers raised on TV, videogames, and the PC has grown up in
a world where, more and more, images refer only to other images. Denby's
son's friend is at home in the world of disembodied images, playing slip 'n'
slide on a slick of pure surface: self-conscious quotes, appropriated styles,
glib asides.

Utterly unlike the hypersensitive Munchian self, this new psychology is characterized by what Fredric Jameson calls a "waning of affect"—
the vertiginous experience of emotions as "free-floating and impersonal"
sensations "dominated by a peculiar kind of euphoria."[20] This affectlessness
is partly the result of what J. G. Ballard calls "the preempting of any free or
original imaginative response to experience by the television screen."[21] Andy
Warhol, who aspired to a TV-age autism, memorably observed that "once
you see emotions from a certain angle you can never think of them as real
again."[22]

Like Denby, Jameson thinks this psychological weightlessness, at
once terrifying and exhilarating, is the result of our inability to distinguish
between reality and media simulation. He likens it to that split-second when
you can't tell the difference between the photorealistic mannequins in a
Duane Hanson installation and the museum goers among them. In that instant of profound disorientation, says Jameson, the world "momentarily loses
its depth and threatens to become a glossy skin, a stereoscopic image, a rush
of filmic images without density."[23] It's paradigmatic of life lived in the mass-
media centrifuge, where everything, from hemorrhoid-treatment ads to
televised suicides, carries equal weight and where it's getting more and more
difficult to tell the virtual from the actual. Call it Angst Lite.

Jameson calls it the "camp sublime"—camp in the sense that camp
delights in depthlessness, celebrates surface; sublime in the sense that this
"peculiar euphoria" is the postmodern equivalent, for Jameson, of what
Edmund Burke called "the Sublime"—the vertiginous loss of self in the
presence of nature's awful grandeur.

Intriguingly, *The Scream* was inspired by an experience that has all the earmarks of the sublime. "I was walking along the road with two friends," Munch recalled. "The sun set. The sky became a bloody red. And I felt a touch of melancholy. I stood still, leaned on the railing, dead tired. Over the blue-black fjord and city hung blood and tongues of fire. My friends walked on and I stayed behind, trembling with fright. And I felt a great unending scream passing through nature."[24]

Munch's nameless dread suits our millennial mood just fine, but his nineteenth-century melancholia and gloomy introspection are out of tune with our TV irony, our postmodern affect, and the media circus atmosphere of the late twentieth century. A brooding consumptive like Munch, haunted by the death of God, fear of hereditary madness, and the advancing shadow of his own mortality, looks thoroughly out of place against the smirking irony and flip nihilism of our age. It's the difference between the solitary madness of Van Gogh cutting off his ear and the farcical nightmare of Mike Tyson biting off Evander Holyfield's, live and in your living room. Thus, while Munch's Screamer is the perfect totem for our pop angst, we perceive his overwrought hysteria as campy, which may be why he's ended up on a *Scream*-patterned dress worn by the drag comedian Dame Edna, who insists that the schmatte-clad androgyne is really yelling, "Oh no, I've lost my earrings."

The *Scream* meme suggests that we're so ironic that we can't even take our own apocalypse—our lurking sense, on the eve of the future, of social disintegration and simmering discontent—seriously. This is the moment Walter Benjamin warned us of, when humankind's "self-alienation" reaches "such a degree that it can experience its own destruction as an aesthetic pleasure of the first order."[25] We see our own alienation reflected in the dead eyes of Meisel's living mannequins, and think it chic—in an ironic sort of way, of course. In the cynical nineties, says Arthur Kroker, "Melancholy itself becomes a kind of commodity."[26]

For years now, the Denbys of the world have lectured us on the alienating effects of skinning the image from the meat of the matter. A long parade of impassioned critics, from Mark Crispin Miller ("The Hipness Unto Death") to Leslie Savan (*The Sponsored Life*) to David Foster Wallace ("E Unibus Pluram: The Television and U.S. Fiction"), have warned us that irony is a leaky prophylactic against consumerism, conformity, and other social diseases spread by advertising and dumb-and-dumber entertainment fare. "TV preempts derision by itself evincing endless irony," writes Miller. It "protects its ads from mockery by doing all the mocking, thereby posing as an ally to the incredulous spectator."[27] Embracing TV irony is a way of reassuring ourselves that we're in on the joke, says Miller, while simultaneously enabling us to laugh at "the earnest, groggy hipness of the past." At the same time, he maintains, it's a commercial inoculation against critical analysis of the medium and the message.

Critical distance is hard to come by for those of us nursed at the glass teat from earliest infancy. Irony is our birthright: the knowing quotes with which we frame our hit-movie slogans and advertising buzz phrases are our way of distancing our media selves from our true selves (whatever remains of them, that is). The earnest, sober-sided sensibility extolled by Miller is founded on an unshakable faith in the authentic self behind the TV affect and the ultimate truth behind the whirl of images. It seems jarringly out of place in our ever more virtual reality. Irony may be a "leaky condom" as a defense against the advertising virus, as Leslie Savan argues, but it's the only way the generations raised on TV know of preventing themselves from being sucked, *Poltergeist*-like, into the vast wasteland on the other side of the screen.

Besides, what's the alternative? The zero-forehead "optimism meme" ballyhooed by *Wired* founder-publisher Louis Rossetto in the magazine's January 1998 issue? "Is there a happiness gene, and is it dominant?" he asks, offering a decoupage-plaque Deep Thought that sounds like E. O. Wilson's idea of a daily affirmation—the sociobiological version of "Today is the first day of the rest of your life." It's the philosophical equivalent of the new Clinique perfume, Happy, promoted in ads featuring a radiantly white young woman in a white void, dressed all in white, laughing uproariously about absolutely nothing. Calculated to make even Dr. Pangloss cringe with embarrassment, *Wired*'s "happiness gene" offers free-floating optimism as our last, best alternative to free-floating anxiety.

So think of postmodern irony as passive resistance. "With postmodernism, as with drugs and pornography, the only way to get anywhere is to immerse yourself in it as much as possible, as mindlessly and abjectly as possible, and then just sit back and enjoy it," writes the cultural critic Steven Shaviro.[28] (But he's being *ironic*, isn't he?)

Arthur Kroker himself is a prime specimen of this sensibility. When he opines that our "panic culture" is a "floating reality" in which the actual world seems increasingly like a "dream world, where we live on the edge of ecstasy and dread," we have the sneaking suspicion that the "ironic" distance between his giddy tone and his pessimistic politics isn't ironic at all— that he looks forward to cultural meltdown with the eagerness of someone who's got comp tickets to the apocalypse.[29] Settling into his moving vehicle for a theme-park ride through a millennial moment where "what is truly fascinating is the thrill of catastrophe," he eagerly awaits "the ecstatic implosion of postmodern culture into excess, waste, and disaccumulation."[30]

This is the sort of designer nihilism the cultural critic Mike Davis had in mind when he observed, "What was once terrible seems to have become fun." Our world will end, if it does, not with a bang or a whimper but with the violin shrieks from *Psycho,* played for laughs.

SECTION I
DARK CARNIVAL

2 / COTTON CANDY AUTOPSY: DECONSTRUCTING PSYCHO-KILLER CLOWNS

Psycho Bozos at the Cacophony Society's Kakophony
Klown Sex Klub, Los Angeles, 1997. Copyright © 1997
Wild Don Lewis.

What is it about clowns? They seem to be a happy enough bunch, delighted to suffer a pie-in-the-face or a seltzer-down-the-pants just to make us laugh. But what dark compulsion drives these men to hide behind their painted-on smiles and big rubber noses? What madness turns a man into a clown?

—Dave Louapre and Dan Sweetman, *A Cotton Candy Autopsy*

[The clowns] sounded happy and they acted happy, but it was a happiness that danced on the edge of hysteria, a manic joy that threatened, in a second, to slip over into murderous rage.

—Jim Knipfel, "Twilight of the Clowns"

"There's nothing funny about a clown in the moonlight."

—Lon Chaney

Bring Me the Head of Ronald McDonald

All the world hates a clown.

Ronald McDonald terrorists struck twice in 1993, neatly beheading a life-sized statue of the corporate mascot posed near a McDonald's in midtown Manhattan. A magazine item reported that the ceramic mannequin was decapitated "cleanly, violently, with an unknown weapon."[1] At the time of the story, the vandals were still at large. Who could have done such a thing? Tourists gone ballistic? Junk-food junkies driven mad by one too many Happy Meals? Collegiate pranksters? Anticorporate protesters? Disgruntled former spokesclowns?

One group is conspicuously absent from this list of likely suspects: the unacknowledged host of clownaphobes who have only recently begun to make their presence known. "Increasingly, clowns are seen as weirdoes," laments the circus historian Bruce Feiler. "Though some people have always found clowns disturbing—because of the seedy surroundings of the big top or the reliance on physical humor—now many feel that behind the face of a clown there may be a rapist waiting to pounce."[2] Bemoaning the "growing enmity" toward the world's beleaguered Bozos, Feiler places the blame on the "climate of mistrust" whipped up by our hysterical fear of child molestation. In the age of Michael Jackson and a seeming epidemic of pedophilic priests, society casts a jaundiced eye on all who work with children, from clowns to "clergymen, daycare workers, even supermarket Santas."

But there's a millennial motivation for anticlown sentiment as well: the search for a societal scapegoat, a pattern familiar from the plagues of the Middle Ages, when apocalyptic fears erupted into witch-hunts for the wretches who had called down divine wrath on everyone's heads. On the brink of the millennium, the symbolic sacrifice of a pie-facing, pratfalling agent of chaos is a means of appeasing the turbulent forces that seem to be pulling our world off its axis.

Whatever the cause, ill will toward clowns is on the rise. Bruce Nauman's 1987 video installation, *Clown Torture,* uses the clown as a psychic punching bag for nameless animosities. Scattered monitors blare tapes of hapless clowns trapped in no-win, no-exit situations, endlessly repeating the same lame jokes, getting dunked by the same water bucket, screaming "No! No! No!" over and over again. It's existential vaudeville, equal parts Bozo and Beckett, slapstick and schadenfreude.

John Bergin takes the theme of clown-as-whipping boy to extremes. Wedding fantasies of clown abuse to a universal symbol of ritual scapegoating, his 1990 cover painting for the underground comic *Caliber Presents* depicts the feet of a crucified clown, his goofy, oversized shoes transfixed by a nasty-looking nail.

Of course, not all clown abuse is a ritual exorcism of pedophilic panic or millennial dread; some of it is simply a cultural gag reflex in

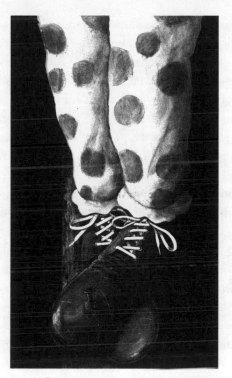

The Fool as ritual scapegoat: "King of Clowns"
by John Bergin. Copyright © John Bergin
1990.

the face of terminal cuteness. The underground movie *Tirez le Cerveau*
(*Shoot the Brains*), a one-joke exercise in splatter slapstick shot in the style
of *Les Enfants du Paradis,* is a clown hate crime played for lowbrow laughs:
A man with a bad attitude encounters an infuriatingly perky clown whose
unwanted attempts at lifting his spirits finally drive the man to blow the
clown's head off. The filmmakers' next effort will be *Blinky Balloon-
Popper,* which they matter-of-factly describe as "the interrogation of a
clown. He finally admits that he's a clown, and is tortured and killed right
away."[3]

Clearly, we're living on top of a cultural landfill of (barely) buried
clownaphobia. The "anticlown" Web site "Clowns Are Evil Incarnate"
includes 30 single-spaced pages of true confessions posted by clowna-

phobes from far and wide. At a cursory glance, "Stories From You: Your Experiences with Evil Clowns" seems like a poker-faced parody of our 12-step culture, where no psychological malady is too preposterous to merit its own support group. Many of the outpourings begin with heart-felt expressions of relief over the fact that others share the writer's afflic-tion: "How wonderful to find all of you! I thought I had a problem that was uncommon in this 'enlightened' day, but now I realize that I'm not alone"; "What a relief it is to find others with the same fear of clowns that I have had all my life."[4]

But it soon becomes obvious that these adult survivors of clown trauma are only half joking. There are harrowing tales of childhood encoun-ters with "garishly dressed, bigfooted monsters with huge smiles . . . painted on their sweating faces," goose-pimply memories of malevolent clowns in episodes of *Scooby Doo, Fantasy Island, Twilight Zone,* and, over and over, the movie *Poltergeist,* where a clown doll inhabited by an evil entity terror-izes a little boy. "If you ever hear about a support group being formed for the unfortunate people like myself that are cursed with clownaphobia, please contact me," writes one participant in dead earnest. "I know that if we join together, we can defeat the diabolic jesters."

"Clowns Are Evil Incarnate" has opened the floodgates of the id, loosing a deluge of clown fear and loathing. So, too, has "Clowns Suck," a discussion topic on the electronic bulletin board the WELL that was inundated by nearly 400 playfully spleen-filled responses before it was "frozen," closed to further comment and rendered read-only. Participants swapped anecdotes about clowns we love to hate, both fictional (Ronald McDonald, Bozo, paintings of weepy Emmett Kelly lookalikes gazing forlornly at flowers) and factual: "a sicko driving around [Washington, D.C.,] dressed as a clown, molesting children," a "made-for-TV movie (based on a true story, of course) about a guy who dressed up as a clown and shot a dad when he came to pick up his son at school."[5] The consen-sus, summed up by "Holly GoDensely," a.k.a. Mary Elizabeth Williams, was that clowns are "sick, drug-addled, disgusting, filthy, murderous creatures from hell."[6] Julia Davy reported, "I just asked my nine-year-old son what he thinks about clowns and he said that 'the only good clowns are the ones that kill each other.'"[7] Evidently, America's kitsch culture love affair with portraits of cheery or teary-eyed buffoons belies a deep-rooted rancor toward clowns.

Killer Klowns from Outer Space (and Crawl Spaces)

Grimaldi [the name of a world-renowned nineteenth-century clown] was . . . short for fun, whim, trick, and atrocity—that is, clown-atrocity, crimes that delight us.

—*The Humorist*, 1839

In a carnival mirror reflection of the growing sentiment that "clowns suck," the archetype of the evil clown—a chortling sadist rather than a whimpering scapegoat—is rapidly attaining the status of a meme in mass culture and fringe media. As the millennium approaches, the psycho-clown who takes his sociopathic slapstick outside the ring is moving stage center in the pop unconscious.

Makers of rubber Halloween masks now sell psycho-Bozos, cadaverous jesters, and razor-fanged Pogo look-alikes. A dwarf who performs at the Coney Island Circus Sideshow, a postmodern gloss on Coney's Freak Street, bills himself as Koko the Killer Klown. The underground cartoonist Kaz's cast of demented characters includes "Demise-O, the Clown of

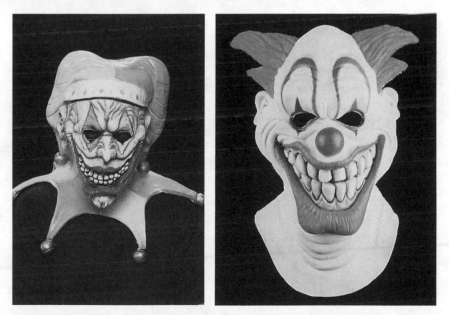

Trick or Trick: Halloween masks. Left: Image property of Cinema Secrets, Inc./Halloween FX. Copyright © Burbank CA. Ph. 818-846-0579, e-mail info@cinemasecrets.com. Right: Copyright © 1993 Altered Anatomy FX/Mask Illusions, Inc.

Death," a rotund, top-hatted clown with a skull necklace who chortles, "Nothing makes me guffaw harder than the eradication of life! With every extinction a chuckle! With every bombing a belly laugh! . . . If we can't laugh at death, we have no business killing people!"[8] Fringe art magazines like *Juxtapoz* and *Art? Alternatives* teem with evil clowns by Robert Williams, Frank Kozik, and R. K. Sloane. In Sloane's "Serial Killers in Circus Land" series, amputee clowns, cannibal clowns, and decapitated clown heads share the stage with two-headed mutations and body parts in jars, lushly rendered in a style somewhere between the Dutch masters and black-velvet Elvises.

The archetype is becoming a fixture in alternative rock and rap, too, where the evil clown appears as a mascot of keg-party hell raising: An acne-splotched clown with a snaggle-toothed grin and HATE scrawled across his forehead leers from the cover of *Groove Family Cyco* by the punk-funk Infectious Grooves; a cigar-chomping, beer-gutted clown cavorts amid burning beer cans on a poster for Ugly Kid Joe's *Menace to Sobriety*. A rap act called the Insane Clown Posse goes even further, sporting stylized clown makeup and brandishing prop skulls.

The evil clown has surfaced in the mainstream as well, in the Joker of Batman fame (*the* quintessential psycho-killer clown) and in Stephen King's novel *It*, about a shape-shifting, child-killing evil that appears in the guise of Pennywise the Dancing Clown, "a cross between Bozo and Clarabell" with "funny tufts of red hair on either side of his bald head," a "big clown-smile painted over his mouth," and a bouquet of balloons in one hand, "like gorgeous ripe fruit."[9]

In the book's opening scene, Pennywise wheedles a little boy into coming treacherously close with the promise of that forbidden balloon fruit, then rips off the child's arm, leaving little doubt in the reader's mind that King's conflation of Bozo and bogeyman is a homicidal pedophile in clown drag—John Wayne Gacy, by another name. Of course, Pennywise is much more than a Gacy surrogate, but King's decision to embody our primal fears in a sociopathic Ronald McDonald who oozes honeyed guile, the better to prey on little boys, is a telling one, as is his reference to *Howdy Doody*'s Clarabell, s/he of the indeterminate gender.

The subject of Gacy is unavoidable in any discussion of the shadow the evil clown casts over the mass unconscious. A sadistic serial killer convicted of

"Comedy for the Criminally Insane" by R. K. Sloane. Copyright ©
R. K. Sloane.

the torture-murders of 33 young men and boys (no one else in American
history has been convicted of killing so many people), Gacy was executed
by lethal injection in 1994. He will live on in pop nightmares as the "Killer
Clown," a sobriquet inspired by the Pogo the Clown persona he adopted
when performing for hospitalized children and at community events. The
image has been fixed in the collective imagination by tabloid newspapers,
serial-killer trading cards, and a lurid biography of the same name. One of
the best-known photos of Gacy captures him in his clown get-up, complete
with tasseled hat and creepy makeup—fiendish arched eyebrows and a smile
that ends in evil, upswept points (professional clowns round off the corners of their smiles to avoid frightening children). One of his favorite songs,
naturally, was the schmaltzy, tear-jerking "Send in the Clowns."

On death row, Gacy parlayed his meager artistic abilities into a lucrative mail-order business, selling crude, cartoony paintings to serial-killer fans: portraits of Elvis, Christ, Snow White and the Seven Dwarfs (!), and, most popularly, clowns: himself as Pogo; a skull in a ruffled collar and clown hat; an empty chair with a clown costume draped over it. The day before he was executed, an exhibition of his work was on view at the Canal Street Gallery in nearby Chicago, the ghoulish clowns among them. (Gacy preferred happier scenes, the gallery's assistant curator noted, but turned out the morbid ones because "he recognizes the market.")[10] On the night of Gacy's execution, the raucous crowd outside the prison walls included pro-death penalty revelers wearing T-shirts that read, NO MORE TEARS FOR THE CLOWN.

Apparently, Gacy's charity work as a clown was more than an ironic counterpoint to the unspeakable acts that turned the crawl space under his house into a graveyard. By all accounts, there was a little Pogo in the psycho-killer. Gacy told police that one of his homicidal parlor tricks was inspired by a clown routine. Cajoling his victim into trying on toy handcuffs, Gacy would switch them for real ones when the victim's back was turned. Once the victim was shackled and helpless, Gacy would subject him to horrific sexual abuse, torture, and ultimately death by ligature strangulation.[11] True-crime writers have conjured up the chilling moment when Gacy morphed from a gregarious big brother, clowning around with his young victim, into a pitiless psychopath who could pause, in the midst of strangling someone, to chat nonchalantly on the phone. As Gacy biographer Tim Cahill imagines it, "His voice has suddenly dropped into a deeper register, and the humor that was there just a moment before has been transformed into a kind of triumphant glee. The man is as merry and malignant as a magpie."[12] It's a moment that cues spooky music in the mind when juxtaposed with Gacy's offhanded observation that one of the reasons he liked clowning was because "you can get away with a lot of things when you're . . . a clown, because people see you as something funny. They don't know what's beneath the greasepaint." As he famously observed, "A clown can get away with murder."[13]

On a lighter note, the psycho-killer clown's close cousin the degenerate clown has capered into the collective consciousness in the form of Homey the Clown, *In Living Color*'s hip-hop riff on the trickster archetype. Krusty the Clown, the foul-mouthed, chain-smoking reprobate who hosts a kiddie show on *The Simpsons,* is another prominent sleazebag in whiteface; so, too, is Shakes the Clown, the embittered boozehound in Bobcat Goldthwait's bizarro black comedy, *Shakes the Clown.*

The image of the evil clown is now ensconced in the library of cinematic clichés as well: The Japanese animated cyberpunk epic *Akira* includes a vicious band of teenage toughs in whiteface, the Clown Gang, and in *Batman Returns* the Penguin's henchmen inexplicably include "terror clowns" in traditional Ringling-type costumes along with others in skull masks reminiscent of *Dia de los Muertos* effigies and George Grosz's famous "Dada Death" mask.

In fact, a little-known but lively horror movie subgenre revolves around the evil clown trope and the related theme that David J. Skal has identified as the "dark carnival" motif, a pathological amusement park whose symbolism often overlaps with that of the psycho-clown. This motherlode of low-budget trashola includes such gems of slapstick splatter as *Clownhouse, The Clown Murders, Out of the Dark* (Divine's curtain closer, as a killer clown), *Funland* (the "abusement park"), *The Funhouse* ("Pay to get in. Pray to get out!"), *Carnival of Blood,* and the unforgettable *Killer Klowns from Outer Space,* a tongue-in-cheek B-movie starring rubber-nosed, fright-wigged grotesques. The *New York Press* writer Jim Knipfel recalls a cubbyhole-sized video store he once worked in, where no matter "how small the stock was, we still carried (I counted one day) 19 films featuring axe-wielding clowns."[14]

So, to return to the question that opened this essay, what is it about clowns? What buried engine drives our clownaphobia?

A facile, pop psych explanation would unearth its roots in childhood traumas. A highly unscientific opinion poll suggests that the Shriners, a fraternal order whose parade appearances in fezzes and miniature cars have endeared it to fans of bad taste everywhere, bear the burden of responsibility for the creation of more than a few virulent clownaphobes. The Shriner tradition of clowning at community charities has apparently left scar tissue on the American psyche. Ken Knutson, a participant in the WELL's "Clowns Suck" discussion group, witnessed Shriner clowns "literally scaring the hell out of the kids" at a Great America theme park, and Jim Knipfel recalls the childhood trauma of playfully grabbing a balloon from a Shriner clown, only to have him wade into the crowd, "a fury burning in his eyes," snatch the balloon away from the terrified seven-year-old Knipfel, and give it to a little girl.[15]

Kafka the Clown (Adam G. Gertsacov), a graduate of the Ringling Clown College who braved the WELL's "Clowns Suck" topic, offered a spirited defense of his red-nosed brethren: "As to why a lot of kids are scared by clowns or don't like clowns, it's because of their parents. OK, you're two years old, you're at a festival, and your parents see a clown. You're scared of the big man with makeup on who's sweating and wearing slightly smelly clothes. You begin to cry. Do your parents get the hint? No, they do not. They stick your face in the face of the clown in hopes of a photo opportunity. And you—you are SCARRED FOR LIFE."[16]

Phil Snyder, a 'zine publisher and longtime clown obsessive, goes to the heart of clown repulsion in his essay "Exorcising Shameful Visions." Recalling his first childhood encounter with clowns at a Shriner circus, he writes, "Somehow, I knew that something was wrong. Why the pasty makeup? Why the funny clothes? They tried so hard to make us laugh that they made me nervous. I was uncomfortable in their presence because I knew that they were really just people in disguise. When you realize that this grotesque creature is another person in makeup, the clown act loses its humor and becomes intimidating. You begin to wonder what they're really up to."[17] Knipfel echoes Snyder's sentiments: "There was something very insidious about [clowns]. You never knew what was going on behind the greasepaint and those hidden eyes, those mouths carved into artificial smiles."[18]

At its roots, clownaphobia springs from the duplicity implied by the frozen grins and false gaiety of clowns. The clown persona protests too much; its transparent artificiality constantly directs our attention to what's behind the mask.

In Hallmark gift-card myth, every painted smile conceals a well of loneliness and private pain. Maudlin clowns, tears streaking their smiling faces, are a staple of kitsch art, from gift-shop ceramics to paint-by-number masterpieces. For the lonely and the lovelorn, sobbing clowns are the patron saints of bathos; they cause a lump of sweetly savored self-pity to rise in the throat. Like the big-eyed weepy waifs painted by the schlockmeisters Margaret and Walter Keane, they give us license to wallow. Gacy, who fancied himself a sentimental soul, collected paintings of sad-eyed clowns; their smile-though-your-heart-is-breaking symbolism appealed to the man who masked his terrifying alienation with selfless acts of community service: director of Chicago's Polish Day parade, Democratic party precinct captain, charity clown.

Of course, as Gacy reminds us, there may be more than a wounded naïf with brimming eyes and a trembling lip behind the whiteface. According to Tim Cahill, "greedy little bastards" who tried to wheedle candy out of Gacy when their pockets were already bulging made the bile rise in his throat. "He'd pinch the kid on the cheek, like clowns will do, only he pinched hard, so that it hurt and he could see the pain in the child's eyes. Smiling and whispering so that no one else but the child could hear, Pogo would rasp, 'Get your ass away from me, you little motherfucker.'"[19]

Clown repulsion is a manifestation of the creeping suspicion that the clown's happy face is Jekyll to a far darker Hyde: an embittered alcoholic with one foot in the grave, perhaps, or a sadistic sexual predator and remorseless killer. But the deepest (if not the darkest) secret concealed in the clown's painted-on smile is our own mortality—the mocking, mirthless grin of the death's head. Clown "mouths carved into artificial smiles" horrify because they embalm a spontaneous expression of happiness; the only other time a human smile freezes is when the mortician fixes it in place, for display in an open casket. Whiteface is just a death mask with a sense of humor.

William Willeford points out in *The Fool and His Scepter* that the characters of the Fool and Death were often interchangeable in medieval mystery plays. The Fool's triumph over death, a triumph reenacted in the resurrection of the circus clown who springs back to life after being konked with a hammer, elevated him to a supernatural status not unlike Death's. At the same time, he was frequently the agent of death: Willeford notes "the similarities between the fool as jester and the figure of the Revenger in many Elizabethan and Jacobean plays."[20]

For example, in works by Dürer and Holbein, the Fool and Death were subsumed into Death the Fool, a skeleton in jester's cap and motley who literalized the late-medieval truism that death makes a mockery of life's fleeting joys. Yorick, the dead jester whose grinning skull inspires Hamlet's musings on the worm-eaten end of all our frolics and follies, is a variation on this theme. The image can be read backward, too: By casting the Grim Reaper in the role of the Fool, life thumbs its nose at death.

As Snyder, Knipfel, and the posts in on-line discussion groups like "Clowns Suck" make abundantly clear, the Fool/Death duality survives in contemporary culture, explicitly in the psycho-killer clown of pop mythology, implicitly in the uncanniness of all clowns.

But we still haven't sounded the depths of clownaphobia. Delving deeper, we find that the clown disturbs because he—it—is uncanny in the Freudian sense of the word, vacillating disconcertingly between human and nonhuman, animate and inanimate. The clown's fixed expression and pixilated antics confuse the human with the wind-up doll, the marionette, the robot. And the living dead: with his cadaverous pallor and blood-red lips, the clown invites comparison to the vampire, a correspondence brought to the fore in the Batman comic *Bloodstorm,* where the legions of the undead rally around the Joker in a pitched battle against the Caped Crusader.

But whether they are conceived of as children of the night or children of paradise, clowns are popularly regarded as nonhuman, an alien nation moving among us, as in *Killer Klowns from Outer Space.* Snyder is haunted by the suspicion that clowns are "a completely unique species, not mere humans in disguise as they try to make us believe."[21] Knipfel likewise concludes, after attending a series of seminars on clowning called Clownfest, that clowns "aren't normal people. They speak a secret clown language and think secret clown thoughts. They see the world in a completely different way."[22]

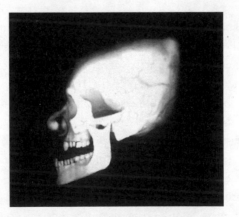

Clown as subhuman: Homo sapiens scurra
bozus, by Randy Johnson. Copyright © 1990
Randy Johnson.

The artist and sideshow-banner historian Randy Johnson uses the clown-as-subhuman theme in works that can be read as a Dadaist spoof of the recent resurgence of genetic determinism. By digitally manipulating a series of photos, he has engineered the subspecies *Homo sapiens scurra bozus*— clowns, by any other name. A jarringly realistic image of a clown skull in profile reveals a macrocephalic head, a curlicue-shaped septum (the anatomical cause of the bulbous clown nose, apparently), and a lantern jaw studded with jagged teeth. Johnson's clown hovers uncannily between opposites: At once ape and angel, he has the prognathous lower jaw of a subhuman caveman and the bulging braincase of a superhuman alien.

Snyder's notion of clowns as a species unto themselves; Knipfel's conspiracy theory of clowns as a secret society, impenetrable to "normal people"; and Johnson's vision of clowns as a mutant offshoot of *Homo sapiens* are all founded on the assumption that clowns are cultural, even biological, freaks. Seen in this light, clowns bear a close resemblance to the freaks in Tod Browning's movie of the same name, a secret society that ritually accepts a normal human as "one of us" in a key scene. The clown/freak analogy harks back to the clown's historical origins in the court jester—the hunchbacks, dwarves, and cripples whose misshapen bodies and grotesque gaits, as much as their jokes, amused nobles from Egyptian pharaohs to Renaissance princes. William Willeford counts among the earliest clowns "the entertainers who wandered the European Continent after the fall of the Roman Empire, among them cripples, the blind, paralytics, amputees, prostitutes, and quack doctors"—in short, all who violated the human image through physical or psychic deformity and who came "to a *modus vivendi* with society by making a show of that violation."[23] The tradition survives in Jerry Lewis's classic character, the spastic, geeky schlemiel, a clown act so freakish it inspired Lenny Bruce's wisecrack that the Muscular Dystrophy Telethon was Lewis's attempt to cure the disease he caused. In the eighties, out-of-control comics like Bobcat Goldthwait, his strangled, speed-freak whine pushing his words to the very brink of intelligibility, and Pee-Wee Herman, a grade-school sissy trapped in a grown man's body, rendered the clown/freak connection explicit.

Thus the lingering perception of clowns as abnormal or nonhuman beings—a notion that informs Dave Louapre and Dan Sweetman's bitterly funny, unbearably sad *A Cotton Candy Autopsy,* the illustrated short story collection from which this essay takes its title. In *Autopsy,* a chronicle of the descent into death and madness—and, ultimately, the deliverance—of a band of clowns fleeing a circus fire one of them set, the clown is depicted as scapegoat, alien, and naïf in the *Forrest Gump* mold, gifted with the wisdom of idiots and children but prey to their infantile impulses as well.

Here, as in Phil Snyder's writings, clowns are "a completely unique species": They have natural enemies (bikers and, as in *Shakes the Clown,* mimes), retain only the dimmest recollections of their parents, and can't recall being named anything but their clown names. When they're in agony, they scream "like only a wounded clown can scream"; when they're aggrieved, they moan a moan "made only by tortured clowns." For them, the world is *King Lear*'s "great stage of fools": they wear their clown costumes and outsized, floppy shoes onstage and off, and their greasepaint seems permanent, less like makeup than natural coloration.

In addition to the disdain invited by his nonhuman or freakish status, the clown stirs up animosity through his apparent condescension. Transformed by his whiteface into a mirror for the reflection of human foibles, he seems to observe the human condition from on high, like Puck wryly musing on "what fools these mortals be." The Olympian scorn implied by the clown's burlesque of mortal follies is at the heart of the resentment that boils over in Randy Newman's "Laughing Boy":

> "Find a clown and grind him down
> He may just be laughing at you
> An unprincipled and uncommitted
> clown can hardly be permitted to
> sit around and laugh at what
> the decent people try to do."[24]

Finally, the clown hate that delights in the comic humiliation and cartoon brutality endured by clowns is a contemporary echo of the fool's ancient role as scapegoat. Thus, Nauman's tortured clown and Bergin's crucified clown can be seen as symptoms not only of millennial panic but of pagan ritual as well. In *A Dictionary of Symbols,* J. E. Cirlot notes that the fool and the clown "play the part of scapegoats in the ritual sacrifice of humans" in "the period immediately preceding history."[25]

Clownaphobia, crystallized in the ubiquitous image of the evil clown, is a meshwork of childhood traumas, the secrets buried in Gacy's crawl space, and the cultural memories that swirl around the image of the clown: the fool's traditional association with death and the uncanny, his pre-Christian role as a scapegoat, his sneering mockery of human follies, and his longstanding status as abnormal or nonhuman Other.

Strange Attractions, Strange Attractors: Psycho-Clowns and Chaos Culture

In millennial culture, the Joker's wild. More and more, the psycho-clown is positioned not as the object of our fear and loathing but as the crazy-funny mascot of our chaos culture, with its random acts of senseless violence, its tabloid feeding frenzies, its mad bombers and millenarian cults.

The evil clown embodies the black comedy of a society in which giddily amoral bystanders cheer "Go, Juice, go!" during O. J. Simpson's slow-motion getaway. A society in which people buy white Broncos like Simpson's, in homage to the accused double murderer, or immortalize their pilgrimages to the Simpson mansion with smiling snapshots. A society in which Colin Ferguson, a mass murderer who "seems more like a clown than a killer," acts as his own attorney, cross-examining the survivors of his Long Island Rail Road shooting spree about "Mr. Ferguson" as though someone else were on trial.[26] The evil clown puts a manic face on an America where the average teenager purportedly knows the names of more serial killers than senators, and where Jeffrey Howorth, a 16-year-old boy who shot his parents dead for no particular reason, left a note that read, "I want a movie to be made for me after I kill everyone."[27]

The psycho-killer clown encapsulates what Stephen King has identified as the have-a-nice-day/make-my-day dualism that typifies postwar American culture. "We're not happy and sad," says King. "We're happy and violent."[28] Obviously, sweeping generalizations about a country as full of economic disparity, ethnic diversity, and geographical dissimilarity as the U.S. are almost always as wrong as they're right, dead on target and miles wide of the mark. Even so, there's no denying the truth of King's words. All over the world, America stands for fun and death: Disneyland and the death penalty, Big Macs and murder (the highest rate in the industrialized world). It's surely significant that, as of 1992, America's top two export items were military hardware and "entertainment products," in that order.[29]

As King suggests, the collective personality of the nation is a split one. The American psyche is characterized, on one hand, by a Teflon optimism and a clench-jawed cheerfulness so impervious to reality it's scary and, on the other, by a coiled violence, just beneath the surface. Think of Ronald Reagan, whose on-camera persona alternated between the aw-shucks innocence of Jimmy Stewart and the tough-guy rasp of Clint Eastwood (he actually threatened to veto legislation for a proposed tax increase with Eastwood's *Dirty Harry* catchphrase, "Go ahead; make my day"). Stewart himself was a cherished national monument to the Capra-esque smalltown virtues that, we're forever told, made this country great. But the transformation of the Christmas broadcast of *It's a Wonderful Life* (1946) into a teary-eyed reaffirmation of family values denies the sense of soured hopes and smalltown claustrophobia that permeates the story. In the warm afterglow of the movie's ending, we forget that the George Bailey belting out "Auld Lang Syne" with brimming eyes is the same George Bailey who collared Uncle Billy after the wool-gathering old man misplaced the bank's money, shrieking, "Where's that money, you silly, stupid old fool? Where's that money? You realize what this means? It means bankruptcy and scandal and prison! That's what it means. One of us is going to jail. Well, it's not going to be me!"

George Bailey is a kinder, gentler predecessor of Stephen King's American psycho; he's suicidally despairing, whereas later incarnations such as King's own evil clown, or the happy-and-violent Jack Torrance in *The Shining* (1980), are gleefully vicious. The difference between Jimmy Stewart's Bailey and Jack Nicholson's Torrance isn't just a matter of short-circuit psychoses and cackling, cartoon violence; there's a jump-cutting, channel-surfing quality to Torrance's madness. It's a postmodern psychosis, mugging for an imaginary camera, framing its brutality in pop culture quotes. Stalking his terrified wife, Nicholson hacks their bedroom door to bits with an ax, then deadpans the signature line of all fifties sitcom patriarchs: "Honey, I'm home." In his snapped mind, he's starring in a campy, splatter-movie send-up of *Father Knows Best*. When he shatters the flimsy door of the bathroom where his hysterical wife cowers, he pokes his head through the hole and grins, "Heeere's Johnny!"

Nicholson's Torrance is an evil clown, emblematizing the off-the-rails, media-giddy mind-set of America late in the twentieth century. Appropriately, pop culture has embraced him as a gonzo antihero: ads for

T-shirts emblazoned with the "Here's Johnny" Nicholson, all wild eyes and vulpine smile, have been a fixture in the back pages of magazines like *Rolling Stone* for some time now. That smile is a metonymy for the have-a-nice-day/make-my-day psychology of King's America. We've seen it before, or variations on it, on the faces that float in the darkness of our collective dreams: Robert De Niro as Travis Bickle, the walking time bomb with the dorky grin in *Taxi Driver;* Woody Harrelson as Mickey Knox, the mad-dog killer with the twinkle in his eye in *Natural Born Killers;* Michael Madsen as Vic Vega, the smirking psychopath in *Reservoir Dogs,* who tortures a cop "not to get information, but because torturing a cop amuses me."

More than any other nineties filmmaker, Quentin Tarantino (who wrote the latter two movies) captures the schizoid mix of horror and hilarity, grotesque and burlesque that is the spirit of our times. The smiling psychopath—an evil clown by another name—attains a giddy apotheosis in his movies, where killers are jokers, torture is clowning around, and a bullet in the head is the rimshot for a laugh line. In *Reservoir Dogs,* Vic sings along with Stealer's Wheel on the radio as he slices off the cop's ear with a razor: "Clowns to the left of me, jokers to the right, here I am, stuck in the middle with you." In *True Romance,* an Elvis-cool kid says to the jivey, wise-cracking killer-pimp he's about to shoot at point-blank range, "Open your eyes, laughing boy." When the petrified lowlife finally does, the kid quips, "You thought it was pretty funny, didn't you?" and splatters his brains. Why do you think it's called a punch line?

Tarantino is intoxicated by the giggly anomie of the tabloid self, the sick-funny moral vertigo induced by life on the media merry-go-round of postmodern culture. Moral judgments, in his world, are so *over,* as they say on the Net. He told an interviewer that he doesn't take the violence in his movies very seriously. "I find violence very funny," he said, "especially in the stories that I've been telling recently. Violence is part of this world and I'm drawn to the outrageousness of real-life violence. . . . Real-life violence is . . . crazy and comic-bookish."[30] Life's a snuff cartoon, equal parts *Henry: Portrait of a Serial Killer* and "The Itchy & Scratchy Show" from *The Simpsons.*

The night I saw *Pulp Fiction,* the audience guffawed when a bump in the road caused John Travolta to inadvertently blow a man's head off at point-blank range, chuckled when Travolta and Samuel L. Jackson traded laugh lines while swabbing up the man's brains, sniggered when a drug lord was sodomized by a sociopathic S&M freak. Here, again, is the "euphoria of weightlessness" that troubles unfashionable moralists like the movie critic Anthony Lane, who like David Denby is worried by the fact that the younger moviegoers at a preview of the latest *Halloween* sequel "didn't care to feel." To them, the blood-splattered slasher movie was "a comedy—a little black around the edges, sure, but basically a scream." Like the audience at *Pulp Fiction,* they "laughed at the gore, whooped at the shocks, and left the theatre in merriment. All those George Bush-period warnings about media desensitization suddenly seemed a little less crusty than before."[31]

Admittedly, the latest return of *Halloween*'s deathless villain, Michael Myers, is comic-strip stuff compared to *Pulp Fiction.* Tarantino exults in the carefree, conscienceless pleasures made possible by our ever more virtual reality, where disembodied images precede experience and media fictions float free from human lives or history or anything else that would bring them down (in both senses of the word). He liberates us not only from the ponderous burden of historical meaning into a Retro Now, where the past is a grab bag of skinned images to be mixed and matched at whim, but also frees us from the dreary adult responsibilities of citizenship.

A profoundly American filmmaker, Tarantino holds up a mirror to a dark-side America unseen in Frank Capra's paean to participatory democracy, *Mr. Smith Goes to Washington,* where freedom and civic life are intertwined. Tarantino's is Timothy McVeigh's America, a survivalist Frontierland where everyone talks about civil liberties and no one mentions social responsibility, where the social Darwinist verities of race and gender are the only laws that matter and freedom means the right to own belt-fed weapons and armor-piercing bullets. It's a teenage boy's fantasy, where the American Dream means a blonde sex kitten, a suitcase full of coke, and a snub-nosed .38, and where Twain's utopian vision of Huck Finn lighting out for the territories has been updated to Charlie Starkweather's thrill-kill spree through Nebraska with his 15-year-old girlfriend in a hot-rodded Ford (the ur-text for Terrence Malick's *Badlands,* which begat *True Romance,* which begat *Natural Born Killers*).

More and more, Tarantino's America is the land we live in, a fun house pushed way past the point of fun. Ironically, for all its carnival-midway abandon to thrills and chills, our Coneyesque consumer culture is founded on a desperate repression of the real, what Ralph Rugoff calls the denial of "our capacity to take on the full spectrum of emotional life which exists beyond the confines of 'fun.'"[32] Ultimately, he warns, "Compulsive infantilization encompasses a sly and pernicious form of violence." He quotes the serial killer Richard "the night stalker" Ramirez's creepy, clownish salutation as he left the courtroom en route to death row: "See you in Disneyland"—a glib, Tarantino-esque one-liner that means everything and nothing.

It's a received truth of Op-Ed punditry and books like James B. Twitchell's *Carnival Culture: The Trashing of Taste in America* that our *Dumb and Dumber* culture has become a bizarre carnival in which Americans will pay to watch Howard Stern read from his memoir astride a toilet, pants around his ankles, the headliner on a pay-per-view bill that also features a topless woman eating maggots. But the fringe culture appropriation of the evil clown trope reminds us that the carnival, a sinister symbol of the loss of innocence in Ray Bradbury's *Something Wicked This Way Comes* or the monsters of the id in Hitchcock's *Strangers on a Train,* can also be understood in the sense that the Russian literary theorist Mikhail Bakhtin understood it. To Bakhtin, the feasts and spectacles of the Middle Ages, with their parody liturgies and their temporary suspension of rank, were brief-lived utopias in which societal mores were subverted and hierarchies inverted through humor and chaos.

As I argued in my introduction, the tradition of what Bakhtin called the "carnivalesque" lived on, in somewhat less Rabelaisian form, in turn-of-the-century Concy Island. According to the historian Jane Kuenz, Coney's appeal "depended in part on the thrill of doing something you otherwise couldn't but may have wanted to."[33] Revelers smashed ersatz china dishes in a booth bearing the sign, IF YOU CAN'T BREAK UP YOUR OWN HOME, BREAK UP OURS!; a prim "schoolma'am" walked, fully dressed, into the ocean, explaining that the sight of "everyone with the brakes off got the better of me."[34] Not coincidentally, Steeplechase's trademark "funny face" was an impishly evil clown, a demented jester whose ear-to-ear grin insinuated that propriety, perhaps even sanity, ended at the park's gates.

Bakhtin's carnivalesque endures in the lewd, uncouth clowns of the Cacophony Society, a San Francisco-based "network of free spirits" whose hit-and-run public pranks recall the Dadaists' antibourgeois art attacks, Situationist provocation, and the anarchic outbursts of seventies punk. The group's L.A. chapter, which claims a membership of 200, specializes in terrorist clowning, or "klowning," as they call it. The group's crack-brained ringmaster, more often than not, is Asswipe the Klown (né Adam Bregman), whose characteristic garb consists of a disheveled polyester clown suit topped by a two-and-a-half-foot-high, bright-orange cowboy hat. Bregman and his coconspirators have crashed corporate meetings, singing warped versions of "Happy Birthday" to bewildered executives; informed customers in a Victoria's Secret store that "the fragrances they were sampling were tested on clowns"; and button-holed patrons in the Los Angeles Museum of Contemporary Art, ranting, "My dead monkey could paint better than this—let's find the guy who did this and give him a knuckle sandwich!"[35] According to the Cacophonist klown Reverend Al, the carnivalesque qualities of "the grotesque and the irrational are exactly the qualities that we Cacophonists want to celebrate. . . . Man escapes the mundane through violation of his regimented world of scientific, aesthetic, and social law. We sell the tickets."[36]

Increasingly, of course, the violation of social codes is all too commonplace, a fact made painfully clear by Howard Stern holding forth from his porcelain throne and Marilyn Manson reminiscing gleefully, in *The Long Hard Road Out of Hell,* about covering a naked groupie with raw meat, then washing her off with urine. Mindful of that fact, some in fringe culture embrace the evil clown not as a standard-bearer for the carnivalesque but as a poster boy for the only sane response to the postmodern media fun house: insanity. Torn between information anxiety and information overload, the psychokiller clown embodies that queasy mixture of horror and hilarity that characterizes the info-vertigo of our moment.

   At the same time, he offers a blueprint for psychological survival at a time when what the philosopher Jean-François Lyotard calls the "grand narratives"—the stories about God, Marx, and progress that we used to tell ourselves in order to live—are in a shambles. By example, evil clowns admonish us to relax into the cultural vortex, to exult in our status as decentered subjects. The only way to survive and even delight in what Fredric Jameson calls "the fragmented and schizophrenic decentering and dispersion" of the individual ego that supposedly results from everyday life in our hyperaccelerated, media-saturated world is to ride it as if it were the out-of-control carousel in *Strangers on a Train* or, better yet, the hyperkinetic roller coaster in *True Romance.*[37]

The method to the evil clown's madness is not unlike the radical strategy for survival under capitalism proposed by the French philosophers Gilles Deleuze and Felix Guattari; in their two-volume work, *Anti-Oedipus,* the authors celebrate the schizophrenic, whose fragmented personality supposedly stands in radical opposition to the closed, centered subject required (and reproduced) by capitalist society. "The code of delirium . . . proves to have an extraordinary fluidity," write Deleuze and Guattari. "It might be said that the schizophrenic passes from one code to the other, that he deliberately scrambles all the codes, by quickly shifting from one to another, according to the questions asked him, never giving the same explanation from one day to the next, never recording the same event in the same way."[38]

Deleuze and Guattari's idealized schizophrenic is a mirror image of the schizoid Joker in recent Batman comics, who never records "the same event in the same way": in the graphic novel *The Killing Joke,* he says of his origin, "Sometimes I remember it one way, sometimes another. . . . If I'm going to have a past, I prefer it to be multiple-choice!"[39] The evil clown's newfound status as a role model for decentered subjects was evinced by Tim Burton's *Batman* (1989), where the control-freak Dark Knight was effortlessly upstaged by that agent of chaos, the Joker, a.k.a. the Clown Prince of Crime. If the comments of Bat-fans are any indication, the Joker was widely viewed as the movie's real hero. One moviegoer reflected, "It's bizarre, because you are feeling, you know, 'What a great guy!' for a madman."[40] The cultural critic Christopher Sharrett points out, "There seems to be an attitude now that the Joker is at least as appealing as Batman in terms of the dark forces he represents. His kind of madness seems associated with the Ted Bundys of society, who seem to hold a powerful fascination for people in the '80s and '90s."[41]

The jester has always been the king's dark doppelgänger, his symbolic inversion. Hence, writes Cirlot, "the clown is the victim chosen as a substitute for the king, in accord with . . . primitive ideas of the ritual assassination of the king."[42] In *The Golden Bough,* James Frazer notes the correlation between the King of the Saturnalia, who reigned over the Roman revels only to be sacrificed at their conclusion, and the Bishop of Fools, who presided over Carnival feasts and spectacles. But in postmodern media culture, where the carnival never ends, the reign of the evil clown is permanent.

In the graphic novel *Arkham Asylum,* Batman pays the Joker a visit in the Gotham City sanitarium of the same name. In a wonderful soliloquy that speaks volumes about the ascent of the evil clown in postmodern culture, a psychotherapist explains the Joker's case to his longtime adversary: "We're not even sure if he can be properly defined as insane. . . . It's quite possible we may actually be looking at some kind of super-sanity here. A brilliant new modification of human perception. More suited to urban life at the end of the twentieth century. Unlike you and I, the Joker seems to have no control over the sensory information he's receiving from the outside world. He can only cope with that chaotic barrage of input by going with the flow. That's why somedays he's a mischievous clown, others a psychopathic killer. He has no real personality."[43] Though Batman has beaten the Joker in the short run, the zeitgeist is going the Joker's way. He's the man of the hour, perfectly adapted to life in a hall of media mirrors where reality and its fun house double are increasingly indistinguishable.

Send in the clowns.

3 / RETURN TO ABNORMALCY: FREAKS, GAFFES, AND GEEKS AT THE FIN-DE-MILLENNIUM

We accept you, one of us: A family portrait from Tod Browning's
Freaks. David J. Skal collection.

On the eve of the millennium, we're witnessing an upwelling of freakish-ness; anomalous bodies, born and made, seem to be everywhere. "It's the era of freakiness!" proclaims a letter writer to the magazine *Muscular Devel-opment,* unknowingly echoing Donna Haraway's observation that "by the late twentieth century, our time, a mythic time, we are all chimeras, theo-rized and fabricated hybrids of machine and organism."[1] When a fan of hyperbolic bodybuilding and a feminist academic who dwells in the nose-bleed zone of high theory agree on what the zeitgeist is, it's official.

Of course, the evidence is all around us, from the sanitized carny culture of the Broadway musical *Side Show* to Coney Island U.S.A., a post-modern revival of the sideshow that features Zenobia the Bearded Lady, a dwarf named Koko the Killer Klown, and Helen Melon, "550 pounds of female pulchritude." We're fascinated by "living curiosities," from literal anomalies like the Hensel sisters, their twin heads sprouting from a shared body on the cover of *Life,* to figurative oddities like John Leguizamo, whose autobiographical Broadway show *Freak* uses the term as a badge of pride for the defiantly deviant Other.

As Leslie Fiedler points out in his classic study *Freaks: Myths and Images of the Secret Self,* Leguizamo isn't the first to brand himself a freak in an act of countercultural chutzpah. Hippies were self-styled "freaks" who read underground comics like *The Fabulous Furry Freak Brothers* and listened to records like *Freak Out!* by the Mothers of Invention. The counterculture embraced the term, Fiedler theorizes, as a way of trumpeting the fact "that they [had] *chosen* rather than merely endured their status as Freaks."[2] Sev-enties punks freaked out, too. Bands took names like the Bizarros, the

Weirdos, and Devo, as in "devolution," the Darwinian nightmare literalized in "missing links" like Barnum's notorious "What Is It?" a microcepha-
lic black man in a fur suit. The anthem of the genre's godfathers, the
Ramones, was a song called "Pinhead" whose "gabba, gabba" chorus was a
mangled version of the chant of the freaks in Tod Browning's *Freaks*:
"Gobble, gobble; we accept you, one of us, one of us!"

Since the advent in the early nineties of the alt.culture fad for tattooing and piercing, American teenagers have been turning themselves into
gaffes, or self-made freaks—mall-crawling versions of illustrated marvels
like the Great Omi, obviously, but also ethnological "freaks" like the plate-
lipped "Ubangi savages" and "Burmese giraffe-neck women" exhibited by
the Ringling Brothers, Barnum & Bailey Circus as late as the 1930s.

In a parallel development, Jim Rose is reinventing the sideshow
for the Lollapalooza generation. A carny barker and sideshow performer
who eats lightbulbs, pounds nails up his nose, and performs as a human
dartboard, Rose leads the Jim Rose Circus Sideshow, a troupe of geeks and

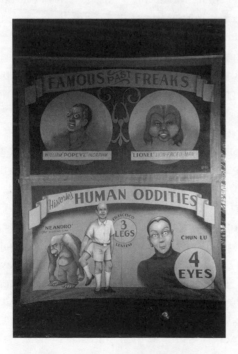

Step right up: Sideshow banner. Banner by Johnny Meah, Bannerline Inc.

gaffes like the Human Pincushion, Slug the sword-swallowing insectivore, and the Amazing Mr. Lifto, who hoists a concrete block hanging from chains fastened to his pierced nipples.

Meanwhile, for the first time since the late fifties, the Ringling Brothers, Barnum & Bailey Circus features a sideshow, albeit one with the family values seal of approval. Performed in the circus's center ring, it features Mighty Michu, a midget who claims to be only 33 inches tall, and Khan, a giant billed as being eight feet tall—but no pinheads, limbless wonders, or conjoined twins.

Even the rarefied art world has gone slumming on the midway. Antique sideshow banners are suddenly hip, their mongrel mix of folk art and advertising legitimated by the vogue for "outsider" art. In art books like *Freak Show: Sideshow Banner Art* and *Freaks, Geeks, and Strange Girls: Sideshow Banners of the Great American Midway,* the "very special people" of the age before television wow the rubes again: Tirko the Monkey Boy, Zoma the Sadist, Popeye ("the Man with the Elastic Eyeballs"), Dickie the Penguin Boy ("Looks and Walks Like a Penguin"), Toad Man with Two Noses, and the Iron-Tongued Marvel (who could lift a 25-pound anvil suspended from his tongue).

Despite their flaking paint and quaint primitivism, sideshow banners seem strangely contemporary for the simple reason that the Great American Midway is where we live these days. The very mass media credited with rendering the freak show obsolete have reinvented it. Local TV news, a quintessentially American mix of Puritan sanctimony, peep-show titillation, and graphic gore, recalls carnival girlie shows and the ubiquitous "chamber of horrors," which featured staged reenactments or waxwork tableaux of historical atrocities, accompanied by a blood-curdling bedlam of taped shrieks and moans.

Barnum's Odditorium lives on, as well, in supermarket tabloids like *The Weekly World News.* The *News*'s Web site features a "human toothpick," a dog-faced girl, a man with a 40-inch horn sprouting from his head, and a hilariously unconvincing human-alligator mutation—a "missing link" between *Homo sapiens* and reptile that "jumped off the evolutionary ladder and blazed its own trail into the modern era" where (hungered, no doubt, by its evolutionary exertions) it scarfed up a piece of chocolate cake and some fried chicken, "bones and all, like there was no tomorrow." Best of all, there's Bat Boy, a pointy-eared, razor-fanged masterpiece of brazen

Barnum in the supermarket: Bat Boy and the missing link between human and reptile, alive!, in the *Weekly World News*. Photo courtesy *Weekly World News*.

fakery. He's a digitally retouched upgrade of the zoological oddities exhibited in decades past, when enterprising showmen used taxidermy to create four-legged ducks and bear-monkey hybrids.

As the eruption of freakery from Broadway to sideshow banner art to alt.culture to supermarket tabloids suggests, the freak has taken his place in the public mind, alongside the cyborg, the serial killer, the evil clown, and Munch's Screamer, as a cultural totem of the late twentieth century. Freaks are made-to-order poster children for an age of extremes: extreme sports, extreme fighting, extreme weather, extreme science (pigs that produce human hemoglobin), extreme TV (*World's Scariest Police Chases*), extreme diseases (flesh-eating bacteria), extreme sex (the mainstreaming of S&M via *Basic Instinct* and bondage couture), extreme art (performance artist Bob Flanagan nailing his penis to a board), extreme toys (*Postal,* a thrill-kill videogame that enables kids to waste innocent bystanders as they beg for mercy), extreme beliefs (the white supremacist Larry Wayne Harris's dream of unleashing bubonic plague in the New York subway), extreme behavior (Mike Tyson biting off Evander Holyfield's ear), and, most profoundly, economic extremes: the yawning income gap between the economic elite and the overworked, overdrawn millions.

Freaks are living symbols of the nineties trend toward X-large, hyperbolic everything. As this is written, the women's shoe du jour is a huge, chunky heel—the disco platform on steroids. The status symbol of the moment is the hulking sport-utility vehicle, the acromegalic giant of the automotive world. Dizzy extremes are becoming commonplace in the guise of the 300-pound offensive linemen on today's football fields, the blow-up-doll bodies of Pamela Anderson and Anna Nicole Smith, the hyperthyroidal massiveness of bendable action figures and comic-book superheroes.

Tracking the nineties obsession with hyperdevelopment, the art historian George L. Hersey notes that the 1970 Batman, while buff, was still relatively normal, "with only a few negligently indicated blobs of fiber at the shoulders, on his chest, and on his upper legs."[3] The 1992 Batman, by contrast, is a hypertrophied grotesque, with huge arms, almost as long as his legs, and shoulders nearly half his height in width. Even so, he looks positively scrawny alongside the latest version of the Incredible Hulk, a green-skinned mountain of brawn whose massive arms are thicker than his head, which has dwindled to "a vestigial polyp on the hero's bright green landscape of muscle."[4]

Freaks of nature emblematize this cultural tendency toward physical extremes. Of course, some self-made oddities, or gaffes, legitimately
earn the label "freak" themselves. The obvious, shopworn example is Michael
Jackson, a plastic-surgery addict whose slow-motion morphing from black
to white, gendered to androgynous, adult to man-child, human to alien has
earned him pride of place in the Congress of Curious People convened at
the supermarket checkout stand. "Wacko Jacko," as the tabs have dubbed
him, is a grotesque gaffe whose ill-fated makeovers have inspired a headline worthy of the midway: MICHAEL JACKSON'S PLASTIC FACE IS MELTING."[5]

His purported vitiligo, a skin disease that causes a blotchy loss of
pigment in blacks, links him to the "human leopards," "spotted families,"
and other blacks with mottled skin once exhibited in carnivals, circuses,
and dime museums throughout America and Europe. He recognized a kin-
dred spirit in the monstrous Elephant Man, whose bones he allegedly
attempted to buy, and in P. T. Barnum, whose book of "theories and phi-
losophies" he once called his "bible."[6] Barnum appears on the cover of
Jackson's record Dangerous, accompanied by the midget Tom Thumb, whose
paramilitary trappings and honorary title of "General," bestowed on him
by Barnum, prefigure Jackson's own penchant for mock-military costumes
and his self-appointed status as the "king of pop." David D. Yuan believes
that Jackson, taking a leaf from the self-styled "prince of humbugs," has
hoaxed the tabs with fabricated tales of sleeping in hyperbaric chambers and
bidding for the Elephant Man's bones in a calculated attempt to "be freakish enough to arouse the restless public's interest, but not so freakish that
fans are shocked or repulsed by him."[7] As Jackson fatefully observed, "I want
my whole career to be the greatest show on earth," and it has been, though
in a way closer to Nightmare Alley, Edmund Goulding's 1947 horror movie
about a carnival geek, than to the Ringling Brothers' big top.[8]

Hard-core bodybuilders, whose bulging physiques have been un-
forgettably described by the cultural critic Andrew Ross as "condoms stuffed
with walnuts," are postmodern gaffes as well. They're "able to push their
muscles and eliminate body fat to a degree well beyond anything seen earlier in human history," writes Hersey. "Today, the muscles of the legs and
upper body can be mounded into huge, intricate sculptural masses interwoven with hoselike arteries."[9] In a posthuman parody of physical fitness,
these self-declared "freaks" pump themselves into Schwarzeneggerian
hulks with the aid of specialized diets, weight-training machines, and, most

important, steroids. According to Dr. Charles E. Yesalis, a professor of "human development" at Pennsylvania State University, "People just don't look like that without steroids."[10]

Nor do many women look like Wendy Whoppers, Lisa Lipps, or Topsy Curvy without surgery. These porn stars' humongous breast implants seem poised for liftoff from gravity, even humanity. Ms. Curvy's purported measurements, for example, are 101-24-34. Fetishized by the heavy-breathing fans known in the trade as "raincoats," she and others like her epitomize a freakish ideal born of the techno-logic of our age. Like the early nineties rage for digital morphing in commercials and music videos, the current trend toward hyperdevelopment is the product of technological advances in steroids, exercise machines, and new techniques in cosmetic surgery that not only make posthuman body modification possible but promote it, as well. The Los Angeles surgeon Garry Brody noted in 1986 that breast augmentation was becoming more extreme simply because surgeons had discovered that breasts would tolerate larger implants than was previously thought possible.[11] Invention is the mother of necessity. "Big-top girls" like Wendy Whoppers have 80 HHH bustlines because they *can*.

Whoppers's fans seem curiously unconcerned that her zeppelin-sized breasts are surgical falsies, a self-evident truth flaunted by her cartoony stage name, which she says means "a 'whopper' like when someone tells a tall tale, in other words . . . a big lie, like big fake boobs."[12] "Larger than life" and "twice as real," the venerable come-ons of the advertiser and the carny barker, are American mantras, and the implicit promise in both is the eye-poppingly prodigious, the transcendently unreal—an apotheosis of the ridiculous which is at once freak and fake.

Trained to grow toward the centerfold and the supermodel in a sort of media tropism, modern male desire is nourished by images of impossible bodies, digitally airbrushed and surgically reconstructed. But women with waiflike bodies and mammoth breasts are as rare as two-headed babies in the real world, so they must be manufactured, like the fabricated freaks of earlier times: the Chinese infants encased in vases so that their bodies would grow to dwarfish proportions or the self-made monsters of eighteenth-century Europe, who mutilated and even amputated body parts to enhance their earning power as beggars. The cultural critic David J. Skal believes that the current "epidemic of plastic surgery"—and it *is* epidemic, according to *The New York Times,* which recently reported an upsurge in plastic surgery of all types—is creating "a nation of gaffed freaks." Says Skal, "There's got to be a name for the syndrome—Elephant Man Envy? The cosmetic surgeon's operating room has more in common with the sideshow tent than we want to admit."[13]

To those who enforce the no-fly zone between high and low culture, the increasingly freakish nature of late-twentieth-century America is symptomatic of advanced culture rot. "If modern culture may be seen in terms of a competition for audience between high and low entertainment, between art and vulgarity, between the Church and the Carnival, then the Carnival is having its day," laments James B. Twitchell, in *Carnival Culture: The Trashing of Taste in America*.[14]

Twitchell is especially exercised about daytime talk shows. "If the sideshow has influenced sports and news," he writes, "it has overwhelmed the TV studio-interview show. Here, truly, is the land that taste forgot."[15] He traces the Descent of Man from the *Today* show in the fifties, when the host, Dave Garroway, shared the stage with a chimpanzee named J. Fred Muggs, through Mike Douglas and Merv Griffin, Dick Cavett and Dinah Shore, to *The Phil Donahue Show,* the syndicated "homemaker" entertainment that gave birth in 1967 to daytime talk as we know it. Phil begat Oprah, with her "discussions on penis size, vaginal orgasm, and porn queens," and Oprah begat Geraldo Rivera and Geraldo begat Morton Downey, Jr., who enjoyed 15 minutes of infamy in the late eighties as the pugnacious king of "garbage and guts TV" before publicly imploding with deeply satisfying messiness.[16]

Twitchell isn't alone in his belief that the vulgarians are at the gates, or at least in the raucous, hectoring studio audiences of Jerry Springer and Jenny Jones and Sally Jessy Raphael. George Gerbner, a professor of communications, thinks that daytime talk shows "are virtually destroying the goodness of America."[17] The media critic Howard Kurtz decries viewers' voyeuristic obsession with the "endless freak show" of daytime talk. The shows numb us, we're told, sacrificing people's pain on the altar of the almighty Nielsen ratings, and "defining deviancy down"—a pet phrase lifted from Daniel Patrick Moynihan's essay of the same name and worn threadbare by pundits everywhere.

The best-known opponent of "cultural rot" is, of course, the nation's self-appointed virtues czar, William Bennett, who initiated a campaign against daytime talk shows in 1995. "We've forgotten that civilization depends on keeping some of this stuff under wraps," said Bennett, a fervent believer in the neo-Victorian ethic of "constructive hypocrisy." Talk shows, with their warts-and-all true confessions about "sex and violence and sleeping around," are "a force of decomposition," he declared, "a tropism toward the toilet."[18]

In many ways, the critics are right. At their worst, daytime talk shows *are* freak shows, parading the deviant and the dysfunctional for the titillation, revulsion, and ridicule of the peanut-crunching crowd. They open emotional wounds, then treat them with the vacuous platitudes of recovery-group culture, stripping vulnerable people who have no one else to turn to naked in front of millions, all in the name of market share. "I felt like a freak in a circus sideshow," said one former talk-show guest.[19] They expose latch-key kids to the puerile and the prurient and toss unprepared teenagers, like the 12-year-old on *Sally Jessy Raphael* who claimed she had slept with 25 guys, to the tender mercies of the mob.

In their frenzied competition for the lowest common denominator, talk shows earn the ubiquitous comparison to carnival sideshows. They have featured a man who said he was raped by an alien and a woman who claimed she and Elvis were from Venus, and have focused on necrophilia (Sally Jessy Raphael), "Jell-O Wrestling: Is it sexist?" (Jerry Springer), and two strippers whose claim to fame was having the biggest breasts in America. David Skal suggests that "Oprah Winfrey herself, in highly publicized bouts of weight fluctuation, manage[s] to embody the spirits of both the fat lady and the human skeleton" familiar from the carnival sideshow.[20] Back when Geraldo Rivera was in "the freak-show business" (his words), before he donned the spectacles of respectability as the host of the current affairs program, *Rivera Live,* he submitted to on-air liposuction in which fat was vacuumed out of his butt and transferred to his forehead. To the best of my knowledge, no talk show has yet featured a "glomming geek," a wet-brained sideshow performer who bites the heads off live chickens, but Phil Donahue did campaign (unsuccessfully) to televise the execution of a murderer. Hope springs eternal.

At their worst, then, daytime talk shows are equal parts geek show, peep show, and *Gong Show,* made morally palatable by a gooey icing of psycho-babble. The deeper questions are: What is the chattering class *really* saying when it reviles these programs as "freak shows"? Who decides who's a freak? And why are freaks so threatening?

Looking past the sideshow-banner slogans of the mainstream crusade against "trash TV," we quickly realize that behind all the yelling about moral decay and our lost capacity for shame lurk the old, familiar specters of class, gender, and race (along with the modern frisson of sexual preference) that haunted James Huneker's fulminations against Coney Island. "What a sight the poor make in the limelight!" Huneker's torchbearers seem to be saying. Like Huneker, many, if not most, of the voices raised against daytime talk are white, male, and upper middle-class. In sharp contrast, the guests, studio audiences, and home viewers of these shows are a racially diverse group of mostly housewives and lower-income working-class women with little or no higher education. More than half of them live in households with annual incomes under $30,000.[21]

It's hard, in light of this cultural chasm, not to read the high-minded outrage of the media elite as a paroxysm of class revulsion. Who *are* these people, anyway, with their bad hair and their uncouth yawp? It's the return of the repressed, again—in this case, the "trailer trash" and subway lumpen denied a seat among the Beltway oracles on Jim Lehrer's *NewsHour* or the beautiful people on *Late Night with David Letterman*. "Talk shows . . . let people who have been largely excluded from the public conversation appear on national TV and talk about their sex lives, their family fights, sometimes their literal dirty laundry," writes Ellen Willis, in *The Nation*. "On talk shows, whatever their drawbacks, the proles get to talk."[22] The cultural critic Donna Gaines is less equivocal: "Bennett's morality squad may see talk shows as carnival freak shows, but all that means is that the shows have the power to drag us statistical outcasts in from the margins."[23]

Freaks of nature are boundary crossers, prodigious beings who violate norms. In the electric carnival of daytime talk, freaks of culture challenge the media elite's exclusive right to Explain It All For Us. Privileging firsthand experience over abstract knowledge, they countervail the scientific "objectivity" of the expert with the boisterous commonsense opinions of ordinary people. Moreover, they shift the focus of discussion from the president's approval ratings and the congressional floor to women's and working-class issues, up-close and personal.

As well, daytime talk-show audiences upend the middle-class conventions of polite public discourse cemented into place in the late nineteenth century, when social reformers like Huneker were condemning Coney and calling for working-class amusements that promoted the bourgeois values of restraint and respectability. Contrast the black or Hispanic woman in *Ricki Lake*'s audience admonishing a guest, "Girlfriend, your self-respect is in the toilet," with the WASP-y reserve and to-the-manor-born air of superiority that pervades Sunday morning political talk shows like *This Week with David Brinkley*.[24] Noting that the Brinkley show rarely features black, Hispanic, Asian-American, or openly gay journalists, Kurtz observes that sometimes the show's regulars often sound "truly insular, clucking over the unruly behavior of the mob beyond the gates." "The whole country needs to be sent to bed without its dessert," sniffed the conservative columnist George Will, a defender to the death of a Merchant-Ivory social order in which a gentleman nobly bears the burden of noblesse oblige and the underclass knows its place.[25]

Not only does daytime talk TV give the rabble a turn at the microphone, but it also provides a forum for women's issues, which are pushed to the margins or ignored entirely in male-dominated arenas like Sunday morning political talk shows and talk radio. Eighty percent of daytime talk TV's audience is female, and show staffs are heavily populated by women. Daytime talk intuitively embraces the feminist assumption that the personal is political, rejecting the Brinkley gang's elite-oriented, Capitol Hill definition of politics in favor of one that spotlights the political struggles of everyday life, at home, on the job, or just about anywhere. "Years ago, when we were doing stories on date rape, artificial insemination, homophobia, sex bias crimes, and spousal abuse, serious news programs wouldn't touch them," says Phil Donahue. "Now they're doing these kinds of stories routinely, and they're giving them quite a bit of time, too."[26]

The personal is especially political for gays. Daytime talk provides what was, until the very recent fad for "lipstick lesbians" and upscale white gays on broadcast TV, a rare form of public address for homosexuals, transvestites, transsexuals, and others who defy the sexual norms of mainstream America. Talk shows offered gays a chance to take charge, however briefly, of their representations in the media, "playing themselves" on national TV. As Vito Russo argues in *The Celluloid Closet,* movie and TV portrayals of gays and lesbians as villains and victims reinforce pernicious stereotypes and perpetuate political powerlessness. "Representation in the mediated 'reality' of our mass culture is in itself power," he writes.[27] Talk shows, argues Joshua Gamson in *Freaks Talk Back: Tabloid Talk Shows and Sexual Nonconfor-*

mity, "are a fabulous chance to see what happens when lesbian, gay, bisexual, and transgender people *are* highly visible in a commercial cultural realm."[28]

Daytime talk shows also made room for gays in their espousal of a postpuritanical morality that values self-acceptance over social respectability. "It's no coincidence that talk shows were the first mass-cultural arena where homosexuals could get beyond polemics and simply justify their love," writes the gay cultural critic Richard Goldstein. "As Bennett (an opponent of gay rights) knows, there is nothing more dangerous. Like the closet, his standard of 'constructive hypocrisy' requires the active denial of a deviant's humanity. Talk TV shatters that pretense, and its popularity suggests an enormous hunger for freedom from the shackles of duplicity." Goldstein sees *The Jenny Jones Show* and other electronic encounter groups, with their overwhelmingly female, multi-ethnic audiences, as badly needed correctives to the Angry White Male demagoguery of Bob Grant and other evangelists for the new (moral) order. True to their carnival roots, daytime talk shows "revel in deviance" and thus "subvert the moral order" envisioned by neoconservatives.[29]

Obviously, the unapologetic, in-your-face display of freakery—in this case, alternative sexualities—poses a threat to the status quo, which accounts for the moral hysterics of Bennett and his vice squad. When media crusaders inveigh against the "sexual perversity" of daytime talk, the time-honored equation of gays, cross-dressers, and gender switchers with perverts is presumed. After Jonathan Schmitz killed Scott Amedure, a gay man who had confessed his crush on Schmitz before an audience of millions on *The Jenny Jones Show,* the media laid the burden of guilt at the show's doorstep for giving airtime to what one commentator called "crazed people whose worst secrets are being exposed to a live audience."[30] The "crazed" person in this little cautionary tale from the Book of Media Virtues, unbelievably, is not the pathological homophobe who blew a man away with a shotgun blast, but the gay who eschewed constructive hypocrisy and blurted out his "worst secret"—being in love with another man—on national television.

Needless to say, *Donahue* segments on dwarf tossing or the staged fights on *The Jerry Springer Show* "revel in deviance" in a manner that isn't exactly a great leap forward for the voiceless minorities marginalized by the mainstream media. But neither are such shows the cancer on the body politic, eating a hole in the soul of America, that, say, daytime talk *radio* is.

Oddly, we haven't heard much from Bennett about the nightmare midway of talk radio, though it feeds on social pathologies that make the blood congeal. The New York radio hate monger Bob Grant observed, after a gay pride parade, that "it would have been nice to have a few phalanxes of policemen with machine guns and mow them down." Welfare mothers are "maggots," he believes, who should be subjected to "the Bob Grant Mandatory Sterilization Plan."[31] Meanwhile, in our fair nation's capital, G. Gordon Liddy exercises his First Amendment right to froth about the Bureau of Alcohol, Tobacco, and Firearms, which he thinks is conducting a "terror campaign" against gun dealers. "Head shots, head shots—kill the sons of bitches!" he foams.[32]

Bennett's deafening silence on the subject of hate radio looks even stranger when set alongside the fact that the Eliot Ness of media decency has been a guest on Grant's show, and Bennett's group, Empower America, provides tip sheets to conservative jocks. The explanation for Bennett's moral myopia may lie in the fact that the talk-radio audience is the virtual obverse of daytime talk TV: mostly white, suburban men over 45 who come from households earning more than $50,000.[33] And—big surprise—they're overwhelmingly Republican. In other words, they're guys like Bennett.

Which brings us full circle, back to the question of who wields the power to name a freak. A freak, apparently, is one of *them*—the mongrel masses, "half child, half savage," as Huneker put it. Lower-class black and Hispanic women. Trailer trash. Unashamed, unapologetic homosexuals, transvestites, and transsexuals who don't have the decency to stay in the closet.

The most terrifying thing about freaks, of course, is that they jar loose definitions of normality and abnormality we thought were set in stone. The battle lines of deviance and normality are drawn, in the media crusade against daytime talk shows, with an absolutism tinged by fear. It's the fear that "they" might have some claim to normalcy, too, and that, horror of horrors, there might be a little of their abnormality in us. This is the essence of homophobia: Schmitz killed Amedure because he "fucked me on national TV," making him, Schmitz, homosexual, too, until the queer within was ritually exorcised by that most macho of acts, killing a queer.[34]

Normality hangs in terrifyingly precarious balance with deviance, it seems, and which is which is at least partly a matter of perspective. "Freaks are what you make them," said Clyde Ingles, who managed the Ringling

Brothers sideshow in the twenties. "Take any peculiar-looking person whose familiarity to those around him makes for acceptance, play up that peculiarity and add a good spiel," and you have a freak.[35] Gamson, a gay man, writes, "I identify with the misfits, monsters, trash, and perverts. From that perspective, talk shows look rather different."[36] Conversely, to the so-called misfits and monsters in the talk-show audience (8 million of them on a good day for Jerry Springer), a neocon crusader for normalcy like, say, George Will must seem decidedly abnormal.[37] With his signature bowtie and Eton collar, his airy disdain for pop culture, and blithely bloodless sentiments like his remark that the homeless should be moved "off to someplace where they are simply out of sight and no longer a visible . . . public nuisance," Will looks positively freakish from the other side of the footlights.[38]

The return of the freak in millennial culture signals a crisis in the dominant culture's authority to decide who stands in the center and who sits on the fringes. As well, it celebrates values that flout the puritanical commandments of Bennett and his New Victorians.

For the marginalized, the widening gyre is a carnival ride—a Tilt-a-Whirl for chaos culture. Looking back from an imagined near future, the feminist theorist Sadie Plant recalls the nineties, when "women were becoming mothers on their own terms, or not at all. Heterosexual relations were losing their viability, queer connections were flourishing, the carnival had begun for a vast range of paraphilias and so-called perversions, and if there was more than one sex to have, there were also more than two to be. Anything claiming to be normal had become peculiar."[39]

Challenges to accepted norms aren't limited to mores and social conventions; timeless standards of physical normalcy are being questioned as well. Jennifer Miller, a bearded lesbian, has starred in a nude calendar that turns conventional notions of feminine beauty and lesbian style inside out. Helen Melon, the feminist fat lady at Coney Island U.S.A., delivers a caustically funny monologue during her performance, skewering stereotypical attitudes toward fat women. Growing numbers of multiracial Americans are checking "none of the above" rather than perpetuate the fiction of a single racial identity. An increasing number of scientists believe that race is a social construct, not a biological verity, a historical means of anchoring power and privilege that has no basis in genetic fact.[40]

Zoe Leonard, "Pin-up #1 (Jennifer Miller Does Marilyn Monroe)", 1995. Courtesy Paula Cooper Gallery, New York.

Anne Fausto-Sterling, a professor of medical science at Brown University, believes there are at least five sexes. Intersexuals (a term they prefer to "hermaphrodites") are questioning the routine surgical "correction" of ambiguous external genitalia at birth. Conjoined twins like Lori and Reba Schappell, profiled in a *New York Times* feature, wouldn't be surgically separated if they could be.

The scalpel cuts both ways: The medical miracles that offer people with anomalous bodies the possibility of a more mainstream existence also transform an irrevocable accident of birth into a matter of conscious choice. The decision to remain as they are is an act of quiet defiance. It dramatizes society's profound discomfort with the Other who won't submit to the normalizing knife, from small-time offenders like Barbra Streisand, who famously refused to "fix" her nose, to threats to the social order like the Schappell sisters.

The realization that we share the human continuum with beings as utterly other as the Schappells unsettles our sense of normality; even as the freakish body sets our own (relative) normality in reassuring relief, it makes us suddenly conscious of our own deviance, be it physical or psychological. Confounding the neat, binary oppositions between male and female (hermaphrodites), black and white ("leopard" children with vitiligo), self and other (conjoined twins), human and animal (the mule-faced woman, the dog-faced boy) that have underwritten Western thought since the Enlightenment, freaks dramatize the extent to which these and other distinctions are—and always were—social conventions, not eternal truths.

In so doing, freaks remind us, disquietingly, that as the freak-show historian Robert Bogdan argues, "'Freak' is a way of thinking about and

"Freak is a frame of mind." Banner by Johnny Meah, Bannerline Inc.

presenting people—a frame of mind and a set of practices."[41] Though we stand on the other side of the footlights, we're freaks as well, in the sense that we have internalized the cultural codes that make a freak. In our inability to see extremely tall or short people as just that, our insistence on viewing them in the fun house-mirror distortions of myths about giants or dwarfs, we participate in a psychology that adequately earns the term "freakish." In her 1995 novel, *The Mirror of Monsters and Prodigies,* Pamela Ditchoff warns, "You can't gaze into a mirror without your image mingling its own nature with that which is contained within the frame."[42] Collaborating on the consensual hallucination that is the freak, we become what we behold.

4 / ANUS HORRIBILIS: JIM CARREY'S EXCREMENTAL EXCESS

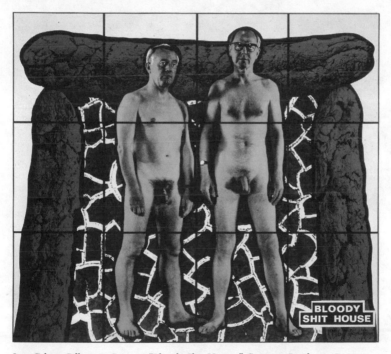

Log Cabin: Gilbert & George, "Bloody Shit House." Courtesy Prudence Cuming Associates Limited.

Jim Carrey is Georges Bataille's Solar Anus, with a change of underwear.

Bataille (1897–1962) was a renegade French philosopher who deplored the subjugation of our "animal" nature by bourgeois culture and industrial modernity. He extolled the delirious excesses of ancient or primitive societies, with their human sacrifices and orgiastic festivals, and excoriated the repressive culture of the modern bourgeoisie, a class whose true face he found "so rapacious and lacking in nobility, so frighteningly small, that all human life, upon seeing it, seems degraded."[1] He celebrated what he called the *heterogeneous:* the incommensurate, the inassimilable—in short, everything *other* that threatens the homogenizing forces of bourgeois culture.

As examples of the heterogeneous, Bataille offered erotic words and deeds; dreams and neuroses; lawless mobs like the ones that swarmed through the nightmares of James Huneker and Gustave Le Bon; murderers, madmen, and self-mutilation. But the heterogeneous *par excellence* is "the waste products of the human body and certain analogous matter (trash, vermin, etc.)."[2] For Bataille, nothing says "primal animality" like excrement. Bataille's concept is closely related to Julia Kristeva's notion of the abject, which encompasses everything society excludes or represses in order to sustain itself: filth, waste, bodily fluids, corpses—all that we "permanently thrust aside in order to live." Human waste is especially abject. "Excrement and its equivalents (decay, infection, disease, corpse, etc.) stand for the danger to identity that comes from without: the ego threatened by the non-ego, society threatened by its outside, life by death," writes Kristeva.[3]

Bataille's writings are fraught with scatological imagery, so much so that the appalled pope of surrealism, André Breton (a textbook anal-retentive), excommunicated Bataille from the movement, condemning him as an "excremental philosopher." Groping toward an impossible philosophy, one "opposed to any homogeneous representations of the world, in other words, to any philosophical system," Bataille pushed the rhetorical envelope to the bounds of rationality, often breaking through into wild conceits, surrealist poetry, pure fiction.[4] Among the strangest of his strange writings was his antimyth of the Solar Anus, an "excremental fantasy" elaborated in a trio of essays written between 1927 and 1930.

In them, he fantasizes a parodic utopia in which the bestial unreason and sacred horrors of "savage" societies come back with a bang—"a sudden, bursting eruption, as provocative and as dissolute as the one that inflates the anal protuberance of an ape."[5] Using the diminution of the bulging, brightly colored simian anus in the course of our evolution from ape to human as a metaphor for the repression of primitive impulses by bourgeois culture, Bataille envisions the triumphant return of the repressed, symbolized for him by the surreal image of a radiant anus.

In Bataille's excremental fantasy, the constipated forces of animality (what he calls the "urges of the ape") bubble up into the brain of *Homo sapiens*. The rational mind is overwhelmed by that sublime butt-head, at once cosmic and comic, the Solar Anus. This metamorphosis culminates in the birth of the Pineal Eye, a polymorphous perversity that is equal parts primate anus, cosmic hard-on, and creature from the id. The Eye usurps the Cartesian seat of reason, the pineal gland, and bursts out of the Solar Anus's head "with the shady and comical character associated with the rear end and its excretions."[6]

The Bataille scholar Allan Stoekl describes Bataille's vision as an evolutionary fantasy involving "the movement of a tremendous erotic force up from the ape's provocative anus to the erect human's head and brain. The next stage of evolution, manifested by a kind of parodic Nietzschean superman, posits a 'pineal eye,' a final but deadly erection, which blasts through the top of the human skull and 'sees' the overwhelming sun."[7] Bataille's antimyth inverts Freud's fable, in *Civilization and Its Discontents*, of the ascent of humankind, up from the anal eroticism that supposedly comes from walking on all fours to the repression of the anal that follows naturally from walking fully upright.

At one point in Bataille's hallucinatory allegory, he notes that on the long, hard, Darwinian haul from simian to *Homo sapiens,* the ape's obscene anus tucked itself discreetly between the buttocks. Now, the primitive emotions that in early hominids made the anus swell and flush find release in the human face, which functions, in Bataille's mind, as a surrogate anus, expressing feelings "that up to that point had made the anal orifice bud and flame."[8]

Jim Carrey, whose signature gag is ventriloquizing his butt, returns us to that glorious moment when naked apes emoted with their hindquarters. Carrey is an air-freshened, family-friendly version of Bataille's excremental fantasies, a rubber-faced icon of vulgarian fun whose abiding themes are feces and flatulence and the brain deposed by the body—the seat of reason usurped by the seat of the pants. Wherever Carrey goes, the smell of methane is never far behind: In *The Mask,* he declares, "This is the moment of truth, when a man shows what he's really made of: crap!"; in *Dumb and Dumber* he megadoses Jeff Daniels with Turbo-Lax, causing him to let loose with a truly biblical movement; in *Ace Ventura: Pet Detective,* he warns people away from the toxic fallout of his trips to the bathroom ("Do *not* go in there!"). Carrey's rear view of the world even follows him into the noncanonical *Batman Forever,* where he exclaims "Spank me!" in a spasm of evil glee.

Often, he seems to be channeling Le Petomane ("the fartiste"), the nineteenth-century cabaret sensation who could blow out candles with a well-aimed blast and break wind in tenor, baritone, and bass registers. In *Ace Ventura,* Carrey mimes singing an aria out of his ass ("O sodomy-a") and pretends that his butt has a mutinous mind of its own, a scene that is weirdly reminiscent of the "Talking Asshole" routine in *Naked Lunch* (inspired by Le Petomane). "You've really pissed him off now—I can't hold him much longer," snarls Carrey, wrestling his rump into submission; in the Burroughs novel, a "man who taught his asshole to talk" ends up battling the treasonous orifice for control of his body, "screaming at it to shut up, and beating it with his fist, and sticking candles up it."[9] Ultimately, the Burroughs character undergoes a bizarre metamorphosis: Tissue grows over his mouth, sealing it off, and, as with Bataille's Solar Anus, the ass infiltrates the brain until "the brain [can't] give orders anymore." The triumph of animality over rationality is complete.

Burroughs's obscenely funny little fable is partly about the victory of the abject—the Other—and partly about the dethroning of language,

which Burroughs viewed with a jaundiced eye. As the nephew of the
public-relations Svengali Ivy Lee, he knew that language could be an ap-
paratus of social control. A student of the semanticist Alfred Korzybski,
he believed that language drove a wedge between mind and body, substi-
tuting words for things, disembodied abstraction for embodied knowledge. For Burroughs, excrement symbolized both the irrepressible abject
and the irrefutable real. When *Naked Lunch* was on trial for obscenity,
the court asked a witness whether the book's title pertained to "a descrip-
tion of a person eating excrement, served on a plate."[10] It doesn't; Burroughs
has said that it refers to reality seen with brutal, cold-turkey clarity, "the
frozen moment when everyone sees what is on the end of every fork."
But it might as well: what better symbol of the repressed, of everything
other, of all that we "permanently thrust aside in order to live," than a
turd on a plate?

Of course, Burroughs is also a wildly obscene social satirist and
scatological humorist, part of a tradition that includes Juvenal, Rabelais,
Henry Miller, and, in its Mall of America manifestation, the Jim Carrey of
fecal follies like *Dumb and Dumber* and *Ace Ventura*. It's hardly a revelation
that humor, especially broad physical comedy like Carrey's, is rooted in
what Mikhail Bakhtin delicately referred to as "the material bodily lower
stratum," which he defines as "the human body with its food, drink, defecation, and sexual life."[11] But the raunchy posts on the Net, in usegroups
like rec.humor and alt.tasteless, have nothing on the bawdy graffiti on the
walls of Pompeii, and Aristophanes' *The Frogs* (405 B.C.) features fart jokes
and a demented bit about being publicly sodomized with a radish that
wouldn't be out of place in *National Lampoon*.

That said, the rising tide of excremental excess is seeping further
into the mainstream than at any other time in recent memory. We live at a
moment in history when a man best known for "yodeling out his ass," as
Premiere inimitably described Carrey, is the $20 million face of family fun
in cineplexes across America. *Entertainment Weekly* recently announced the
"return of the grown-up gross-out," noting that "goopy bodily substances
and odors are the happiest of happy topics among moviegoing *adults* again,
enjoying a popularity unparalleled since the eras of Molière, Swift, and the
Zucker brothers" (*Airplane!* and *Naked Gun* fame).[12]

The box-office hit of the moment, *There's Something About Mary,* is
a raunchy comedy whose sight gags include a hapless schlemiel with a long,

gooey gob of semen dangling from one ear. Another comedy, *Henry Fool,* includes a scene in which a woman accepts a wedding proposal after seeing her lover's bowel movement swirling down the toilet. *The New York Times* claims that mainstream TV, in 1998, is "flaunting the most vulgar and explicit sex, language, and behavior that it has ever sent into American homes."[13] To the endless consternation of both the left and the right, *South Park,* a Comedy Central cartoon about potty-mouthed third-grade boys, is a huge hit with the jejune and the jejune at heart. Episodes have featured aliens probing a fat kid's butt, explosive diarrhea, and a wise-ass talking turd named Mr. Hankey the Christmas Poo.

Meanwhile, off-screen, there are "Barf-O-Rama" books like *Dog Doo Afternoon* and *The Legend of Bigfart,* a desperate attempt to engross young boys with tales of boogers and "buttwurst"; Jenny McCarthy sitting on a toilet, for no discernible reason, in an ad for Candie's shoes; and, always and everywhere, the man whose name is synonymous with the cathartic cleaning of the collective colon, Howard Stern. Simultaneously, fringe culture's predictable interest in scandalizing the Moral Majority has escalated subcultural hostilities, examples of which include 'zines like *Poop, Scatology,* and *We Like Poo; The Re/Search Guide to Bodily Fluids;* and *A light at the End of the Tunnel: Writers, Artists, and Poets on Feces.*

It's not only the commercial mainstream and fringe culture that are going down the toilet. The body politics that has obsessed the art world throughout the nineties—issues such as AIDS, abortion rights, the beauty myth, eating disorders, death, and the puritanical denial of bodily functions and carnal pleasures—has inspired abject art such as Kiki Smith's sculpture of a woman crawling on all fours, an impossibly long turd trailing behind her (*Tale,* 1992), Gilbert & George's proud photos of their movements (*The Naked Shit Pictures,* 1995), and Todd Alden's *Collectors' Shit* (1996) which consists of the titular product, canned and accompanied by certificates of authenticity.

The art historian Hal Foster argues that infantile artistic personalities appear in turbulent times as semaphores of alienation and defiance, presumably of the status quo. "In the early 1990s, this defiance was manifested in a general flaunting of shit," he writes, invoking Freud's observation that "anal eroticism finds a narcissistic application in the production of defiance"—canning and selling the shit of one's patrons, for example, or yodeling out one's ass.[14]

Kiki Smith, "Tale," 1992. Collection of Jeffrey Deitch.

Of course, the equation of artistic expression with evacuation has become a pop psych cliché, buttressed by pop culture caricatures of the temperamental artiste as an overgrown infant, arrested in the anal phase. Undeniably, much of this century's art seems to take an anal delight in playing with society's waste products or thrusting our industrial excreta back in our faces: Think of Arman's *Poubelles,* the contents of garbage cans displayed in Plexiglas boxes; Nancy Rubins's *Worlds Apart,* a 45-foot-tall tree fashioned from thrown-out appliances; and John Chamberlain's exhibition of a crushed car chassis as sculpture.

Such works can be read as critiques of the throw-away society, an artistic response to the sociological truism that one can judge a society by its waste products, or a Duchampian armpit-fart in the face of highbrow notions of beauty and quality in art. But there's also an excremental alchemy at work in the transmutation of base materials into art. Freud reminds us that in dream logic the worthless often stands in for the priceless; hence the association of excrement and gold in folktales and alchemy. Patti Smith, no stranger to the "material bodily lower stratum," writes, "The transformation of waste is perhaps the oldest preoccupation of man. . . . Inherent within us is the dream and task of the alchemist . . . to create from the excretions of man pure and soft then solid gold."[15] The Italian artist Piero Manzoni, notorious for *Merda d'Artista* (1961)—his canned excrement, sold for its weight in gold—would surely agree.

Just as art can be seen as a regression to the anal phase, excretion can be seen as artistic expression. Gilbert & George contend that playing with feces is a child's first artwork. A bowel movement, says George, is "the only sculpture that exists naturally. It's people's first adventure in form, and it's one that everybody in the world understands." Gilbert adds, "It's the first clay that you have. Children naturally make sculptures out of shit."[16]

And, as every child knows, shit is a surefire shocker, guaranteed to set authority figures in an uproar. "Children are, indeed, proud of their own excretions and often make use of them in asserting themselves against adults," writes Freud.[17] Thus, it seems only natural that the enfants terribles of the avant-garde would use excremental imagery (and sometimes the real thing) to outrage the bourgeoisie and give the art world the finger. Modernist avant-gardism has been anal-expulsive from its opening salvo in 1896: the character Père Ubu barking *"Merde!"* ("Shit!") at the premiere of Alfred Jarry's play *Ubu Roi*. The artistic landscape of this century is littered with scatological droppings: Marcel Duchamp's notorious *Fountain* (1917), a urinal signed and submitted to an exhibition as sculpture; Salvador Dali's *The Lugubrious Game* (1929), an explosion of dreamlike images prominently featuring a man in shit-stained boxer shorts; Hannah Wilke's terra-cotta sculptures of stools; and Sam Goodman and Boris Lurie's matter-of-factly named *Shit Sculptures,* towering mounds of papier-mâché feces splattered with brown paint. ("I'd like it understood this is my final gesture after thirty years in the art world," said a disgruntled Goodman. "This is what I think of it.")[18]

As we near the end of the century, ever-greater outrages are required to jerk the chains of conservative art critics like Hilton Kramer and jolt to attention an art world whose nerve endings have been numbed by a hundred years of the shock of the new. Hence Gilbert & George's 1997 broadside, "The Fundamental Pictures," blown-up images of human waste in all its emetic glory, with titles like *Piss on Us, Piss on Piss, Piss Piss Piss,* and, for variety's sake, *Shit and Piss.*

* * *

So what, exactly, is Jim Carrey's talking butt trying to tell us? What does it mean when our cultural plumbing backs up into the art world, alternative culture, and the mega-malled, cineplexed mainstream all at once? When Bataille's anality and Kristeva's abject and Bakhtin's lower stratum seem to be bubbling up everywhere?

Some see doomy portents of cultural decline in the excremental excesses of the late nineties, a creeping moral decay brought on, they say, by the coarsening of the social fabric, the death of shame, and the moral and intellectual bankruptcy of a mass-media marketplace in thrall to the lowest common denominator. The *New York Times* critic Michiko Kakutani bemoans the "teen-aging of America," pop culture's descent into gross-out antics and sniggering adolescent lewdness. "We're all Beavis and Butt-head now," despairs the *New Yorker* essayist Kurt Andersen. "What was too coarse for polite conversation a few years ago has become the mainstream's vernacular."[19] James B. Twitchell dolefully declares that contemporary culture is coming full circle, shucking off the social codes developed between the fifteenth and eighteenth centuries, during the rise of bourgeois culture, to manage the products of the body and what Bataille called "the urges of the ape."

The butt-talking Carrey, who once lamented, "I've been dubbed responsible for the dumbing of America," is a made-to-order whipping boy for such critiques.[20] But seen from the upside-down worldview of Bakhtin's carnival, Carrey looks more like a mainstream poster boy for excess and ecstasy—Bataille's Solar Anus redux. According to Bakhtin, "Carnival celebrated temporary liberation from the prevailing truths and from the established order; it marked the suspension of all hierarchical rank, privileges, norms, and prohibitions. . . . The utopian ideal and the realistic merged in this . . . experience, unique of its kind."[21] It's a vision that resonates sympathetically with the impermanent anarchotopias, online and off, real and imagined, that have captured the subcultural imagination in recent years: Hakim Bey's notion of the "temporary autonomous zone," the pirate utopias romanticized by the "outsider" philosopher Peter Lamborn Wilson, underground raves and techno-pagan bacchanals like the "Burning Man" festival staged yearly in Nevada's Black Rock Desert. To fringe-culture dwellers, Carrey's anal yodel in the face of propriety sounds a hopeful note at a time when the *true* infantilization of America proceeds apace, through the father-knows-best paternalism of William Bennett's *Book of Virtues,* the V-chip, and legislation like the Communications Decency Act, Congress's ill-advised 1995 attempt to criminalize "obscene" speech on the Internet.

He wouldn't put it in such politically charged terms, but Michael Hirsh, executive producer of an animated version of *Ace Ventura* that aired in 1995 on CBS, wouldn't deny that Carrey is a leading indicator of larger trends. "We're at the end of the century, so we've got this fin-de-siècle thing going," he says. "There's a breakdown of society's false expectations of people. We're allowing ourselves to be more honest about who we are, and we're a people who like basic humor, which includes bathroom humor—the most primitive sort of humor. We're allowing what we like to be successful rather than saying, 'Uh oh, this is not acceptable.'"

In the final analysis, Carrey embodies *both* aspects of millennial America, the loathsome and the liberatory. The excremental carnival he epitomizes is simultaneously a symptom of a *Dumb and Dumber* culture *and* an upwelling of the popular desire to wriggle out of the social straitjacket of bourgeois culture and our puritan legacy. Carrey's "talking asshole" routine can be seen as lamentable evidence of just how low we've sunk as a postliterate, attention-deficit-disordered TV nation. But it can also be read as a carnivalesque mockery of the social order and an uncrowning of the rational mind.

Carnival culture's subversive "sense of the gay relativity of prevailing truths and authorities" is often manifested, says Bakhtin, in irreverent gestures that turn the symbols of the official culture inside out or roundabout (the baseball cap worn backward, the once-radical act of hip-hop style rebels, is a contemporary example). Inverting the social hierarchy and behavioral norms, the folk culture of the carnival (which was also a marketplace culture, a nascent version of our pop culture) inducted celebrants into a "world inside out," says Bakhtin, an observation that throws a revealing light on William Bennett's aghast remark that daytime talk shows represent "the world turned upside down." Bakhtin notes that the comic logic of the carnival, which drags all that is sacred or exalted down to the "material bodily lower stratum," is often expressed by themes and images in which the face is replaced by the buttocks or, conversely, the rump is presented as the face, as in Carrey's talking butt. The kiss-my-ass gesture of displaying the buttocks is "one of the most common uncrowning gestures throughout the world," writes Bakhtin.[22]

To be sure, even Norman O. Brown would be hard-pressed to defend a smiling Jenny McCarthy astride the crapper, hawking shoes, or to see Gilbert & George's Godzilla-sized turds as hopeful signs of libidinal liberation, just around the millennial bend. Brown, a countercultural icon in the sixties, was a radical Freudian who argued that liberation lay not in Marxist economics but in giving the body politic an enema, freeing it from its pathological repression of anal eroticism and unleashing a "Dionysian ego" charged with "an erotic sense of reality." But where's the Dionysian radicalism in a shoe ad that uses sex, shock, and potty humor to cut through the clutter of competing ads? Or in up-close-and-personal photos of feces calculated to stir up the controversy essential to economic success in today's media-driven art market? Gilbert & George are among Britain's richest artists because, like Dali and Warhol before them, they have shrewdly managed to keep themselves at the eye of the media storm. McCarthy freely admits that her descent into the lower stratum was a career move. "[I] had to concentrate on my demographic," she says, which consists almost entirely of young males. "They love *Beavis and Butt-head,* so what do you do?" she says. "You burp and all that stuff."[23] Tastemakers reviled her Candie's ad. The company's sales skyrocketed from $45 million in '96 to $93 million in '97.

Marx, the Oedipal father Norman O. Brown is always trying to slay, urged us to follow the money when we're in search of the truth about how our world works. When we do, we discover that the new openness has as much to do with market share as it does with the obsolescence of Victorian morals and a cultural coming-of-age. When the famously anal-fixated cartoon *Ren & Stimpy* became a pop phenomenon, "the networks started wondering how they were going to compete with these cable shows," says Gary Hartle, the producer of a now-canceled Saturday morning cartoon version of *The Mask.* "Rather than being creative, executives said, 'Hey, that hit, let's [imitate that formula] until it's used up.' Now things are going to extremes, where everybody's trying to do [bathroom humor] as much as possible."

The "tropism toward the toilet" (to borrow William Bennett's pungent phrase) represented by *South Park* and *Dumb and Dumber* is partly a product of a national market geared toward the boys aged 12 to 19 who, according to one marketing survey, spend twice as much time watching MTV as reading and who will constitute a significant chunk of the 30 million status-conscious, trend-driven teenagers who will be looking for a way to spend their disposable income in the year 2010.[24] It's the partial result, too, of the globalization of consumer capitalism, which means that American domestic products must do double-duty in a multinational, multilingual marketplace where broad physical comedy stomps witty dialogue and the dance of ideas every time.

At the same time, a hardheaded economic analysis of the cultural logic of excremental excess gets us only so far. There's a kernel of truth in Brown's argument that our society's most virulent pathologies are rooted in our repression of the body and, by extension, the material world. In *Let Us Now Praise Famous Men,* James Agee notes the middle class's "worship of sterility and worship-fear of its own excrement," a deep-seated complex of neuroses amply evidenced by the evolution of the American bathroom into a brightly lit shrine to personal hygiene and an operating theater for the elimination of waste.[25]

Our fear of the flesh and the material world is obvious, too, in advertising's image of the body as a nightmare landscape of enlarged pores and unsightly blemishes, a cesspit of bad breath and underarm odor, and in its vision of the home as a fallout shelter besieged by germ warfare: bacteria, bad smells, ring around the collar, untidy toilet bowls, and worse. These phobias reach their hysterical crescendo in the yuppie vogue for "colonic irrigation," in which tubes are inserted into the patient's rectum and the colon is flushed with 15 to 20 gallons of distilled water. The procedure— whose health benefits are nonexistent, according to medical authorities— is a New Age charm against "toxins," that undefined cloacal evil lurking in the deepest, darkest recesses of the bowels.

In a crowning irony, consumer capitalism is all about waste— conspicuous consumption, planned obsolescence, disposable products, excess packaging. Now, the waste matter in our overflowing landfills and Superfund sites is coming back to haunt us. In America, the twentieth century began with the rise of a system based on mass production, its gears greased by advertising's promotion of the ceaseless pursuit of status through passing styles and the notion of waste as an economic motor. "The major problem confronting us is . . . stimulating the urge to buy!" wrote the industrial designer J. Gordon Lippincott in the late forties. "Our willingness to part with something before it is completely worn out is . . . truly an American habit, and it is soundly based on our economy of abundance. . . . The prime job that national advertising, research, and the industrial designer are doing in common is . . . convincing the consumer that he needs a new product before his old one is worn out."[26] Lippincott and his fellow mesmerists worked their magic. Our century ends amid a solid-waste crisis symbolized by the *Mobro,* a garbage barge that sailed haplessly from port to port in 1987 in search of a dumping ground for its 3,100-ton cargo of refuse.

If there's a message here, it's that we're going to have to make our peace with the repressed, whether it's the body and all it implies (defecation, sex, disease, old age, and death) or the solid waste and toxic runoff of consumer culture and industrial production. In his drily funny 1992 essay on L.A.'s Hyperion Waste Treatment Plant, Ralph Rugoff suggests that one can judge a society by the way it disposes of its waste products. "Whatever the sources of our uneasiness, our attitudes toward shit generate concrete consequences," he writes.

> Because of our obsessive desire to separate the pure and impure, we waste billions of gallons of reusable water. . . . Preying on our collective denial, real estate developers push for faster urban growth without considering necessary increases in sewage capacity. The recent pipeline disaster in San Diego . . . suggest[s] that infrastructural decay has been routinely ignored. Apparently, no one wants to deal with the amount of shit we've got on our hands.[27]

It's high time we *grew up,* already. Almost a century after the end of the Victorian era (a period whose moral corset was always more tightly laced in the States than in England), we still live in a society where it took until 1985 for a tampon manufacturer to utter the P-word ("period") on national TV and where the former surgeon general Jocelyn Elders was nearly ridden out of town on a rail for her public mention—and, even more unthinkable, sanction—of masturbation. Naturally, the custodians of common decency swimming against the cultural currents swirling us into the flushing toilet are also the ones who endorse William Bennett's belief that "civilization depends on keeping some of this stuff under wraps." Ironically, as Trey Parker, one of the creators of *South Park,* points out,

"As soon as we advance into beings evolved enough to speak freely about farts and barf and anuses, this stuff won't be funny anymore and we'll move on to higher-minded topics. Until then, we're just capitalizing on America's immaturity."[28]

The pathological puritanism that forbids the advertising of condoms on TV, despite an epidemic of teenage pregnancies and the slow death march of AIDS, is a willful blindness we can no longer afford. Nor can we sustain a market economy whose upbeat theme song of runaway production, giddy consumption, and guilt-free waste is also the planet's funeral march. Our relationship with our bodies and the natural world are inextricably knitted together. At its most profound, says Bakhtin, the descent into the "material bodily lower stratum" is a "mighty thrust downward into the bowels of the earth, the depths of the human body"; not for nothing is scatological humor called "earthy."[29] On a similar note, Bataille has traced the connections between womb and tomb, the melting away of the boundary between fetus and mother in utero, self and other in sex, one and the universe in death. Patriarchal culture's swooning, Oedipal horror at the dripping maw of the vagina and the gory spectacle of birth (vividly illustrated in the movie *Alien*) and its shuddering recoil from old age and death are joined at the root. In a culture shaped by the Protestant contempt for the weak flesh, advertising's evocations of the vile body, and the capitalist dictum that the physical world is valuable only as raw material for the machinery of production, all matter is waste matter.

Writing about our relationship to our excreta in his preface to John Bourke's *Scatological Rites of All Nations,* Freud observes, "Civilized men today are clearly embarrassed by anything that reminds them too much of their animal origin. They deny the very existence of this inconvenient trace of the earth, by concealing it from another, and by withholding it from the attention and care which it might claim as an integrating component of their essential being. The wiser course would undoubtedly have been to admit its existence and to dignify it as much as its nature will allow."[30]

Bataille's vision of the Solar Anus represented just such an attempt to come to terms with our animal origins, our lower stratum. According to Allan Stoekl, Bataille intended the Solar Anus as a rallying point for "a cult, a secret society, or perhaps even . . . an entire civilization at the end of history."[31] There's a sense of millennial madness to the excremental excesses of nineties America that hints at a point where scatology and eschatology meet, where Yeats's widening gyre is reimagined as a downward spiral, a vortex of cultural currents that looks, to fans and foes of the Solar Anus alike, like a flushing toilet at the fin-de-millennium.

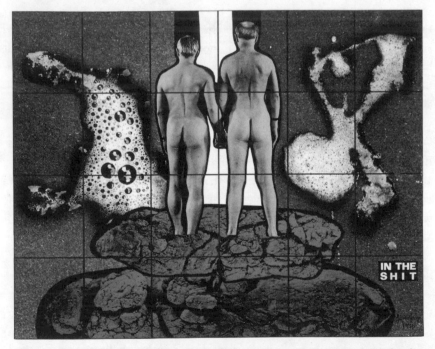

Gilbert & George, "In the Shit," from *The Fundamental Pictures*, 1997. Courtesy Sonnabend Gallery, New York City.

SECTION II
DEAD MEAT

5 / MAD COWS AND ENGLISHMEN: READING DAMIEN HIRST'S ENTRAILS

Damien Hirst, "Philip (The Twelve Disciples)," 1994. Steel, glass, formaldehyde solution, and bull's head. Courtesy Jay Jopling/White Cube, London. Photographer: Stephen White.

Standing in front of the meat animals, neatly sectioned and suspended in formaldehyde, that have earned the English artist Damien Hirst a bad-boy reputation, the viewer feels a pickled numbness. After the initial jolt of their sheer weirdness wears off, the conceptual emptiness of these hunks of too, too solid flesh makes us wonder: Where's the beef? What's the point, beyond ontological shock treatment, of a couple of cows sliced into vertical sections, shuffled around, and displayed in a row of narrow, upright vitrines? Of a pig buzzed in half lengthwise and mounted in two parallel cases, one of which slides along a track to reveal the animal's marinating entrails in a queasy striptease?

The catalogue to Hirst's 1996 show at New York's Larry Gagosian Gallery tries to help. The exhibition's title, "No Sense of Absolute Corruption," refers to the corruption of the flesh that follows death, says Hirst, as well as the moral decay that hollows out lives spent chasing dreams that money can buy—what he calls the "world of desire that you meet in advertising." In addition to dead animals, "No Sense" also included elbow-in-the-ribs pop art jokes such as a *Land of the Giants*-sized ashtray littered with normal-sized cigarettes that looked like dollhouse props in contrast, and a 40-foot billboard depicting a cucumber of heroic proportions, provocatively posed beside a jar of Vaseline. Says Hirst, "All the sculptures contain both [physical and ethical] senses of corruption. . . . Advertising is corruption, so there is the big billboard sculpture. Everything is rotting, even sculptures. And the idea of hoarding, selling artwork is corrupt."[1] Of course, we hold these truths to be self-evident: that dead livestock is about, well, death, and that the subtext of media-savvy shock art might be the unrelenting commercialism that has reduced art to niche marketing.

Damien Hirst, "This little piggy went to market, this little piggy stayed at home," 1995. Steel, glass, pig, and formaldehyde solution. Courtesy Jay Jopling/White Cube, London. Photographer: Stephen White.

Meaning, here, is in the mind of the beholder. Are Hirst's pickled pigs and cows memento mori, with animals in the role of human remains? Or are they a melancholy memorial to the forgotten body, snidely derided as "meat" on the subcultural fringes of our ever more disembodied, on-line world? Or evidence, perhaps, of a growing fascination with the dark secrets of the body's penetralia at a time when CAT scans, MRI, and endoscopy have turned our interiors into alien landscapes—*Star Trek*'s proverbial "final frontier" for an Information Age that has consigned its dreams of interstellar exploration to the garden of mothballed rockets at Kennedy Space Center?

Then again, maybe Hirst's dismembered carcasses are just a canny career move, calculated to snap the artistocracy out of its been-there, done-that trance. In our mass-mediated environment, where increasingly we reach out and touch the world with virtual-reality DataGloves, so to speak, the virtualization of everyday life is undermining our sense of what's real and what's not. The cultural critic Susan Willis recalls her stay in Disney World, where she saw "two children stooped over a small snake that had crawled out onto the sun-warmed path. 'Don't worry, it's rubber,' remarked their mother. Clearly, only Audio-Animatronic simulacra of the real world can inhabit Disney World. A real snake is an impossibility." The next morning, it rains. A hotel neighbor wonders, "'Oh! Did they turn the sprinklers on?'"[2]

Obviously, Willis's droll anecdote speaks volumes about the willing suspension of disbelief inside Disney's "imagineered" reality. But her postmodern fable is relevant beyond the park's gates. In a world of media fictions and high-tech simulacra, finding oneself nose-to-nose with a flayed bull's head—in the upscale, high-culture vacuum of a Soho art gallery, of all places—can be a jarring reality check. In many ways, Hirst can't lose. Thrusting into our faces a raw, goggle-eyed reality most of us have only seen on TV, if at all, he bypasses the intellect and goes straight for the gut. It's the difference between the robotic beasts of the jungle in Disneyland's Jungle Cruise and the real-life Big Bad Wolf ripping into the child in *When Animals Attack* on the Fox network. At the same time, Hirst's art does an end run around the critics. Heavily freighted by art-historical baggage and French philosophy, contemporary art criticism tilts toward the formal, the theoretical, the cerebral; it has no idea what to do with a pig sawed in two.

Even so, lines of connection can be drawn between Hirsts's formaldehyde horrors and the use of meat as metaphor in fine art and pop culture. Often, meat brings the atrocities of the death camp and the killing field home by transporting them to the slaughterhouse and the butcher shop, as in the paintings of Francis Bacon. Likewise, Chaim Soutine used bloody carcasses to evoke the slaughter bench of Jewish history.

In a far lighter vein, meat plays the part of the abject in black comedies about our estrangement from the natural world and what Bataille would call our "animal" nature. Dead meat represents an eruption of the unspeakably real into our freeze-dried, vacuum-packed lives; only a little alienation is needed to produce the shift in perspective that reveals the

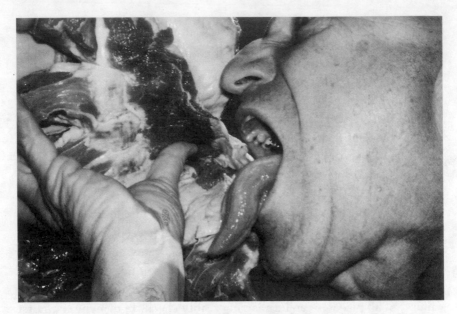

Gwen Akin and Allan Ludwig, "Meat Boy,"1997. Copyright © Akin/Ludwig 1997.

mind-wrenching weirdness of cow's tongues and pigs' feet reposing under fluorescent lights at the supermarket meat counter, amid the anes-
thetic strains of Muzak.

　　David Lynch uses meat as an emblem of the abject in *Eraserhead,* in
the scene where the nerdy protagonist is trying to carve a roast bird and
the creature comes horribly, hilariously to life, twitching spastically and
spouting black bile out of its decapitated neck. So, too, did the art prank-
ster Robert Delford Brown in his notorious 1964 "meat show," a neo-Dada
gag at the expense of the tragically hip New York art world. Brown rented
a meat locker in New York's meat-packing district and exhibited cows' and
pigs' heads, beef hearts, and other sundry animal parts, hung from hooks,
as a pop art "happening." He used livers dipped in animal blood to make
"limited edition" prints, and had a nurse draw some of his blood, after which
a Chinese cook fried it and Brown *ate* it. When dazed spectators emerged
from the show, Brown served them sausage, which some thought was "a
bit much," he admits.[3]

Meat also triggers our deep-rooted body loathing, as in Allan Ludwig's hilariously over-the-top photos of his surrealist hijinx at a suburban barbecue, cavorting with raw meat. When he exhibited his photos, he writes, "People who would not think twice about eating turkey parts were appalled to see them represented on a wall. People who ate fish were upset when they saw pictures of fish gills. A close-up of sliced roast beef made people turn away in disgust. People found the images distressing because they did not want to be reminded that they were themselves meat and would eventually end up as dead meat."[4]

Conversely, meat can stand for the bloody rebirth of Bataille's heterogeneous: the carnal body and the primal animality sublimated by bourgeois society. In 1964, the performance artist Carolee Schneeman

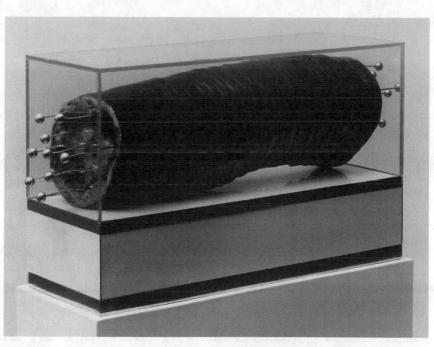

Paul Thek, "Untitled Sculpture" from "Technological Reliquaries," 1965. Wax, formica, Plexiglas, and metal. Courtesy of Alexander and Bonin, New York. Photograph: D. James Dee.

staged *Meat Joy,* a celebration of eros and ecstasy in which participants smeared their nearly naked bodies with blood and cavorted with chicken parts and raw sausages. Similarly, in the seventies the Austrian artist Hermann Nitsch invoked the catharsis of Dionysian ritual and the joyous savagery of primitive cultures in a series of performances called "Orgies, Mysteries, Theatre," where a slaughtered lamb was disemboweled and its blood and guts poured over naked celebrants. On occasion, meat metaphors oscillate irresolvably between attraction and repulsion, as in Paul Thek's "meat pieces" of the mid-sixties, fastidiously realistic wax sculptures of human and animal flesh, all gore and gristle, encased in Plexiglas boxes. They're simultaneously a Norman O. Brownian celebration of polymorphous perversity and an extended meditation on the body's otherness, its instant transformation into inanimate object once consciousness flickers out.

Damien Hirst, "Mother and Child Divided," 1993. Steel, GRP composite, glass, silicone sealants, cow, calf, formaldehyde solution. Courtesy Jay Jopling/White Cube, London. Photographer: Stephen White.

But despite their connections to Thek, Bacon, and the like, Hirst's "pets in formaldehyde," as he jocularly calls them, have more in common with the midway than the gallery. They recall the barnyard oddities that were a staple of state fairs and carnival sideshows: two-headed calves and rhinencephalic monsters like the CYCLOPS PIG WITH ELEPHANT TRUNCK bally-hooed on one old banner. At the same time, their flat, factual presentation in unadorned display cases suggests a natural history museum—or, more accurately, an *un*natural history museum. (In fact, Hirst's title for his "zoo of dead animals" is *Natural History*.)

Of course, there's no avoiding the association of Hirst's cows with mad-cow disease. As any tabloid reader knows, the mad-cow epidemic sparked near panic in England, where authorities linked it to an outbreak, among British beef eaters, of the deadly brain disorder Creutzfeldt-Jakob disease. When Hirst's pickled cows were shipped to the States for his Gagosian show, USDA officials expressed concern. The artist's representatives assured them that the animals on display had died of natural causes and that the meat, soaking in its formaldehyde bath, was obviously not for consumption.

CJD is one of a class of neurological maladies called spongiform encephalopathies because they turn the diseased brain into a spongelike mass, riddled with microscopic holes. It's a body invader straight out of a Cold War sci-fi movie, worthy of an *X-Files* episode. As a matter of fact, it *was* an *X-Files* episode: "Our Town," about workers in a small-town chicken processing plant who contract CJD by eating chickens that had eaten feed made from chicken offal, like the British cows that ate feed made partly from sheep brains. The fact that the townspeople were also eating each other may have had something to do with it, too: there's a proven link between ritual cannibalism and spongiform diseases like kuru, the ghastly plague that was devastating the Fore tribe in Papua New Guinea before it was traced to their funeral custom of eating the brains of the deceased.

Its status as a sign of the times certified by *The X-Files*, the mad-cow scare has become tabloid shorthand for a host of anxieties gnawing at the public mind, themselves a sort of brain-eating virus (albeit one made of information: a meme). Haunted by the shadow of an incubating plague, Hirst's cows play on fears of our processed world, where the raising, slaughtering, and even the eating of meat animals is an assembly-line operation, and where growth hormones, chemical additives, and contamination make every bite of McFood a potential toxic adventure. In the United States, whose food supply is reportedly one of the world's safest, salmonella bacteria kill more than 4,000 people a year and sicken as many as 5 million. In most deadly outbreaks of food poisoning, many of which involve the intestinal bacterium *Escherichia coli,* red meat is the culprit.[5]

In our highly industrialized, increasingly denatured culture, the indelicate sights and sounds of the slaughterhouse are kept far from the public eye, perpetuating the consumer fantasy of a shrink-wrapped, bar-coded product that was made, not born. The corporatization and globalization of the food industry have alienated us from the meat on the ends of our forks, and there's a creeping unease about the dirty details. Most of us would rather not know how that McDonald's Happy Meal began its life, and what happened to it on the way to our plate.

Hirst's cows and pigs also turn our thoughts to the dark side of a shrinking planet where jet travel can spread disease with terrifying speed, turning the global village into one vast petri dish for the culturing of strange new pathogens, mutant microorganisms that can leap species barriers and survive blasts of radiation. "A hot virus from the rain forest lives within a 24-hour plane flight from every city on earth," writes Richard Preston in *The Hot Zone,* his best-selling book about the horrific Ebola virus.[6]

Intriguingly, a prominent subtext of the viral nightmares of the late twentieth century is the anxieties spurred by out-of-control technological change: disquieting leaps in machine intelligence, the information overload brought on by the shrinking of the globe through jet travel and telecommunications. Often, information itself is seen as a postmodern encephalopathy, as in computer viruses, which eat their way through our prosthetic brains, and in Dawkins's memes. "When you plant a fertile meme in my mind you literally parasitize my brain," writes Dawkins, "turning it into a vehicle for the meme's propagation in just the way that a virus may parasitize the genetic mechanism of a host cell."[7]

Appropriately, the publication in 1994 of *The Hot Zone* unleashed the "virus" meme, inspiring a slew of trend-hopping nonfiction books and at least one movie (*Outbreak*) and showcasing the mass media "at their recombinantly contagious worst," in the words of the critic Colin Harrison.[8] The term "mad-cow disease" is itself a meme; like the sexy buzz phrase "road rage," it has infected the circulatory system of the mass media by virtue of its sheer weirdness (the *X-Files* factor) and the way it rolls trippingly off the tongue. Finally, the title of this essay is a meme, used as the headline for stories on bovine spongiform encephalopathy in *The New Yorker, The Detroit News, The Washington Times, The Economist,* the *Washington Post, The Baltimore Sun,* and the *San Francisco Examiner.*[9] Clearly, something's in the air. An air-borne media pathogen?

In *Virus Hunter,* C. J. Peters's chronicle of "thirty years of battling hot viruses around the world," the media are parasitic life-forms, infectious agents locked in symbiosis with the toxic invaders Peters is fighting. He conjures the horrors of "trying to battle a killer virus and a media frenzy at the same time," of contending simultaneously with hot viruses and "publicity hot buttons."[10] The "handling of information," he discovers, is "just as important from a public health standpoint as the job our field epidemiologists [are] doing."[11] Through spin, damage control, and the coordinated message that White House media strategists call a "line of the day," Peters and his colleagues contained epidemics of media frenzy and mass hysteria.

Similarly, in Preston's *Hot Zone,* viruses often look and act like metaphors for technology. Like artificial-life programs, they "seem alive when they multiply, but in another sense they are obviously dead," mere machines, "subtle ones to be sure, but strictly mechanical."[12] They're "ambiguously alive, neither alive nor dead," like the uncanny expert programs, software robots, and other artificial intelligences multiplying around us, which, we're told, will one day attain silicon sentience. Viruses—promiscuous pieces of molecular code that make copies of copies of copies of themselves inside a cell, ad infinitum, until the cell explodes—seem to act out in miniature the drama of what Hillel Schwartz calls our "culture of the copy," where the dizzy proliferation of simulations, recreations, surrogates, duplicates, and, any day now, clones has all but buried predigital conceptions of the authentic and the original.

On a deeper level, mad-cow disease has become a screen for the projection of popular anxieties about the free-floating, indeterminate nature of things in postmodern culture, where quotation, hybridization, and mutation are the order of the day. Joanne Reynolds, an American Op-Ed writer living in England, despairs of finding anything uncontaminated to eat. Even the most unlikely items, from Polo mints to Fruit Fool desserts, contain beef by-products; not even chicken is safe to eat, because "the chickens eat fish" and "the fish eat beef." It's a "food chain gone awry," says Reynolds.[13] To many, science and industry are begetting an ever more Frankensteinian world; the consequences of their unnatural acts seem increasingly gothic, though not even Mary Shelley could have imagined a brain-devouring contagion like CJD. Transmissible spongiform encephalopathies are extremely rare in nature, but so are injections of a growth hormone derived from the pituitary glands of human cadavers (the cause of 62 cases of CJD worldwide), or instances of herbivores eating feed made from ground-up slaughterhouse waste (a practice one prominent scientist calls "high-tech neo-cannibalism").[14] Such human interventions "may radically alter the picture," notes the neurologist Oliver Sacks, causing "a galloping transmission of these diseases of a sort that never occurs in nature."[15]

Not only is the natural order in disarray, but the philosophical bedrock of Western civilization is eroding. *The Times* of London lamented the passing of "a nation of beefeaters . . . handy with a knife or sword, prosperous and free" and bemoaned the dark day when "beef has become 'another national institution in which the nation has no confidence.'"[16] In Britain as in America, beef is "real food for real people," as the ad tagline had it, mythically associated with red-blooded manhood, freedom from want, and the libertarian autonomy of cowboys and yeomen, home on the range.

Long before the Wendy's commercial asked where it was, beef was shorthand for hard-boiled masculinity and a just-the-facts-ma'am view of the world, shorn of "feminine" frills. "Panty-waist stuff burns me," says a ball-busting big boss man in "I'm Tough," a forties ad for Bond suits reproduced in Marshall McLuhan's *The Mechanical Bride*. "Gang at the plant call me 'Chief,'" he says. "Sure I've made money. Not a million—but enough to buy steak when I can get it."[17] A slab of steak, "good clothes with plenty of guts"—What more could the well-dressed Neanderthal want? But times have changed: Our national institutions are crumbling and the beef-eating tough-guy is in danger of dissolving into a quiche-eating "puddle of indecision," as Robert Bly shuddered in *Iron John*. Even our meat isn't what it used to be, the Freudian implications of which will be obvious to any American male.

Although he was writing about the Unabomber, the *Time* essay-ist Lance Morrow gave vent to such fears when he inveighed against the "deconstruction of American public authority" that left "boundaries eroded and crumbling" in the aftershocks of the sixties. Working himself into a fit of neoconservative spleen, he wrote, "Individual roles melted into one another. Older distinctive identities and purposes grew confused." Now, "Men and women interchange roles on a horizontal axis. Children and parents switch places on the vertical."[18] (Men and women are swapping traditional roles? Next thing you know, the weaker sex will want the vote.)

In contrast, the feminist historian of science Donna Haraway cham-pions the "transgressed boundaries, potent fusions, and dangerous possi-bilities" symbolized by the monsters and marvels of biotechnology and bionics. She dreams of a "cyborg world" where "people are not afraid of their joint kinship with animals and machines, not afraid of permanently partial identities and contradictory viewpoints."[19] Glimpsing a window of political opportunity in the cultural chaos all around us, she celebrates the utopian potential of a historical moment when, for example, "the bound-ary between human and animal has been thoroughly breached."[20]

It's no coincidence that Hirst's deconstructed, reconstructed crea-tures appear at the very moment that "transgenic" animals engineered in biotech labs and cross-species transplants promise—threaten?—to literal-ize a century's worth of surrealist collage, pop assemblage, and postmodern appropriation. A surrealist "exquisite corpse" come to life, the monstrous hybrid Hirst created for his sculpture *Some Comfort* has eight legs and a head at each end. One head looks back on Frankenstein's monster, the organic collage that prefigured our recombinant century; the other gazes ahead, toward the sci-fi future augured by genetically altered pigs that produce human hemoglobin, transgenic mice with human breast cancer genes, and the animal-to-human xenotransplants that some worry could give rise to species-leaping viruses.

Then, too, the "twenty centuries of stony sleep" of Yeats's "Rough Beast" are a catnap to natural agents like Ebola, which having "flashed its colors, fed, and subsided into the forest," is dormant for the moment, says Preston. Nonetheless, like Schwarzenegger's implacable Terminator, "It will be back."[21] What rough beast is being born in the central African rain forest or, for that matter, the negative-pressure, spacesuits-only confines of a biosafety-level-4 high-tech lab, even now? Rumor has it that one of the cows in *Some Comfort* died giving birth, a bit of trivia that seems portentous as we search for a glimpse of things to come, reflected in its eyes. But they're closed, sealed shut in the moment of death; only the merest glimmer of eyeball peeks out. Try as we might, we can't meet its clouded gaze.

Damien Hirst, "Some Comfort Gained From the Acceptance of the Inherent Lies in Everything," 1996. Steel, glass, cows, and formaldehyde solution. Courtesy Jay Jopling/White Cube, London. Photographer: Stephen White.

6 / MYSTERIES OF THE ORGANISM: *THE OPERATION*

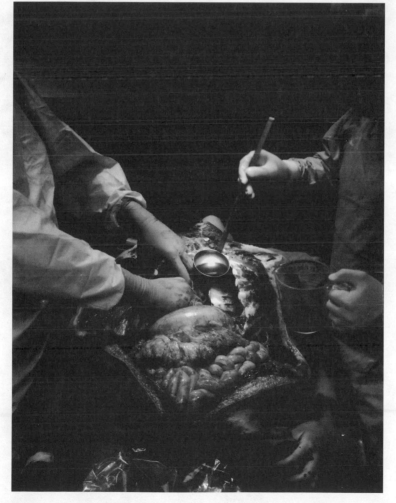

Autopsy. Copyright © Max Aguilera-Hellweg.

At the end of Poe's gothic horror story "The Facts in the Case of M. Valde-mar," the protagonist's body dissolves, in an image worthy of *Tales from the Crypt,* into "a nearly liquid mass of loathsome—of detestable putridity." In truth, *all* bodies are "nearly liquid" masses of blood, bile, and soft tissue, as any who have seen *The Operation,* on the Learning Channel, know too well.

The cult-fave cable show offers more or less unabridged documen-taries of actual operations, from brain surgery to bunion correction, heart reduction to hair transplant, bookended by before-and-after interviews with the patient. There's at least one gut-clencher per episode, and moments of jaw-dropping surrealism, like the shot of steam swirling around an abdomi-nal incision, in the hot camera lights, as the narrator informs us, "Dr. Gross is now putting temporary staples in the abdominal wall . . ." On occasion, there are unintentional laugh lines, like the surgeon's offhanded observa-tion, in the vasectomy episode, that "this operation was used in a more radi-cal form to create eunuchs in the golden age of the Greeks." Er, exactly *how* radical, doctor?

One episode documented what might be called an in-your-facelift, replete with close-ups of yellow fat globules being squelchingly pared off muscles, bloody slivers of skin peeled off eyelids, blobs of fat tweezed from the bags under each eye—fat which "on its own, without any prompting from us, is about ready to launch itself out of her eye," as the surgeon matter-of-factly remarks. It's Naomi Wolf's worst nightmare, as directed by David Cronenberg. At one point, the surgeon slips his gloved fingers under the anesthetized woman's face and peels it back. After a lifetime's exposure to the prosthetic horrors of special-effects artists like Tom "Night of the Liv-ing Dead" Savini, the patient's limp, sallow skin seems somehow *less* real than painted latex, her glassy-eyed, slack-jawed face *less* convincing than the fake corpses in most horror movies.

It's the body's job, these days, to be a symbol of "detestable putridity" in the eyes of an information society characterized by an exaltation of mind and a contempt for matter, most of all the body—that aging, earthbound relic of Darwinian evolution that Net junkies sneeringly refer to as "meat." In late-twentieth-century America, Descartes's mind/body split has widened into a neognostic chasm. When artificial intelligence theorists like Hans Moravec speculate about transferring human consciousness to robot ships and heading for the stars (the flesh being, you know, "so messy," as Moravec puts it) or UFO cultists like the Heaven's Gaters disparage their bodies as unworthy "vehicles" and the Earth as a cosmic discard destined for the recycling bin, they're speaking the language of gnosticism, an early Christian heresy that reviled the body as a "corpse with senses" and the material world as the creation of an evil demiurge.

The Operation is part of a cultural undercurrent cutting across the neognosticism of mainstream society. As we shift from a manufacturing base to an information economy, from embodied sensation to electronic simulation, from RL to VR, the cultural logic of digital disembodiment is countered by the return of the repressed, abject flesh. Images of morbid or monstrous bodies haunt our collective dream life in the subgenre of viral horror typified by *The Hot Zone,* with its Lovecraftian descriptions of the "sludging" of the brain with dead blood cells, the sloughing of the gut, the "shock-related meltdown" of the diseased corpse into a puddle of gore. Apparitions of the visceral have materialized in the art world as well, in Hirst's pickled animals and the morgue-slab art of Anthony Noel-Kelly, the British sculptor-turned-body snatcher arrested for making plaster casts of stolen human body parts.

But *The Operation* has other tales to tell, other lessons to teach. It's a glimpse of the TV subconscious, one of those twilight zones where the medium talks in its sleep, like the bizarre public access sermons of the cult leader John-Roger or the late-night infomercials of the motivational guru Anthony Robbins, he of the vacuformed hair and acromegalic jaw. It's one of the weirder scopophilic pleasures afforded by a media landscape where seemingly everything is reflected in the camera's eye, from the nonchalant atrocities of stocking-masked thugs caught by surveillance cams to the natural disasters, police beatings, and *Candid Camera* hijinx captured on home video to the fantastic voyages relayed, live, from the innermost recesses of our bodies by laparoscopic cameras.

The Operation, which often features laparoscopic images, is a living-room initiation into the dark, wet mysteries of a body that each of us inhabits but few of us know much about. In that regard, it's also a pitiless deconstruction of our most cherished assumptions about ourselves, disquieting on a level far deeper than the pop-eyed gross-out experienced by the uninitiated, grazing past the show. J. G. Ballard underwent just such a revelation in med school. "Doing anatomy was an eye-opener," he recalled, in a 1970 interview. "One had built one's whole life on an illusion about the integrity of one's body, this 'solid flesh.' . . . Then to see a cadaver on a dissecting table and . . . to find at the end of term that there was nothing left except a . . . heap of gristle and a clutch of bones . . . was a tremendous experience of the lack of integrity of the flesh."[1]

The Operation is one of the Learning Channel's top-rated programs, the object of greater viewer response than any other show on the network—a hopeful sign in these times of ethical cleansing, when advocates of the Disneyfication of cyberspace and the gentrification of urban space insist that the adult mind should abide by preschool standards. Still, the "Gag me!" theatrics of disgust that typically greet The Operation bespeak a stunted emotional maturity born of puritanical mores, bourgeois notions of good taste, and our culturally inbred reluctance to look beyond the free trial offers and the bonus prizes to the severed ear on the suburban lawn, to put it in Blue Velvet terms.

The severed ear is a fitting metaphor, because this pervasive squeamishness about the meat—about what goes on in the operating theater, the funeral parlor, or the slaughterhouse—betokens, again, a cringing inability to confront the inescapable fact that beneath the hard, dry exoskeleton of our technology, we're still soft, wet biology, a "nearly liquid mass" of soft tissues and bodily fluids that mocks the escapist fantasies of the age we live in by growing old, dying, and decaying, the prayers of AI experts, UFO cultists, and plastic surgeons notwithstanding. Suction, please.

7 / NATURE MORTE: FORMALDEHYDE PHOTOGRAPHY AND THE NEW GROTESQUE

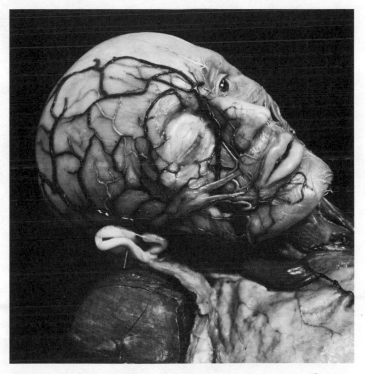

Arne Svenson, "Untitled, 1993." Wax anatomical model. Copyright © 1993 Arne Svenson.

I have heard tell

That in a museum in Atlanta
Way back in a corner somewhere
There's this thing that's only half
Sheep   like a wooly baby
Pickled in alcohol . . . his eyes
Are open   but you can't stand to look

—James Dickey, "The Sheep Child"

It is conventional to call "monster" any blending of dissonant elements. . . .
I call "monster" every original, inexhaustible beauty.

—Alfred Jarry

A partial listing of my interests: physical prodigies of all kinds, pinheads,
dwarfs, giants, hunchbacks, pre-op transsexuals, bearded women . . .
women with one breast (center), people who live as comic book heroes,
Satyrs, twins joined at the foreheads, anyone with a parasitic twin . . .
living Cyclopes, people with tails, horns, wings, fins, claws . . . Sex masters
and slaves . . . People with complete rubber wardrobes. Geeks. Private
collections of instruments of torture, romance; of human, animal, and alien
parts . . . Hermaphrodites and teratoids (alive and dead). A young blonde
girl with two faces. Any living myth. Anyone bearing the wounds of Christ.

—Joel-Peter Witkin

If the Enlightenment ushered in "the disenchantment of the world," as Max
Horkheimer and Theodor Adorno put it, postmodernism returns us to the
age of wonder—and terror. In *Mr. Wilson's Cabinet of Wonder*, Lawrence

Weschler's book about a postmodern cabinet of curiosities called the Museum of Jurassic Technology, Weschler suggests that the pendulum of history swings back and forth between modernist and postmodernist tendencies. Actually, he prefers to think of our moment not as postmodern but as one of the cyclical recurrences of the *pre*modern, a time whose hallmarks are deliriously heterogeneous tastes and a boundless appetite for the marvelous and the monstrous.[1]

Societal attitudes toward extraordinary bodies chart the historical movement from what the cultural critic Rosemarie Garland Thompson calls a "narrative of the marvelous" to a scientific worldview founded on reason and empirical proof, which transforms human and animal anomalies, by sleight of mind, from prodigy into teratological specimen, monster into mutation.[2] Now, as we return to a world of gods and monsters, there's a burgeoning fascination on the cultural fringes with congenital deformities, pathological anatomy, and other curios from the cabinet of wonder.

The postmodern/premodern obsession with dark matter is joined at the hip to the eruption of freakery examined earlier. Like freak chic, the resurgent interest in medical grotesquerie centers on human oddities, but it's drawn to the darker corners of the cultural midway as well. If the evil clown and the freak of nature incarnate the infernal carnival, the poster child for the aesthetic known as the New Grotesque is the pickled punk. ("New" in contradistinction to the grotesque aesthetic of the last fin-de-siècle, manifested in the Victorian fondness for the droll and the deformed.) "Pickled punk" is the less than reverent carny term for the malformed fetuses—hydrocephalic babies with enormous light-bulb skulls, anencephalic monsters born with only brain stems, sirenomelic "mermaids" with fused legs—exhibited in sideshows under the legitimating banner of scientific education and moral instruction about the Miracle of Life. Misbegotten siblings of the premature infants nursed back to health before rapt crowds at Dreamland's famed Baby Incubator, pickled punks were a legacy of the "museums of anatomy" that traveled the country in the late nineteenth century. Ballyhooed as a high-minded public service, these itinerant museums exploited the Victorian fascination with "improper matters," exhibiting abnormal fetuses, skeletal remains, photos of disease and deformity, and wax models of tumors, wounds, and skin diseases, the latter rendered with a fever-dream clarity that still freezes the viewer in his or her tracks when chanced on in a medical museum.

The current preoccupation with the deformed unborn, severed limbs, pickled viscera, diseased flesh, and medical museums as public-address systems for official ideologies harks back to what the art critic Brooks Adams has called "a whole specialized genre of formaldehyde photography [which] emerged in the mid-'80s."[3] The photographic aesthetic of the New Grotesque as we know it springs, arguably, from the brow of one man, the photographer Joel-Peter Witkin, renowned for baroque tableaux starring costumed freaks, sexual fetishists, and, most notoriously, the borrowed heads and limbs of forlorn cadavers. "Repulsion: Aesthetics of the Gro-

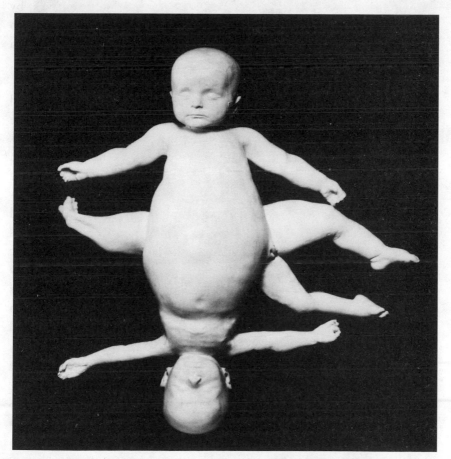

Arne Svenson, "Untitled, 1994." Plaster cast of conjoined twins. Copyright © 1994 Arne Svenson.

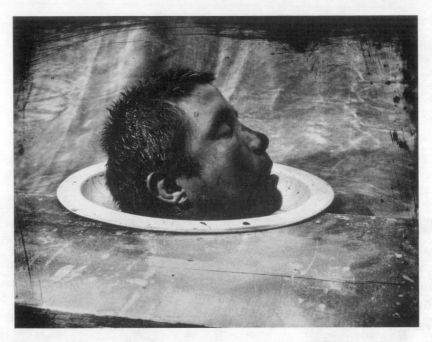

Joel-Peter Witkin, "Head of a Dead Man, Mexico," 1990. Copyright © Joel-Peter Witkin.
Courtesy PaceWildensteinMacGill, New York.

tesque," a 1986 exhibition at New York's Alternative Museum that was
curated by Allan Ludwig, spotlighted the genre, as did the 1987 collection
Masterpieces of Medical Photography: Selections from the Burns Archive, edited by
Witkin, and the "Repulsion" exhibition catalogue, *Grotesque: Natural Historical and Formaldehyde Photography* (1990).

    Less than a decade after the "Repulsion" exhibition, the New Gro-
tesque went mainstream via the 1994 video *Closer,* by Nine Inch Nails. Shot
by sunlight with hand-cranked cameras on grainy film stock, *Closer* looks like
a bondage film for Victorian doctors. The antique tech lends a sickly cast to
fleeting, dreamlike impressions of an infant's skeleton, laboratory glassware
crawling with beetles, moldy tomes in an antique cabinet. In large part, the
video is a devoted homage to Witkin. The director, Mark Romanek, borrowed the photographer's technique of scratching and splotching his pictures
to give them the patina of age and quoted several of his signature images: a
monkey tied to a crucifix, a still life with a severed head.

    David Bowie's restless, magpie eye caught the telltale glint of the
Next Big Thing in *Closer.* A year later, he released the video for *Heart's Filthy*

Face, medical museum, Krakow. Julie Dermansky.

Lesson, a sepia-toned study in stylish grotesquerie, with vitrines of shriveled organs and pickled tarantulas and Bowie ventriloquizing a mutilated mannequin (or is it a corpse?). That same year, the director David Fincher took the New Grotesque into the abyss with *Seven,* a harrowing movie whose obsession with murky depths and grisly details partook equally of MTV-style avant-pop (jerky flashes of sprocket holes and film leader) and Witkin (rude sutures on the autopsied belly of a freakishly obese man). By 1996, when Marilyn Manson's video *The Beautiful People* subjected the MTV audience to a bad-acid flashback of weirdos in leg braces, a fat man in bondage, and Manson in a dental torture device that stretched his mouth into a lunatic rictus, the New Grotesque had been fixed in mortician's wax as a rock-video and Hollywood style.

Meanwhile, the aesthetic has flowered darkly in the world of fine-art photography, where it first took root. Nancy Burson's wrenching portraits of children with craniofacial disorders are undeniably grotesque, though it's a grotesquerie shot through with a profound empathy utterly absent in Witkin's work. Julie Dermansky's photographic gaze, on the other

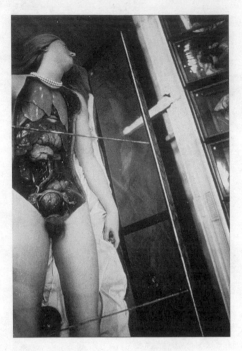

Zoe Leonard, "Wax Anatomical Model, Partial
View from Above," 1990. Courtesy Paula
Cooper Gallery, New York.

hand, is at once rapt and dispassionate. She is untouched by sentiment but
unapologetically fascinated by nature's endlessly inventive cruelty—the
teratological oddities that Aristotle called *lusus naturae,* or "nature's sport."
The snapshots she took in a medical museum in Krakow have a matter-of-
factness to them that lets the air out of high-flown philosophizing. We are
what we are and nothing more, they seem to say, though what the gaping
mask of a preserved face and the fish-eyed infant with the hideous grin *are*
is more than is dreamt of in most of our philosophizing.

    By contrast, Zoe Leonard's use of the anatomical grotesque is
overtly political, focusing the feminist gaze on eighteenth-century anatomical models of women with their viscera laid bare. It is poles apart from the
mediagenic grotesqueries of the British New Wave represented by neo-
conceptual shockers such as Marc Quinn's bust of himself, cast in nine pints
of his frozen blood, and Jake and Dinos Chapman's horrifically hyperrealistic
sculptures of Goya's *Disasters of War* and their mannequins of nude mutant

Lolitas with penis noses, vaginal (or is it rectal?) mouths, extra limbs, and too many orifices in all the wrong places.

The New Grotesque attained a sort of nightmarish sublimity in the late, much-lamented Mutter Museum calendar. Ensconced in the College of Physicians of Philadelphia since 1863, the Mutter Museum is Hannibal Lecter's idea of family fun: a museum of pathology, open to the public, whose track lighting casts a warm glow on the joined livers of Chang and Eng, the original Siamese twins; the naturally preserved Soap Lady, so-called because her obese body decomposed into a fatty wax not unlike soap; and exquisite wax models of faces and limbs gnawed by gangrene, ravaged by syphilis, disfigured by tumors. The calendar is "late" because Marc S. Micozzi, M.D., the college's current executive director, decreed in 1996 that the college would produce a less gothic calendar, one that didn't associate it in the public mind with the gross and the grotesque. Subsequent editions have been inoffensive enough to satisfy

"Fetal Pig in Boiler Room." Fetal pig with rhinencephaly, a form of cyclopia. Copyright © Max Aguilera-Hellweg.

even the 19th century surgeons whose bewhiskered visages frown down from the college's walls.

In contrast, the museum's 1995 calendar featured fine-art photographs of a neoclassic plaster bust of a woman with an enormous neck tumor, a murderer's brain floating dreamily in a jar, and a hyperreal wax model of the puffy, pustulant face of a man suffering from erysipelas, a contagious infectious disease of the skin. Bizarre as it is, such imagery struck a resonant chord: Stocked at bookstores around the country, the first (1993) Mutter calendar sold out, and subsequent editions did brisk business as well, according to the museum director, Gretchen Worden.

Two of the 1995 calendar's most quietly disquieting images are by Max Aguilera-Hellweg, an acclaimed photojournalist whose longtime preoccupation with "dark psychological matter" was inspired by Diane Arbus and the lurid Roman Catholic imagery of his Mexican-American upbringing in Los Angeles—Jesus' Sacred Heart hung over his grandmother's fireplace, "bleeding, wrapped in thorns, engulfed in flames." The quintessentially Mexican sense of one's own mortality, archetypically expressed in the *Dia de los Muertos* ("Day of the Dead"), informs his work as well. "Mortality has always been my greatest of interests," he says. For the past six years, Aguilera-Hellweg has explored the dark continent of the body's interior in a series of surgical photos published in 1997 as *The Sacred Heart: An Atlas of the Body Seen Through Invasive Surgery*.

The first of his Mutter calendar photos is a dreamlike scene that looks like an outtake from *Eraserhead:* a deformed fetal pig in a jar, plunked incongruously on the floor of the college of physicians' grim, industrial boiler room. Hunched as if in agony, its misshapen snout strangely human, it stirs up conflicting reactions: revulsion, fascination, and—because of its weirdly humanoid appearance and the raging debate over abortion—something approaching pity. It makes poetic sense, somehow, that this misbegotten creature is hidden away in the shadowy basement of the Freudian subconscious.

Aguilera-Hellweg's second offering is even more unreal: one half of a human head sliced vertically and suspended in a glass container, sitting on a table in a dank-looking, dimly lit room. Two chairs are drawn up to the table; a pair of shoes sits in front of one, as if a spectral presence is communing with this forlorn fragment of a human being. The photographer calls the surreal séance a "narrative of objects." He says, "Sometimes I've thought, 'How come I can't photograph beautiful women? I must be crazy!' But it's about going into a forbidden world; this is who we are, this is *us*." His words

The Widow Sunday. Copyright © 1993 Rosamond Purcell.

recall the Roman playwright Terence's deathless line: *Homo sum: humani nil a me alienum puto*. "I am a man, and nothing human is alien to me."[4]

The Widow Sunday, one of Rosamond Purcell's contributions to the 1998 Mutter calendar, puts Terence to the test. It depicts a human conundrum whose deformity blurs the boundary between human and animal, medical anomaly and ancient myth: a wax model of Madame Dimanche (French for "Sunday"), a nineteenth-century woman who had a ten-inch horn shaped like a banana jutting from her forehead. The ghost of a smile haunts her lips; for someone who looks like the unfortunate object of divine wrath, she exudes an air of quiet dignity and wry sweetness. She holds her head high despite its unwanted adornment, as if to remind us that someone once loved her, horn and all.

For 12 years Purcell has prowled the backrooms of mostly European medical and natural history museums—"the dustiest corners of the furthest reaches of the oddest places"—in search of the perverse and the poetic, the sublime and the unspeakable. In *Finders, Keepers: Eight Collectors,* a meditation on collectors of human and animal artifacts with text by the paleontologist Stephen Jay Gould, Purcell provides a peephole on Peter the Great's *Wunderkammer* ("cabinet of curiosities"), a baroque treasure house whose contents include the pickled remains of a four-legged rooster and a two-headed sheep.

Purcell and Gould also explore the *Wunderkammer* of the renowned seventeenth-century Dutch anatomist and preparator Frederick Ruysch, whose cabinet of wonders rivaled Peter's. (Ultimately, the Russian monarch bought Ruysch's entire collection of anatomical preparations.) Gould notes that Ruysch, like Peter, was driven by "a willingness to act and explore in realms that most people would shun as macabre or gruesome. . . . For both men, the need to explore and capture the bizarre found ideal expression in the tradition of collecting then current—the *Wunderkammer,* with its emphasis on the exotic, and its keen understanding that fascination often arises from fear."[5]

Wunderkammern were personal collections assembled by seventeenth-century gentlemen-scholars that prefigured the modern natural history museum. Not for nothing were they called cabinets of curiosities: these private museums were often a hodgepodge of patent fakery and palpable fact, their motley, jumbled contents born of a desire to astonish, rather than to classify and systematize. "In those old collections," writes Umberto Eco in *Travels in Hyperreality,* "a unicorn's horn would be found next to a copy of a Greek statue, and, later, among mechanical creches and wondrous automata."[6] During the Enlightenment, when natural history came to prominence as a premier science and a popular fad, the *Wunderkammer,* purged of its unicorns' horns but still showcasing the rare, the exotic, and the wondrous strange, survived in the form of the natural history cabinet. According to the historian Londa Schiebinger, a "cabinet of natural history, containing any number of curiosities—perhaps the brains and genitalia of both sexes, a skeleton, embryos at different stages of development, or a monstrous fetus—was a prized possession of members of the cultivated leisured classes" in the eighteenth century.[7]

Among the stranger items in Ruysch's collection were baby's heads in jars, their beatific expressions beautifully preserved, lacy bonnets (sewn by Ruysch's wife or daughter) added as a last, loving touch. But the strangest of all Ruysch's creations—most of them lost to the ravages of time— were his phantasmagorical tableaux, constructed by arranging human fetal skeletons in landscapes fashioned from preserved organs and other anatomical remnants: Gallstones and kidney stones counterfeited "geological" elements, veins and arteries injected with preservatives afforded a convincing facsimile of "trees" and "bushes." Embellished with inspirational quotations and moral admonitions, Ruysch's dioramas treated allegorical themes familiar from the memento mori: Skulls lamented the transience of mortal existence, weeping into "handkerchiefs" made of brain meninges or mesen-

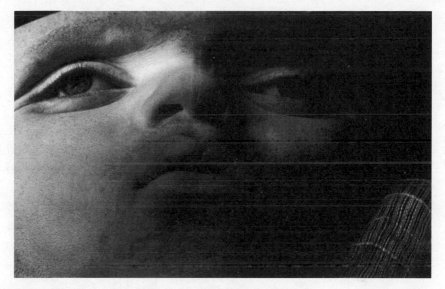

"Baby with Open Eyes." Copyright © 1990 Rosamond Purcell.

tery; a fetal skeleton played a violin with a bow fashioned from a dried artery, lamenting, "Ah fate, ah bitter fate."

Purcell is fascinated by human monsters, all that stands "at the rim of the natural world, at the edge of human tolerance."[8] She says, "You see heads and limbs in scenes of war or murders, but to actually come upon a beautifully presented and preserved artifact that consists of a truncated bit of a human being is a really moving experience." A reflective pause, then: "It *is* very odd," she concedes. "I mean, it's eccentric, obviously, and—when taken out of cultural context—perverse, I suppose."

Indeed, there is something of Freud's uncanny in Ruysch's *Baby with Open Eyes,* which appears in *Finders, Keepers.* Like a waxwork or a china doll, it hovers disconcertingly between animate and inanimate; we can't quite convince ourselves that no spark of life lingers in those unseeing eyes. It's close kin to the vampire, forever young but older than anything living; its clouded eyes contain centuries. In her "Photographer's Afterword" to *Finders, Keepers,* Purcell writes, "I think of the children in alcohol as having come to us in a time capsule. I, for one, had never seen the eyes of a person who lived in the 17th century until I saw the girl with the lace collar."[9]

Gwen Akin and Allan Ludwig have teased an aesthetic out of the "keen understanding that fascination often arises from fear," as Gould describes the mixed feelings that underlie the uncanny allure of the *Wunder-*

kammer. It's the sensation Emily Dickinson had in mind when she wrote, "'Tis so appalling—it exhilarates. . . ."[10] In their essay "The Aesthetics of Attraction and Repulsion," Akin and Ludwig theorize a photography of the "dreadfully beautiful" in which an exquisite dissonance reverberates between the macabre, grotesque, or stomach-churning nature of their subject matter and the sensuous elegance of their medium, the platinum-palladium printing process, which yields stunningly detailed, almost painterly images. They seek to return us to the sense of wonder we experienced as children in the presence of death, before the social conventions of the adult world drew a moralistic scrim over the "fascinating horrors" of "insects crawling through putrefying flesh," the mouth of a dead animal "drawn back by decay" in a "macabre grin."[11] Like Witkin, who dreams of an "egalitarian consciousness" beyond good and evil, one that finds "beauty in a flower and in the severed limb of a human being," Akin and Ludwig strive to create a

"Sliced Face No. 1." Copyright © 1985 Gwen Akin and Allan Ludwig.

momentary Bataille-ian utopia in which the (culturally) irreconcilable opposites of attraction and repulsion become one and, the theory goes, social
conditioning falls away, leaving the viewer's vision unclouded by manners
and mores (if only for an instant).[12] When "beauty and its opposite . . .
merge," they argue, "socially conditioned responses are shattered."[13]

Akin and Ludwig attempt to jolt the viewer out of his culturally
induced trance through the galvanic shock of images such as *Skeleton No. 1,*
their 1995 Mutter calendar photograph of the spindly, balloon-headed skeleton of a little boy who died from hydrocephaly, and the tragicomic mask of
an eyeless, gaping face that reveals itself, from behind, to be one half of a
dissected head (*Sliced Face No. 1* and *Sliced Face No. 1—Verso*). "In confronting death, all of our illusions are finally shattered," says Ludwig. "You can't
hide behind nature or culture or anything else. Splat!—there it is, you know?
It's like the Baroque *vanitas,* a portrait of someone staring at a skull."

Akin and Ludwig's aesthetic of attraction and repulsion—an aesthetic
shared, to varying degrees, by Purcell and Aguilera-Hellweg—mortises neatly

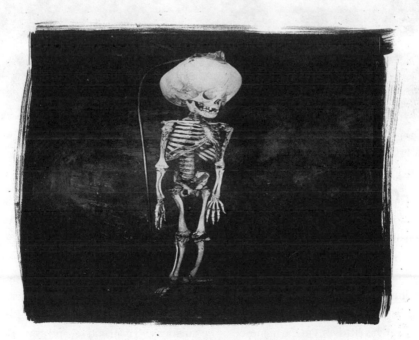

"Skeleton No. 1."Copyright © 1985 Gwen Akin and
Allan Ludwig.

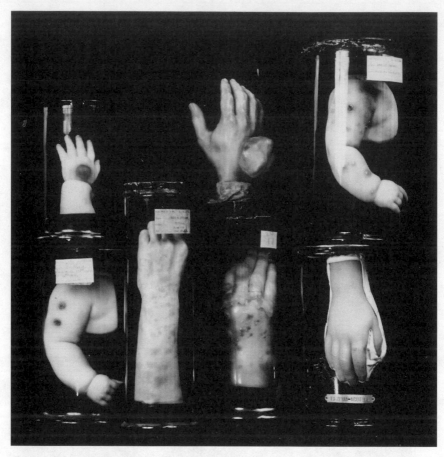

The pathological sublime: Wax models of diseased limbs. Arne Svenson, "Untitled," 1995.
Copyright © Arne Svenson, 1995.

with Edmund Burke's sublime: that which defies rational understanding by
evoking a mixture of pleasure and terror in the viewer. It recalls the rarified
sensibility extolled in an unsigned item, addressed to "worshippers of morbid nature," that appeared in an 1845 issue of the *Boston Medical and Surgical
Journal*: the pathological sublime. Writing anonymously, Oliver Wendell
Holmes exhorted his colleagues to visit an exhibition of paintings "representing a great variety of surgical disease, principally tumors." They were, he
assured his readers, "in the highest degree curious and instructive, and as works
of art they may challenge the admiration of artists themselves."[14]

Akin and Ludwig's aesthetic also harmonizes with Kristeva's abject: that which calls into question the accepted order of things by occupy-

ing an ambiguous position between opposites (a concept not unrelated to Freud's uncanny). The abject is the "in-between, the ambiguous, the composite"—anything that hovers uncannily between states, upsetting the on/off, either/or binary logic of Western culture. In a coincidence that nicely suits our purposes, the corpse, neither human nor nonhuman, is the ultimate abject. Corpses, Kristeva writes, "*show* me what I permanently thrust aside in order to live." Worse than a pustulant wound, worse even than human waste, that notably revolting marker of the boundary between the me and the not-me, "the corpse, the most sickening of wastes, is a border that has encroached upon everything," extinguishing the me for all time. "It is no longer I who expel," as in defecation. "'I' is expelled. . . . In that compelling, raw, insolent thing in the morgue's full sunlight, I behold the breaking down of a world that has erased its borders. . . . The corpse . . . is death infecting life."[15]

Clearly, Akin and Ludwig, Purcell, and Aguilera-Hellweg invest the New Grotesque with their own meanings. But beyond their elaborations on the theme, there are other stories to be told about the sympathetic vibrations touched off, in the culture at large, by the Mutter Museum calendar, Nine Inch Nails' *Closer,* the formaldehyde photographers mentioned in this essay, and comrades-in-arms such as Damien Hirst.

Most immediately, the New Grotesque resonates at the same frequency as the zeitgeist. Writing in the late fifties, the critic Wolfgang Kayser had already noted "a greater affinity to the grotesque" between the art and literature of his day "than that of any other epoch."[16] In the grotesque, the natural order is subverted in feverish fantasies that are at once playful and sinister: human and nonhuman elements fuse in unholy union; the laws of symmetry and proportion are mocked; the solid melts and the sharply defined blurs and nothing is what it seems to be; a profusion of perverse confusions is the (dis)order of the day. "Structurally," Kayser argues, the grotesque "presupposes that the categories which apply to our world view become inapplicable," which is what makes the second half of the twentieth century—the postmodern or, as Weschler would have it, premodern era—grotesque.[17] He writes, "We have observed the progressive dissolution which has occurred since the ornamental art of the Renaissance: the fusion of realms which we know to be separated, the abolition of the law of statics, the loss of identity, the distortion of 'natural' size and shape, the suspension of the category of objects, the destruction of personality, and the fragmentation of the historical order."[18]

At the end of the twentieth century, technology, science, and social trends have literalized this aesthetic trend. We inhabit what Kayser calls the *Millennium* section of Hieronymus Bosch's *Garden of Earthly Delights*, where "a frightful mixture of mechanical, vegetable, animal, and human elements is represented as the image of our world, which is breaking apart."[19] In our age, the grotesque's monstrous conjugation of the human and the inhuman is often expressed in the fusion of the organic and the mechanical, or in inanimate objects that are treated like living things, or in a "'technical' grotesque in which the instruments are demonically destructive and overpower their makers," says Kayser.[20] Hearing this, we think of prosthetic limbs and artificial hearts; of Nicholas Negroponte's fantasies of "smart" houses filled with talking toasters and interactive doorknobs; of the Frankensteinian fears of genetically engineered chimera, computer viruses, and germ warfare that darken our dreams. Kayser mentions the grotesque's signature "withdrawal into a phantasmagoric and nocturnal world," and we think of the nonstop theme-park simulator ride of mass-mediated reality, late in the twentieth century. He tells us that the grotesque is "terrifying and hilarious," "horrible and ridiculous," and we think of Tarantino's slapstick splatter, and of Pennsylvania State Treasurer R. Budd Dwyer's ghastly on-camera gunshot suicide, replayed for laughs on the Web site "Morbid Reality." "For us in the last days the sense of a blending [of the grotesque and the real] is widely shared," writes Geoffrey Galt Harpham in his 1982 study, *On the Grotesque*. As an emblem of the "freakish and absurd nature, the nightmarish malignancy of the modern world," he cites an apocryphal-sounding anecdote about the attempted transfer, in the early days of heart transplants, of a pig's heart to a man. "In the middle of the operation, the story goes, the anesthetized pig woke up and ran squealing around the room with the doctors in pursuit as the man died on the operating table."[21] Not only the man, Kayser would argue, but the belief "in a perfect and protective natural order" died on that table.[22]

The New Grotesque gives twisted shape to the pervasive freakishness of the *Wunderkammer* we live in, a media landscape that sometimes seems to be populated exclusively by the grotesque, the macabre, and the pathological. The Mutter's conjoined twins embody the Janus-faced nature of millennial cultures, as well as the spirit of the age of mechanical reproduction, which began with photography and chromolithography and continues, in our brave new world, with in vitro fertilization and cloning. Madame Dimanche's horn makes us suddenly conscious of our kinship with the ani-

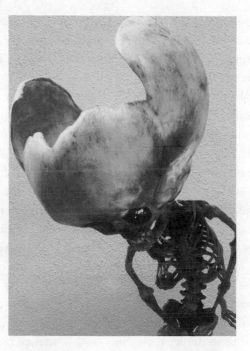

"Hydrocephalic child whose skull has opened like a
flower." Copyright © 1997 Rosamond Purcell.

mal kingdom, a kinship reaffirmed in strange new ways by the baby with
the baboon heart and the lamb with human genes. Looking at Purcell's photo
of a hydrocephalic child who must have died when his ballooning cranium
finally collapsed "with God knows what sound of rushing water in his . . .
ears," as she puts it, we realize just how rare medical advances have made
the truly extraordinary body.[23] The image evokes an irreconcilable mixture of pity and guilty pleasure: pity at the awful sadness of the stick figure
with the outsized head who was someone's child, guilty pleasure at being
allowed to exchange the moral gaze for an aesthetic one that savors the
pathological sublime.

   Then again, the New Grotesque can also be read as a reflexive recoil from the deodorization of death in secular modernity. It speaks to a
subconscious yearning for a resacralized world in which our sense of our
own mortality weaves the threads of our lives into the web of all that lives

and dies. "The rituals of the past which tied all of us to creation and assured us a place in the universe have been replaced by the spiritual vacuity of today," write Akin and Ludwig, in an unpublished essay. "It is this sense of unity we mourn and to which these mysterious and potent relics"—such as their photographs of pickled human curios—"testify." As recently as the nineteenth century, when hospitals were infamously unhygienic, death took place in the home; the funeral too was held there, and family and friends laid out the dead and transported the coffin to the grave. Today, death is an antiseptic, quarantine affair, out of sight and out of mind. In *The American Way of Death,* Jessica Mitford notes that, in the contemporary American funeral, the funeral director stages "a well-oiled performance in which the concept of *death* [plays] no part whatsoever."[24] Max Aguilera-Hellweg insists, "We need to do away with the fantasy of dying with dignity so that we *can* die with dignity. If we knew who we were, then we could make the leaps that we really need to make as a society."

A "narrative of the marvelous," the New Grotesque recalls us to a time when myth and science, the freak show and the natural history museum were closer kin; in so doing, it reminds us that science is partly a cultural construction, a notion that is the keystone of recent philosophical challenges to science's cultural authority as the "value-neutral" arbiter of truth. Drawing connections between "institutionalized science and social power," Akin and Ludwig wonder about "lurid displays . . . sanctified by science." In the unpublished essay cited earlier, they ask, "What cause, other than morbid curiosity, is served by allowing the public to view . . . a penis hanging limply in formaldehyde like a piece of meat?"

The issues they raise go to the heart of the controversy swirling around the new, unimproved College of Physicians calendar that replaced the Mutter calendar. A National Public Radio story noted that the former college president Dr. Alfred Fishman didn't think fine-art photos of the museum's pathological specimens were appropriate fare for general consumption. "It wasn't a calendar that I would send out to six-year-old children to hang and turn pages every month," he said. "On the other hand, I could see very clearly how I would turn pages and I did, curious about what was on each page. I was impressed by some of the anomalies that they showed there—the developmental defects. But, you see, that is a kind of professional curiosity. That's what the museum was intended for. It wasn't intended for artists."[25]

Here, as if preserved in formaldehyde, are the nineteenth-century gentleman-scholar's misgivings about the commonfolk's ability to handle the hard stuff—in this case, to view the Mutter's little shop of horrors from a properly disinterested scientific distance, rather than the prurient, nose-to-the-glass attitude of the unabashedly enthralled laity. As if rapt fascination, mingled with wonder, terror, and the occasional pantomimed upchuck, weren't a perfectly natural reaction to the anatomical grotesque. As if doctors themselves exhibited only dispassionate "professional curiosity" about such specimens. "Among my classmates there was a spectrum of reactions" to

Cephalothoracopagus (conjoined twins fused at head and thorax).
Copyright © 1990 Scott Lindgren.

anatomy class, "from revulsion and nausea to outright horror and sick humor," recalls C. J. Peters in his autobiographical *Virus Hunter*. "I'd like to say most of us are too sensitive to indulge in the latter, passing off severed hands or penises to unsuspecting acquaintances and the like, but I'd be lying."[26]

Then, too, this notion that the world should be child-proofed, that the moral and intellectual sophistication of a six-year-old should be the universal standard of measurement in matters of public decency, bears closer scrutiny. As does the college's desire to move the Mutter into the twenty-first century by removing potentially "offensive" exhibits such as the wall of 139 skulls and the plaster cast of Chang and Eng and replacing them with spiffy, interactive presentations like the recent exhibit "Say Ahhh!," which encouraged visitors to "take a whirl on the wheel of treatment!" or record their thoughts on smoking, safe sex, and AIDS. What the world needs now, at a moment when extraordinary bodies like Chang and Eng's are vanishingly rare and disease and death are increasingly experienced as special effects, isn't more interactive kiosks and video monitors, but a reality check: a face-to-face encounter with the anatomical Other, the inescapably embodied.

The New Grotesque speaks volumes about body loathing in the age of AIDS, flesh-eating bacteria, and hemorrhagic viruses. It constitutes a deliberation on the growing irrelevance of the body in an ever more virtual world, where terminally wired technophiles regard the weak flesh with open contempt, as an evolutionary vestige that should be relegated to the backrooms of natural history museums. Countervailing the cyberpunk rhetoric of etherealization, with its rhapsodic evocations of embodied consciousness supplanted by discarnate, "downloaded" existence in computer memory, the New Grotesque confronts us with the ineluctable fact of our mortality, reminding us that (for now, at least) the politics of the late twentieth century come to ground in physical realities, not virtual ones. "The one question I get asked, more than any other," says the Mutter museum director Gretchen Worden, "is: Is it real?" The bisected heads, decapitated doll babies in lace bonnets, and hydrocephalic skeletons photographed by Aguilera-Hellweg, Purcell, and Akin and Ludwig simultaneously incarnate postmodern media culture and bring it crashing down to earth, anchored by the drag coefficient of the body.

SECTION III
MAIN STREET, U.S.A.: THE PUBLIC SPHERE

8 / PAST PERFECT: DISNEY CELEBRATES US HOME

Celebration, Florida. Author's collection.

Wired: Describe the city of the future.
Bradbury: Disneyland. They've done everything right.

—Ray Bradbury, *Wired* magazine interview

The food court is our new town square, as any mall crawler knows. And our city streets are being theme-parked for mass consumption, as Universal Studios' CityWalk attests.

CityWalk, an ersatz La-La-Land cum-outdoor shopping mall, is a textbook example of the Disneyfication of public space. Located in Universal City, it telescopes L.A., from Malibu to Melrose Avenue, Sunset Strip to Venice Beach, into a few overscaled, overdesigned blocks. Its principal architect, Jon Jerde, insists that, despite its postmodern Toon Town aspect, CityWalk is its own "real-life place," a bona fide neighborhood rather than a theme-malled Los Angeles.[1] The chief project designer, Richard Orne, extols the simulated "patina of use" that implies a lived history behind the pixilated streetscape. "People want to have a communal experience in a place that they feel safe and comfortable [in]," he told *The Los Angeles Times*. "Who cares if it's artificially created . . . ?"[2]

The replacement of landmark neighborhoods by commercial simulacra like CityWalk marks the usurpation of Main Street's civic life by the mall. To many, it's a tolerable, even desirable response to cuts in basic services by cash-strapped local governments and an effective means of exorcising fear of violent crime. It's a solution that seems right for the times, speaking simultaneously to a deepening distrust of big-government solutions to urban blight and an abiding faith in the "free" market. As important, it taps into a growing desire to return to the supposed civility and tranquillity of prewar America, before the fabric of our common dreams and shared values was unraveled (the story goes) by industrialization, urbanization, the automobile, and mass-media culture.

The ritual invocation of the word "community" in media punditry and ad copy bespeaks a widespread yearning for the lost (and for many of us, largely imagined) civic life and social ties of an earlier America: *Our Town* minus the angst, *Huckleberry Finn* with the slave traders and the lynch mobs left out—Disneyland's Main Street, U.S.A. At the root of our wistful hope that we *can* go home again, argues Eric Hobsbawm, is the collapse, in the wake of postindustrialization and globalization, of "the historic structures of human relations which modern society inherited from a pre-industrial and pre-capitalist past. The strange calls for an otherwise unidentified 'civil society,' for 'community' [are] the voice of lost and drifting generations."[3]

More immediately, our fetish for the concept is tied to media-fanned fantasies about crime and the article of Op-Ed faith that America is an increasingly inhospitable place, the mean, every-creep-for-himself urban jungle of the Angry White Guy movie *Falling Down* or the irredeemably sick hell-world of the weirdly reactionary *Seven,* where the sage old detective and the sociopath are united in their revulsion at the depravity—and cultural illiteracy—all around them. There's a pervasive longing for a place where "everybody knows your name," as the *Cheers* theme puts it, although there's an instructive irony in the fact that a bar full of time-killing losers, none of whom seem to *like* each other very much, is our sitcom shrine to misty dreams of lost community.

Wired's executive editor, Kevin Kelly, once remarked in an on-line discussion topic titled "Is Disneyland a Place to Live?" that he'd gladly take up residence in the Magic Kingdom if the rent was cheap.[4] Kelly's comment gives voice to the desire, prevalent among the self-styled "digital elite," to abandon America's hopelessly modern metropolises for the postmodern environs of edge cities and gated communities. To use Robert Reich's term, it's the "secession of the successful," the upper class's flight from public space and social responsibility.

True believers in Alvin Toffler's Third Wave theology anticipate a near future in which the body politic (or at least the economic elite, the only part of it that matters) has dissolved into a networked nation of telecommuting "knowledge workers" who work, play, and socialize from the high-tech comfort zones of their electronic cottages. The computer-industry guru George Gilder, reviling the nation's urban centers in prose worthy of *The Eternal Jew,* anticipates the demise of the "big parasite cities sucking the lifeblood out of America" with undisguised relish. He predicts the arrival of an on-line global village that he calls the "telecosm," a netropolis that will "destroy cities because then you can get all the diversity, all the seren-dipity, all the exuberant variety that you can find in a city in your own liv-ing room."[5] Esther Dyson, a fellow technology booster, sings from the same page. In *Release 2.0: A Design for Living in the Digital Age,* she articulates her hope that as real communities wither, on-line ones will replace them. She'll take cyberspace, where like-minded users congregate in cozy enclaves, over a real world where everything "seems to get more complex and more over-whelming, and public space ever more scary."[6] In *The Road Ahead,* Bill Gates, ever the visionary, proposes an enlightened solution to "many of today's major social problems [that] have arisen because the population has been crowded into urban areas." Breathlessly, the reader wonders what inspired piece of software Gates has in store for us: a new twist on economic devel-opment zones, yoked to a radical plan for reinventing public education? Futuristic visions of mass transportation and architecture that would foster a sense of community and facilitate civic life? The world's most exalted übergeek labors mightily, and brings forth the answer to the social ills that plague our cities: telecommuting.

The digerati's clean-room fantasy of retreating into virtual worlds exudes a Hunekerian fear and loathing of the "mongrel metropolis," where unwanted encounters with lumpenproles lurk around every corner. It par-allels the theme-parking of urban space mentioned earlier, which transforms the city's visual cacophony and chaotic street life into a crowd-controlled, quality-of-life-patrolled simulation of itself: "New York as we would like it to be," in the words of *The New York Times* food columnist Ruth Reichl, "a place of clean, manicured parks, gorgeous architecture, and interesting food."[7] In like mind, New Urbanists like James Howard Kunstler take up the city-bashing refrain, but offer, as their utopian alternative, soft-focus visions of small towns rather than sanitized cities or virtual communities. In *Home from Nowhere: Remaking Our Everyday World for the 21st Century,* Kunstler sympathizes with Americans who love Disney World "because the everyday places where they live and go about their business are so dismal that Disney World seems splendid by comparison."

Who can argue with clean, manicured parks or the kinder, gentler ways of small-town life? As a statistic in the middle-class flight from the big cities to the suburbs, I'm in no position to deny the all-too-familiar litany of woes about urban decay, the death of civility, and the end of community. After a decade in Brooklyn, enduring car alarms, car stereos, and the bigotry that culminated in a gang of bat-wielding goons mobbing a man for the crime of being Asian-American, I lit out for the territories, to a village like the "classic Main Street town in upstate New York" that Kunstler lives in.

Still, there's a Babbittry to pronouncements like "American cities are dismal" that makes my left knee jerk. It's no mere coincidence that our cities' most vocal critics tend to be neocons like Gilder or laissez-faire futurists like Dyson. But the small town mythologized by Americans from Ray Bradbury to Ronald Reagan has a dark side that its enthusiasts conveniently overlook. Its close-knit community and social equilibrium were often purchased at the cost of lost privacy, conformity to the unwritten laws of local custom, and the ugly adhesive of racism. Noting the nostalgia in Herrnstein and Murray's social Darwinist polemic *The Bell Curve* for "the good old days of towns and neighborhoods where all people could be given tasks of value," Stephen Jay Gould drily observes that the authors "have forgotten about the town Jew and the dwellers on the other side of the tracks in many of these idyllic villages."[8] Show me a real-life Waltons' Mountain, and I'll show you the Winesburg, Ohio, locked away in its closets.

Moreover, the doomy pronouncement that American cities are "dismal" evinces a suburban provincialism, a Dockers monoculturalism that simply can't fathom, and therefore fears, the profane pleasures of what Bakhtin might have called the Times Square carnivalesque: urban sleaze, cheap thrills, the pell-mell foot traffic that throws strangers of all colors and classes into momentary proximity, the sheer sensory overload of it all. Opposing the ideal city as imagined by Gilder, Dyson, Kunstler, or even Reichl—sane, spic-and-span, easily navigable, and immanently manageable—is a bohemian vision that embraces the metropolis after dark as a labyrinth of teeming boulevards and trackless back alleys, drunk on its own synesthesia, utterly out of control. From Weegee's *Naked City* to Rem Koolhaas's *Delirious New York,* it's a vision that revels in the very prospect that strikes fear in Gilder and company— the threat of being overwhelmed by the urban id, overcome by the noise and the neon, caught up in a chain of bizarre events, swallowed and swept away by the crowds. The bohemian vision is a vision of the city as infernal fun house, a Luna Park of the subconscious.

In a delicious irony, this vision inspired a New Urbanism of its own in Ivan Chtcheglov's "Formula for a New Urbanism." According to the cultural critic Greil Marcus, Chtcheglov's 1953 essay is an exhortation to his fellow Lettrists to "create their first city, 'the intellectual capital of the world,' a sort of Fourierist Las Vegas, a surrealist Disneyland, an amusement park where people would actually live . . . a city where 'the principal activity of the inhabitants' would be 'the CONTINUOUS DÉRIVE,' a drift through a landscape of 'buildings charged with evocative power, symbolic edifices representing emotions, forces, and events from the past, the present, and the future.'"[9]

Guy Trebay's 1995 *Village Voice* essay on the Disneyfication of Times Square is a eulogy for this vision. Trebay bemoans the passing of "pornville," the disappearance of the smutty novelty shops that sold "'Man's Sexy Squirting Cucumber,' a strange toy gizmo with a rude warty 'joke inside,' or decks of 1960s nudie playing cards, or glass flowers, or dusty nunchakus, or 'jade' elephants the color of limes. . . ."[10] He writes, "Walking past the razed lots of Times Square, I'm feeling grouchy. . . . I've been to Disney World— where the terror of nature, not to mention the subconscious, is so pervasive that even the shrubs are trained into perky shapes—and just now I'm having problems picturing my city reinvented by 'imagineers.'"[11]

Of course, those who resent annexation into the Magic Kingdom are probably in the minority; many, like Ray Bradbury, Kevin Kelly, and the corporate consultant Regis McKenna, would welcome the prospect. In *Real Time: Preparing for the Age of the Never Satisfied Customer*, McKenna enthuses, "Perhaps, we will all someday live inside entertainment—artifacts of fantasy and distraction."[12]

He may soon get his wish. Already, the United States is beginning to look like a simulator ride based on the postmodern philosopher Jean Baudrillard's *America*, a sneering paean to a country that is, for him, the apotheosis of the artificial. Everyday life is being turned into a simulation of itself in restaurants like New York's Television City, where diners are guests on a talk show beamed to 130 monitors throughout the restaurant; in "entertainment retail" like NikeTown, which is really in the business of selling "shopping fantasy"; in *Blade Runner* streetscapes like Las Vegas's Fremont Street, which immerses strollers in an electronic hallucination with the aid of 211 million lights and a 540,000-watt sound system.[13] We live in a "culture of alienated spectacle," contends Ralph Rugoff, "where all aspects of experience, from shopping to warfare, are routinely transformed into thematized entertainment."[14] There's a siege mentality to the *Utne Reader* cover story on "reclaiming real life," which promises "a way out of wonderland" for those who are "fed up with a faux world," then asks, "Is a real life possible anymore?"[15]

By no accident, Disney, the world's most powerful media and entertainment conglomerate and an unequaled retailer of fantasy worlds, is taking the obvious next step in the theme-parking of reality and the corporatizing of the commons: Celebration, the planned community the company is building near Orlando, Florida. It's a New Jerusalem for New Urbanists, a shining city on a swamp.

Celebration welcomed its first residents in June 1996; within 10 to 15 years, the 4,900-acre town will be home to a projected population of 20,000. Residents' houses are in one of six neotraditional styles (Classical, Victorian, Colonial Revival, Coastal, Mediterranean, and French) based on regional prototypes in what a promotional brochure calls America's "best and best-loved small towns" from Charleston, South Carolina, to East Hampton, New York.

If reality follows the Disney script, Celebration's inhabitants will promenade beside the town lake, take in a movie at the faux Deco "picture palace," and socialize in Founders Park ("a civic space where, ultimately, neighbors might congregate after walking their children to school," the brochure suggests, hopefully).[16] Some of those who have moved in are already sending their children to Celebration School, a K–12 facility operated by the Osceola County School Board. As the community takes root, we're told, they'll shop, bank, and post their mail in downtown Celebration, and receive health care at Health Campus, a medical center owned and operated by Florida Hospital.

The *Architectural Walking Tour* guidebook I obtained when I visited Celebration in October 1996 calls Disney's planned community "a traditional American town built anew . . . designed to offer a return to a more sociable and civic-minded way of life." After a stroll through the downtown area, I called it Bedford Falls on Prozac. The town suggests an eerily literal realization of Seahaven from *The Truman Show,* sans sea, or the Privatopias in Neal Stephenson's science fiction novel *Snow Crash,* with their picture-perfect lawns and stately brass fire hydrants "designed on a computer screen by the same aesthetes who designed the DynaVictorian houses and the tasteful mailboxes and the immense marble street signs that sit at each intersection like headstones. Designed on a computer screen, but with an eye toward the elegance of things past and forgotten about."[17]

Taking in the tasteful pastels and witty medley of architectural styles, I couldn't shake the feeling that the buildings had been scaled down, like the ones along Disneyland's Main Street, U.S.A., where everything is built five eighths true size to give reality a whimsical, toylike quality. A vague ontological queasiness settled over me, a postmodern malaise I'll call the *Prisoner* Syndrome: the unsettling suspicion that reality is really theme-park fakery, stage-managed by unseen conspirators with dark designs. Who will live here? The Audio-Animatronic family from GE's Carousel of Progress? A Duracell version of the Mayberry gang? Surveying the near-complete cinema, I bumped into a perky young couple. He was a clean-cut boy next door whose parents lived in Celebration; she was a cute brunette in shorts and a bikini top who bore an unsettling resemblance to Annette Funicello. Is Disney cloning these people from Mouseketeer DNA?

Scratch the surface of Disney's Frank Capra idyll, however, and the cynical truth lies exposed: that Celebration is a company town—a media monolith's vision of privatized governance and democracy overruled by technocracy. The town's seal, a ponytailed girl riding her bike past the proverbial picket fence, a playful pup nipping at her tires, is a registered Disney trademark. Market Street, the town's "primary shopping promenade," would have been named Main Street, as in Disneyland, were it not for the fact that "there already was a Main Street in Osceola County, and street names can't be used twice," the brochure notes, with a sigh of regret. Celebration's welcome wagon will include an official history course that the Celebration Foundation's administrator, Charles Adams, describes as "very similar to what we do when we bring in a new cast member to work for the Walt Disney Company."[18] ("Cast member" is Disneyspeak for "employee.") Of course, Celebration's only "history," to speak of, lies in the CityWalk-ish "slightly aged" look that the town's coplanner Jacqueline Robertson gave some of the downtown buildings, and in the houses' fastidiously historical exteriors. No matter, assures Adams: "We do have some history, really, going back to the original vision from Walt."[19]

Adams's comment unmasks the agenda behind Celebration's Hollywood backlot facade, namely, the reengineering of participatory democracy in accordance with a more corporate-friendly vision of governance. The "original vision" on which the town is based is EPCOT (Experimental

Prototype Community of Tomorrow), a Jetsonian technopolis conceived by Walt in the sixties as a company town populated by Disney World employees. It was to be a brave new experiment in urban planning and social engineering, propelled by the thrusters of American technology—in Walt's words, "a planned, controlled community, a showcase for American industry and research."[20] As realized in Disney World, EPCOT is a corporate-sponsored science fair whose obsolete tomorrows smell more pungently of mothballs with each passing year. Even so, Walt's dream lives on in EPCOT's overarching theme of corporate paternalism and technocratic solutions to social problems, the bedrock conviction "that planning for the future can be left to corporations which will 'maximize the common good,'" as the Disney scholar Alan Bryman puts it.[21]

This, the "original vision from Walt"—the belief that father knows best, be he "Uncle Walt," the self-styled "benevolent dictator of Disney enterprises," or the corporation itself as paterfamilias—is Celebration's ideological cornerstone. Beginning with a misty-eyed evocation of child-hood memories, the town's promotional video promises that "there is a place that takes you back to that time of innocence. A place where the biggest decision is whether to play kick the can or king of the hill. A place of cara-mel apples and cotton candy, secret forts and hopscotch on the streets. That place is here again, in a new town called Celebration."[22] In Disney's "tradi-tional . . . town built anew," residents will entrust the burdensome respon-sibilities of civic life in a participatory democracy to their corporate parents, just as the Disneyesque Reagan left the dreary business of governing to others, "as if government was a boring job best left to the grown-ups," as one critic put it.[23] An unincorporated town under the jurisdiction of Osceola County, Celebration won't be self-governing in any meaningful sense. Disney will exercise veto power over the decisions of the home owners' only representative body, the community association, for 40 years or until three quarters of the master-plan residences are occupied, whichever comes first.

As Russ Rymer argues in his penetrating *Harper's* essay on Celebra-tion, "Back to the Future," Disney's planned community is consecrated to "prevailing nostalgias for a bygone time of life, the life of a carefree child, a civic infant, when the corporation could make the rules and keep the peace."[24] In an America racked by social change and economic inequity, where community and civility are fast unraveling, Disney promises to time-warp an anxious middle class to a revisionist past (or is it a neotraditional future?) where our corporate parents unburden us of our rights and responsibilities as citizens so that we may frolic in secret forts and hopscotch on the streets like the inner children we've always been at heart.

The growing appeal of the corporatized commons is evident in the fact that demand for Celebration's initial offering of homes was almost three times the supply, despite the fact that prospective buyers had nothing to go by but models, videos, and promotional literature—and the Disney name, one of the best-known, best-loved brands in the world. According to the Celebration co-planner Robert A. M. Stern, "People . . . almost glory in the fact that someone runs the show. People love to come to Disney because the very word 'Disney' means a certain authoritative standard that they will succumb to."[25]

To imagineers like Stern, New Urbanists like Kunstler, and digerati like Dyson and Gilder, dystopian forebodings of the public sphere themeparked by the private sector and, ultimately, participatory democracy rendered obsolete by multinational capitalism would doubtless seem like neo-Marxist paranoia. Nonetheless, we would do well to consider Disney CEO Michael Eisner's expressed belief that Celebration "will set up a system of how to develop communities"—presumably, along privatized, postdemocratic lines. "I hope in fifty years they say, 'Thank God for Celebration,'" says Eisner.[26] Consider as well the extralegal status of Disney's Florida fiefdom, an expanse of real estate larger than the island of Manhattan that is the workaday home of approximately 30,000 Disney employees. In 1967, Florida officials passed legislation that granted Disney's holdings, the inoffensively named Reedy Creek Improvement Area, the status of an autonomous county, which empowered it to levy its own taxes and enact its own building codes and exempted it from filing environmental impact statements or abiding by municipal or regional laws regarding development, zoning, and waste control.

"Disney World is, before anything else, a governmental entity," writes Rymer. "Walt's greatest feat of imagineering was his vaulting of a theme park into a polity. . . . Because [Reedy Creek's] powers are allowed only to popularly elected bodies, Disney instituted a 'government' that stayed firmly in company control; voting 'citizens' were a handful of loyal Disney managers. Walt's own enmity for democratic forms was legendary."[27] Indeed, Walt's original vision of Celebration, né EPCOT, was premised on the notion that the company would own the homes, renting them to the town's residents: "There will be no landowners and therefore no voting control," Walt happily declared.[28]

Once, when asked by a journalist if he'd ever considered running for office, he replied that he had no interest in being president of the United States, remarking, "I'd rather be the benevolent dictator of Disney enterprises."[29] Then again, if he'd imagineered a future like the one envisioned by the *Spy* magazine parody in which Michael Eisner was elected president while remaining CEO of Disney, he might have reconsidered.

In *Spy*'s tongue-in-cheek fantasy, President Eisner declares a "national closing time" of 11:30 P.M. on all federally funded streets, highways, and mass-transit systems; turns inner-city black ghettos into themed tourist attractions; and replaces representatives and senators with professional actors. The Disney CEO proves hugely popular with the American people, his sole detractors "cynics and intellectuals who felt constrained by an orderly, cheerful society where the good of the many was placed above the good of the individual."[30] *Spy*'s "speculative history of the near future" ends by noting that "at this writing, ratification is near for a constitutional amendment that would exempt Michael Eisner from the 22nd Amendment's two-term limit and allow him to continue to exercise his benevolent dominion over this happy, happy land."

Today, Celebration; tomorrow, the world.

9 / TRENDSPOTTING: I SHOP, THEREFORE I AM

You are what you buy. Copyright © 1998 Eric White.

TO HELL WITH MORAL VICTORIES

—Nike billboard near Crenshaw High School in inner-city Los Angeles

"Tattooed Ears Cause New Teen Craze," a story that aired on NPR's *All Things Considered* on a recent April 1, caught my ear. As a zero-tolerance critic of the growing encroachment of corporate influence on our everyday lives, I wasn't at all surprised by Noah Adams's report on Laser Splash, a breakthrough technology that used lasers to etch logos on teenage earlobes in exchange for a 10 percent lifetime discount on a company's products. "Alphanumeric bits" embedded in the paint enabled retailers to scan the tattoos at checkout counters. According to Adams, several corporations, Nike among them, had already scrambled aboard the trend du jour.

Laser Splash's glib young CEO defended brand-name branding as a ritual of resistance ("a way to . . . take the idea of being bought and . . . throw it in their face") while maintaining, in the same breath, that logo tattoos were "interactive consumerism," "a way of celebrating" the fact that, in an age of designer lifestyles, we're all "walking billboards," anyway.[1] She sounded all the right notes, harmonizing boomer delusions of youthful rebellion in the Minoxidil years with Generation X's cherished vision of itself as immune to the not-so-subliminal seductions of consumer culture, inoculated by terminal cynicism.

Listening to the report, I took grim satisfaction in the confirmation of my worst suspicions about commodity culture. Here, in the sale of the slacker body as advertising space, was the ultimate justification for anticonsumerist screeds. It was almost too perfect.

Branded. Photo: Shannon Mendes. Courtesy *Adbusters*
magazine (www.adbusters.org/1-800-663-1243).

In fact, it *was* too perfect: "Tattooed Ears" was an April Fool's
gag played by NPR on its listeners, among them me, a supposedly wary
critic who has even written about media hoaxes, embarrassingly enough.
But mortification turned to vindication only a month later, when *The New
York Times Magazine* carried an item about EKINs (spell it backward), the
banzai, mostly twenty-something male Nike employees who tattoo the
company's boomerang-shaped logo (known as the "swoosh") on their
calves or upper thighs. The concept of corporate vassals so gung-ho they
literally tattoo their fiefdom's coat of arms on their bodies makes the fictional CEO's assertion that logo tattoos represent a gonzo "embrace" of
the fact that "the corporation owns our souls" sound a little less laughable
all of a sudden. There's a creepy-funny resemblance, here, to the commodity future of William Gibson's *Neuromancer,* in which Japanese corporate serfs are tattooed with their company logos, and to present-day
Japan, where a salaryman introduces himself by saying, "I am Toyota

Company's Mr. So-and-So," since an employee's corporate affiliation is his core identity.

Meanwhile, Nike, the world's largest footwear manufacturer and a self-styled "guerrilla marketer," is busy tattooing the body politic. My utterly unscientific study of the New York streetscape, based entirely on the evidence before my eyes, is that the swooshing of America is well under way: Baseball caps, sweatshirts, and other items of apparel bearing the Nike emblem, as cryptic and conspiratorial as the mysterious post-horn symbol in *The Crying of Lot 49,* seem to be everywhere. The improbably named Duke Stump, an EKIN quoted in *The New York Times Magazine* blurb, may have been only half facetious when he cracked, "It's a cult. But it's a great cult."[2]

There's an increasing tendency in American culture to define oneself in terms of brand-name affiliation. Spun off its axis by information overload, the introspective psyche of McLuhan's "typographic man" has given way to the postmodern "decentered self." Idiosyncratic purchasing patterns are emerging as a means of reinforcing the shaky boundaries of the self: I shop, therefore I am. Here at the end of the century, when the radical redefinition of gender roles, the family, the nature of work, and other formerly immutable features of the cultural landscape is undermining our sense of who we are in relation to society, nothing reifies like the niche marketer's gaze.

More immediately, in a culture where the semiotics of nonconformity are almost instantly appropriated by the corporate mainstream, the under-25 demographic that accounts for more than half of Nike's sales collages a fierce individuality out of shared pop references, one-minute microfads, and kitschy or whimsical products. The impromptu ruminations of a young black man interviewed in one of the "Mindtrends" marketing videos produced by the New York–based trendspotting firm Sputnik are enlightening. "If Reebok made a line that was, like, a California line, catering more to the lifestyle in California, and then had something different for someone in Texas, that would be a little bit better, you know?" he says. "Because then you're not just falling into the crowd; you can actually set yourself apart." The bar-code consciousness of mass culture is parried by a "nonconformity" fashioned, ironically, from the conspicuous consumption of brands that have earned the elusive youth-culture approbation "cool."

To be sure, there's no denying the guerrilla semiotics at work in kids' refunctioning of mass-produced goods; rave culture's embrace of

pacifiers, cartoon lunchboxes, and other kiddie gear as tokens of psyche-
delic infantilism is playfully perverse. Nonetheless, despite Douglas Rush-
koff's sweet dreams, in his book *Media Virus!*, of the Powers That Be brought
to their knees by "activist memes" such as *Beavis and Butt-Head*, multinational corporations aren't losing any sleep over the hilariously nineties notions of subversion through channel surfing and consumption as rebellion.
As the advertising critic Leslie Savan points out in *The Sponsored Life: Ads,
TV, and American Culture,* "Advertisers learned long ago that individuality
sells, like sex or patriotism. . . . [Commercials tell] the television-imbibing
millions that they are secret rebels, freedom-loving individuals who refuse
to be squished by society's constraints. Corporate America is always advis-
ing us that if we just buy in we can feel like irrepressibly hip outsiders. As
the jingle goes, 'I like the Sprite in you.'"[3]

The fiendish brilliance of American consumer culture is its ability
to shrink-wrap our defiant gestures and sell them back to us as off-the-rack
rebellion, a dynamic exemplified by Nike's notorious use of the thirty-
something button-pusher "Revolution," by the Beatles, to announce "a revolution in fitness." Embodied by CEO Phil Knight, a wild 'n' crazy billionaire
in jeans and mirror shades who just can't drive 55 and who professes to
loathe advertising, the company's public image bristles with attitude, all
never-say-die bravado and no-bullshit street credibility. A virtuoso impro-
viser on the consumption-as-rebellion theme, Nike slam-dunks its message
that rebel cool can be had for the price of a pair of Air Jordans in commercials like the controversial "Search and Destroy" spot that aired during the
'96 Olympics, featuring athletes as punk-rock warriors and a bloody mouth-
piece sailing across the Nike logo. *Forbes 400* approvingly noted that "by
focusing its sponsorships on individual athletes" such as Charles Barkley,
who notoriously declared in a Nike ad that he wasn't a role model, "Nike,
despite its size, maintains its cool, outsider image."[4]

Ironically (though hardly surprisingly), the corporate conduct behind the company's born-to-be-wild image is pure status quo: Nike has taken
hits for its all-too-typical practice of relocating its manufacturing to the Third
World and employing nonunionized workers at less than subsistence wages.
In 1991, the owners of an Indonesian factory that manufactured Nike shoes
refused to pay even the minimum wage of $1.25 a day and called in the
military to crush the ensuing strike.

Knight, whose holdings have been estimated at more than $5 billion, mouthed the laissez-faire canard that Indonesia's economy would be ruined if wages were allowed to get too high.[5] In his documentary movie *The Big One,* the filmmaker Michael Moore has a surreal exchange with the Nike CEO about Indonesian factories that manufacture Nike apparel: "Twelve-year-olds working in [Indonesian] factories, that's okay with you?" Moore asks. "They're not twelve," says Knight. "The minimum age is fourteen." "How about fourteen, then? That doesn't bother you?" "No."[6]

According to the United Auto Workers newspaper *Solidarity,* Cicih Sukaesih, an Indonesian worker who was fired for striking, was stunned when she saw a Nike ad that exhorted, "Go ahead, demand a raise. You have everything to gain and nothing to lose." Notes Sukaesih, "They would never say that on their ads in Indonesia. When we worked in the factory, we thought 'Just do it!' meant 'Work harder and don't question authority.'"[7] A world away from the American legions who want to Be Like Mike, the battle cry of trademarked iconoclasm sounds like an authoritarian admonition to grin and bear the corporate yoke. No pain, no gain.

Far from the sweatshop floor, among the 77 percent of American teenage boys whom a "brand power survey" said would rather be wearing Nikes than any other shoes, the swoosh still stands for an "anti-authoritarian streak," an "athlete-against-the-establishment ethic," according to Donald Katz, author of *Just Do It: The Nike Spirit in the Corporate World.*[8] In a revealing irony, the company synonymous with the maverick miler who runs to a different drummer has the highest levels of "acceptance of company policy ever recorded by the national firm that conducted the study," says Katz.[9] The employees who work on the Nike World Campus, a company town shielded from the outside world by a Disneylandish berm that encircles its 74-acre grounds, display a cultish devotion to the paternalistic corporation that bequeathed them a manmade lake, miles of jogging trails, the state-of-the-art Bo Jackson Fitness Center, a Joe Paterno Day Care Center for Nike tykes, and, best of all, the chance to be part of what one EKIN breathlessly called "some amazing force." And no one is more devoted than the EKINs, the technical experts out in the field whom Duke Stump describes as "the eyes and ears of the company." It is these tattooed road warriors who spring to mind while one absorbs Katz's assertion that "the corporate 'we' is used in place of 'I' with regularity inside Nike, even as the corporate 'we' is lost at most other companies."[10]

Though few, if any, illustrated youth have chosen to embellish themselves with corporate logos (to the best of my knowledge), there's an obvious, ironic parallel between Nike's tattooed EKINS and twenty-something "modern primitives": Both have transformed themselves into "walking billboards," their "Just do it!" individuality a pastiche of symbols pilfered from the cultural memory bank. Moreover, *consumer tribalism* in youth culture—the use of brand names as tribal totems, from Timberland to Stussy to No Fear to whatever this week's flavor is—echoes the EKIN use of the swoosh as an emblem of clan pride.

We may be standing on the threshold of the future imagined by William Gibson in the video documentary *Cyberpunk,* "a world where all of the consumers under a certain age will probably tend to identify more with their consumer status or with the products they consume than with any sort of antiquated notion of nationality."[11] In the Nike commercial where James Carville champions the baseball star and Nike endorser Ken Griffey, Jr., for president, or the one where Dennis Hopper does a postmodern turn on George C. Scott's Patton by delivering an over-the-top ode to football with an enormous swoosh in place of Patton's American flag, we glimpse a tongue-in-cheek vision of a corporate-brand future brought to you by transnational capitalism.

It will arrive, if it does, on the morning after the death of the nation-state so breathlessly anticipated by the laissez-faire futurists and self-styled "cyberelite" who soapbox in *Wired.* Premonitions of this branded, post-national future can already be discerned in the creeping corporate mono-culture that the social theorist Benjamin R. Barber calls "McWorld," a Family of Man created not by the electronic interconnectedness McLuhan extolled but by MTV, Microsoft, and McDonald's. As McLuhan's "retribalized" world of "electronic interdependence" approaches, it looks less like a global village than like Planet Reebok or NikeTown. In *Jihad vs. McWorld: How the Planet Is Both Falling Apart and Coming Together and What This Means for Democracy,* Barber argues that multinational capitalism is hell-bent on stamping "obsolete" on what Gibson would call the "antiquated notion" of the nation-state, which, Barber maintains, "has been democracy's most promising host."

22222

Paradoxically, the waning of the nation state takes place at a time when multinationals are acting more and more like sovereign powers. In fact, the leap from corporation to nation-state has already been taken. In a comic-relief version of Barber's nightmare, the company Cuervo Tequila recently purchased an eight-acre island in the West Indies and declared it the Republic of Cuervo Gold. Tongue firmly in cheek, the company has petitioned the U.N. to recognize its real-life Margaritaville as a legitimate island nation—unsuccessfully, so far.[12]

Obviously, the creation of a corporate-sponsored Fantasy Island where the ruling party's platform is "frozen or on the rocks" is a publicity stunt worthy of Barnum. But the secessionist stirrings among those who have bought a piece of what Evan McKenzie calls "Privatopia," the gated, guarded enclaves described in a 1995 *New York Times* story as "the fastest-growing residential communities in the nation," are no laughing matter. Fed up with paying taxes to local governments as well as to the developer-controlled home owners' associations that are their own private governments, residents have begun to dream darkly about seceding from the towns beyond their walls. Figuratively, of course, they already have, as McKenzie points out, abandoning the cross-class, multi-ethnic "flux and ferment" of the city, with its "spontaneity and diversity and its unpredictable rewards and hazards," for the Privatopia of common-interest housing developments, "where master-planning, homogeneous populations, and private governments offer the affluent a chance to escape from urban reality."[13] In *Snow Crash,* Neal Stephenson imagines a mordantly funny near future in which the bunker-mentality middle-class has incarcerated itself in so-called burbclaves, each "a city-state with its own constitution, a border, laws, cops, everything."[14]

It's a worrying vision, though a science-fictional one for now. But that thought was cold comfort during a recent flight, when my eye landed on an ad for temporary "logo tattoos" in the in-flight magazine. In the photo, a smiling young woman bared her back to reveal a riot of EASY ON, EASY OFF tattoos for Volvo, Gannett, Thrifty, Toshiba, and the like. Distracted by a familiar image hovering in my peripheral vision, I glanced up. A few seats away sat an athletic-looking young woman, her windbreaker proudly emblazoned with the American flag. On the patch of blue where the stars usually go was a white swoosh.

SECTION IV
THE PARENT TRAP

10 / GRIM FAIRY TALES: RENÉE FRENCH'S KINDERCULTURE

"Mitch and the Mole," from *Grit Bath*. Copyright © Renée French.

The more disturbing and violent the fairy tale, some would argue, the more insight into the "primitive" feelings that arise and shape us in early childhood and, in turn, in adulthood. . . . Kinderculture, in this context, inadvertently reveals at a very basic level what is disturbing us in our every-day lives, what irritants reside at the level of our individual and collective subconscious.

—Shirley R. Steinberg and Joe L. Kincheloe,[1] "Kinderculture: The Corporate Construction of Childhood

Renée French's comic books transport readers back to a suburban child-hood whose coordinates lie somewhere between *Lord of the Flies* and *Leave It to Beaver.* It's not the childhood sentimentalized by the soft-focus lens of adult reminiscence, but childhood as seen from a kid's-eye view, a parallel reality of bullies, scapegoats, cruelty to animals, playing with dead things, budding sexuality, and the creepy little secrets adults bury deeply—but never deep enough, it seems, that kids don't dig them up.

In *Grit Bath,* French's girlhood adventures with the gang of New Jersey kids she spent her summers with in the late sixties and early seven-ties are the raw materials of dark, dreamlike narratives that read like David Lynch's idea of bedtime stories. In French's illustrations an impenetrable gloom laps at the edges of everything, marooning her moon-faced charac-ters in a sea of blackness. But the gross-out details—the mess of rubber bands and braces in a kid's mouth, the tumorous growths on Uncle Art's neck—are spotlit and meticulously rendered, giving *Grit Bath*'s world the hyperreal clarity of a bad dream. Dark with cross-hatching and stippling, her fever-

ishly detailed drawings recall the paintings of the American surrealist Ivan
Albright (an avowed influence) and the art of the insane. Stylistically (or,
for that matter, thematically), they have next to nothing in common with
the willfully crude draftsmanship and raw spleen, equal parts feminist wrath
and PMS, of fellow female cartoonists like Julie Doucet (*Dirty Plotte*),
Roberta Gregory (*Bitchy Bitch*), or Aline-Kominsky Crumb (*Twisted Sisters*).

French's stories are set in a twilight zone where the gross and the
grotesque—sexual perversions, family pathologies, schoolyard sadism,
bodily functions—are given free reign. For once, that shopworn adjective
"surreal" is justified. When the story "Silktown" opens, in *Grit Bath* #1, with
a vaguely androgynous young man (winkingly named Wynck) cuddling up
to his brother-in-law Walt and coaxing him to "come on down to the basement with me," most of us have assimilated enough pop Freud to know that
we're off on a dark ride through the id. Sure enough, the two brothers-in-
law engage in mutual masturbation after Wynck notices that Walt is turned
on by his newfound fetish object: a loop of animal intestine he found in the
backyard. "Animal innards really do it for you, huh?" Meanwhile, Walt's
son Gil is distraught over the grisly death of his rabid pet raccoon. Gil consoles himself by making love to a teenager named Eve, who begs him, in
the throes of passion, to bite her nipple; he obliges a little too zealously,
chomping it off and spitting the gory morsel into the bathroom sink. The
only solution, of course, is for Wynck to improvise a Frankensteinian trans-

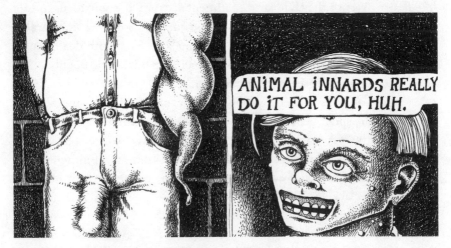

"Silktown," from *Grit Bath*. Copyright © Renée French.

plant, replacing Eve's severed nipple with his dog's hastily amputated penis. (He discreetly saves the nipple in a jar of preservative—for future use, no doubt, as a fetish object in another basement tryst.)

"Silktown," like many of French's stories, is a fractured fairy tale about the beginning of the end of innocence, the dawning of the realization that things aren't always as they seem. Average-Joe family men turn out to be deviates with a thing for dead meat; Gil's cute pet changes into a rabid, slavering beast; and Gil's mother snaps out of her cigarette-puffing ennui and into an erotomaniacal frenzy, practically fellating an éclair at the dinner table. Wiping the creme filling off her lips, she asks Eve, "Tell me, are you still lusting after my son?" French says in two dozen pages what one of her major influences, David Lynch, says more operatically in *Blue Velvet,* a movie about "things that are hidden" (Lynch's words). Lynch told a *Village Voice* interviewer, "That's the horror of the world—so many things are hiding behind things that it's a frightening, sick place."[2]

The lurking horror in both "Silktown" and *Blue Velvet* is the raging libido that turns clean-cut youngsters into teenage werewolves, transforming animal-loving Gil into a nipple-biting sadist and *Blue Velvet*'s all-American Jeffrey Beaumont into a peeping Tom and S&M boy toy. (True, we don't know if Gil, who's old enough to have a mustache, is losing his virginity, but his naïve obliviousness to the concupiscent Eve, whose name says it all, suggests that he's not exactly wise to the ways of the world.) Pauline Kael has called *Blue Velvet* "the only coming-of-age movie in which sex has the danger and the heightened excitement of a horror picture. . . . There's no sticky-sweet lost innocence, because the darkness was always there, inside."[3] There's an eerie echo, here, of the terrifying revelation in *Lord of the Flies:* "'Fancy thinking the Beast was something you could hunt and kill!'" says the savage god of the novel's title. "'You knew, didn't you? I'm part of you? Close, close, close!'"[4]

In French's world, as in *Lord of the Flies* and *Blue Velvet,* the Lucifer rising of adolescent sexuality and adult depravity casts a long shadow over childhood innocence. Always, the Beast is closer than we know, hiding in the basement of the psyche. In "Fistophobia" (*Grit Bath* #1), a gang of kids gathers around to witness the unforgettable spectacle of a little girl forced, for no particular reason, to "fist" an older girl, jamming her hand wrist-deep into the girl's vagina. She pulls it out, trailing goo, the kids applaud, and the gang reverts to the default mode of kids everywhere, battling the ever-present threat of boredom: "What do you guys wanna do now?" In "Tommy and Susan" (*Grit Bath* #2), a grade-school seductress begs a sweet-faced boy to tie her up with scarves she found in the attic. "Now you pretend you're Telly Savalas and you can do whatever you want to me," says the trussed-up girl, more to the reader than the boy. Forcing us to finish the story, French implicates us in her queasy blend of *Babysitters' Club* and bondage fantasy. On the shelf above the girl's head, stuffed animals stare blankly down, childhood totems already gathering dust.

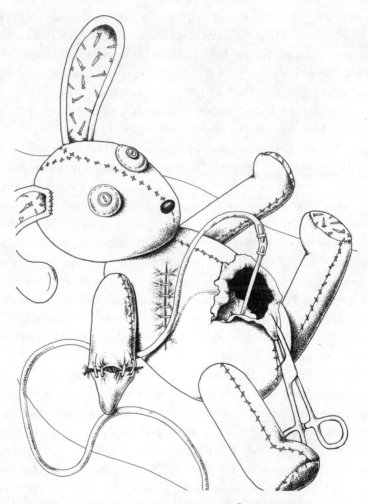

Bunny surgery, from *The Ninth Gland*. Copyright © Renée French.

The stuffed animals and cuddly pets in French's comics are close cousins to the shabby thrift-shop toys the artist Mike Kelley uses to shred our Hallmark visions of childhood. Kelley's *Double Figure (Hairy)*, a shaggy monster with a doll's head grafted between its spread thighs, tongue waggling lewdly, or *Estral Star 2,* twin monkeys joined at the groin, offer mute commentary on incest, child abuse, and the sexuality of children. They remind us that the Nutrasweet cuteness of *Barney,* Raffi, and Disney sugarcoats a world of complexities and contradictions. To Kelley, the gift-card myth of the perfect childhood embalms the messy reality of being a kid; it's the philosophical equivalent of those nineteenth-century daguerreotypes of dead children posed in cardboard wings on cotton clouds.

Kelley uses dolls because a doll is "a dead child, an impossible ideal produced by a corporate notion of the family," as he told Ralph Rugoff in the journal *XX Century*. "To parents," says Kelley, "the doll represents a perfect picture of the child—it's clean, it's cuddly, it's sexless, but as soon as the object is worn at all, it's dysfunctional. It begins to take on the characteristics of the child itself—it smells like the child and becomes torn and dirty like real things do. It then becomes a frightening object because it starts representing the human in a real way and that's when it's taken from the child and thrown away. In our culture, a stuffed animal is really the most obvious thing that portrays the . . . idealization [of childhood]."[5] Equal parts Garbage Pail Kids and inner children, Kelley's "frightening objects" are sociopathic cousins of the teddy bears clutched by sniffling participants in John Bradshaw's workshops.

French's semiotic shorthand for childhood innocence is the rabbit, specifically toy rabbits, which appear in several of her comics. Like Kelley's stuffed animals, they dramatize the tension between mass-produced images of childhood as a pixilated never-never-land and childhood in the real world, haunted by adult sexuality and by the sexual stirrings Freud claims begin in infancy. While bunnies like *Bambi*'s Thumper are enduring images of cuddlesome cuteness, rabbits, from the *Playboy* icon to the Easter bunny, are also symbols of lust and fecundity: In Roman Polanski's *Repulsion,* the decay of the dinner rabbit symbolizes the mental meltdown of the sexually repressed virgin, and in *Fatal Attraction* the pet rabbit, plopped in the family stewpot, is jilted Glenn Close's way of reminding the philandering Michael Douglas that he's still in the soup.

When French's key archetype ventures into the netherworld of adult desire, in "Bunny Man" (*Grit Bath* #1), it's reincarnated as a buck-toothed naïf in a bunny suit, confronted in a public urinal by a menacing masturbator. In "The Chocolate Bunnyhead" (*Grit Bath* #2), a young man who looks a lot like Wynck encounters an older man who looks a lot like Walt in the darkness of a movie theater. In a bizarre come-on, the young man offers his seatmate the severed head of a chocolate Easter bunny: "Want a bite?"

Beyond their sexual symbolism, French's rabbits embody the kitschy grotesquerie that gives David Lynch gooseflesh—the "frightening, sick" fraud of a mainstream reality whose basements and attics hide psychopathologies beyond all imagining. Lynch's shuddering realization that "so many things are hiding behind things" captures the horror of normalcy—not just that there are monsters outside the pages of *Goosebumps* books, but that they're often disguised by false fronts: the clerical collar of a grandfatherly priest can hide a child molester, the whiteface of an amateur clown can mask a serial killer. The spookiest bogeymen are the John Wayne Gacys, support-your-local-sheriff Rotarians who have their pictures taken, smiling, with the First Lady.

In French's private sign language, rabbits emblematize the bait-and-switch dualism of things. "Bunnies, to me, represent this innocent, cute childhood," she says, "but there's also a kind of horror to them—the emptiness in their eyes, the stupidity, the eating-your-own-feces thing." It may have something to do, she says, with her childhood experience of trying to rouse her pet rabbit when he "didn't seem to be as lively as he usually was." Rolling the unresponsive animal over, she discovered that his underside was crawling with maggots. "They were eating him alive. I think he died the next day." Even she couldn't dream up a better symbol of childhood's end, of the inevitable revelation that the shadowy underside of things, where the truth is often hidden, isn't always pretty to look at.

Adrift between toddlerhood and adolescence, the kids in *Grit Bath* are learning that the adults in bedtime stories—those unfailingly warm, wise, and wonderful authority figures—are a collective wish-fulfillment fantasy. In French's stories, mothers radiate the zombie perkiness of Stepford wives; fathers are blank-eyed nonentities. "I killed a mole, dad," confides the tearful little boy in "Mitch and the Mole" (*Grit Bath* #3). "Take some creamed onions," his mother interjects. "That's nice, son," says his father. "Did you hit it over the head with a rock?"

French realizes that to kids, adults are aliens, like the creature in Philip K. Dick's short story "The Father Thing," about a boy who discovers that his dad's body has been taken over by an evil entity. As a child, Dick was troubled by the conundrum that the same parent could be both loving caregiver and angry, arbitrary god. "I always had the impression, when I was very small, that my father was two people, one good, one bad," he wrote. "I guess many kids have this feeling."[6]

Ironically, the view is just as weird from the other side. In the LCD culture of mainstream America, children, as opposed to kids—the difference being one of doe-eyed ideal versus nose-picking reality—are venerated icons of cherubic innocence, a button-nosed, chipmunk-cheeked image enshrined in Joan Walsh Anglund books, Hummel figurines, and collectible dolls such as Cathrine [sic], one of the "Darling Little Ladies" advertised on the Home Shopping Network. Cathrine's catalogue blurb is syrup of ipecac for the soul: "'Bless mommy, daddy, sister . . .' Adorable Cathrine is kneeling and saying her bedtime prayers. She has her brown hair swept up in a pink bow with side tendrils. Her cute little face has brown eyes with real upper lashes and an open mouth. . . . She has her precious rag doll by her side."[7]

But as French's comics emphatically insist, children aren't just adorable little tearjerkers or lovable tykes who say the darnedest things. They're also grubby, intense creatures, a surprising number of whom like to play with—even consume—dirt, boogers, peeling skin, and dead things until taught otherwise. (I'm thinking of my two-year-old daughter squatting on her haunches to get a closer look—and preferably a poke—at squashed bugs or the cat's half-eaten birds, her expression one of rapt fascination, untouched by the repulsion most adults would feel.) The kids in French's stories turn their eyelids inside out, tear the legs off spiders, stuff raisins into corpses' nostrils, and perform unsuccessful operations on stuffed toys and live animals.

But for all their little abominations, they're innocent in the sense that every child is: They're born before the Fall, so to speak, blissfully ignorant of good or evil. Thus the myth of the moral superiority of children. The problem with the Rousseau-ian romanticization of children as noble savages is that there's too much nobility and not enough savagery in this vision of the precivilized mind. "However kids are actually treated in America, we want to think of them as belonging to another race of beings," writes the cultural commentator Tom Engelhardt. "We want to see them as different, more sensitive, somehow more human than ourselves."[8] If they *are* morally superior, it's in the Nietzschean sense of being beyond good and evil, rather than the New Testament sense of spiritual humility. Little kids possess a guiltless amorality, the conscienceless self-interest that makes mothers afraid to leave older brothers or sisters alone with their newborn siblings.

Not for nothing did Freud link children, in essays like "The Return of Totemism in Childhood," to animals and "primitives." Kids, to adult society, are a symbolic threat to the social order, embodying the insatiable primal drives for instant gratification, regardless of the consequences, that

"Fistophobia," from *Grit Bath*. Copyright © Renée French.

Freud argued were held in check by civilization. In their all-consuming self-interest, their *Lord of the Flies* wolf-pack mentality, and their "precivilized" embrace of a reality cobbled together from fact and fantasy (amply evidenced by the lurid imaginings that prompted the witch-hunt for pedophiles at the McMartin preschool in Los Angeles), kids draw our reluctant attention to what the education theorists Steinberg and Kincheloe call "the 'primitive' feelings that arise and shape us in early childhood and, in turn, in adulthood." Underscoring our uncomfortable commonality with what we once were and still may be inside, the kids in Renée French's comics hint darkly that the repressed is always threatening to return, and that our inner children may look more like Chucky, the pint-sized, knife-wielding sociopath in the *Child's Play* movies, than the wounded innocents of self-help myth.

11 / THE *UNHEIMLICH* MANEUVER: *THE DOLL HOUR*

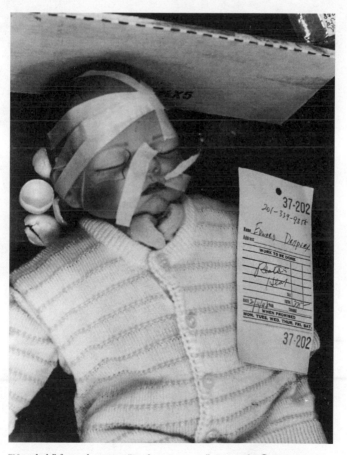

"Untitled," from the series "Broken Dreams." Copyright © Jane Greer.
Courtesy Jan Van Der Donk—Rare Books Inc., New York City.

There you are, clicking drearily around the dial, when it happens: TV performs the *unheimlich* maneuver on you. Without warning, the REM trance of channel surfing is shattered by the creepy, clammy sensation Freud called the *unheimlich,* the uncanny.

The Home Shopping Network's *Gallery of Dolls* is an infomercial for Freud's uncanny, transfixing the unsuspecting grazer with misbegotten moppets like little Ginny, her bovine eyes flesh-crawlingly lifelike, her tongue thrust obscenely between glistening lips. The host, a blonde with a Steinway smile named Alice Cleveland, keeps up a ceaseless stream of patter as she preens the $229 doll, who is "full-body porcelain," "highly collectible," and "absolutely adorable," to boot. To unbelievers, little Ginny looks like a garroted cherub, her goggle-eyed last gasp fixed for all time by the embalmer's art. She crosses the Hummel figurine with the prenatal nightmare floating in formaldehyde.

In his famous essay, "The Uncanny," Freud singles out the doll for special consideration. Whereas children live in an animistic universe where the boundary between living things and lifeless toys is fuzzily drawn, the adult mind is unsettled by such ambiguities. Children treat their dolls as if they were alive, says Freud, while adults are often unnerved by waxworks, mannequins, and other inanimate objects that seem to follow us with their eyes or stir behind our backs. Hence the perennial theme of the evil effigy, from *Twilight Zone* episodes such as "Living Doll," in which Talky Tina makes good on her threat to kill a little girl's hateful stepfather, to the *Child's Play* movies, about a homicidal doll named Chucky possessed by the spirit of a murderer.

With its weird combination of kaffeeklatsch coziness and Polanski-esque repulsiveness, the Home Shopping Network's *Gallery of Dolls* never

fails to unnerve. While many of the dolls on sale are standard-issue faux
Victorians, each show features at least one truly grotesque offering: FayZah
Spanos's Bonnie Boo Boo, a doe-eyed heartbreaker with more streaming
plastic tears than a Madonna dolorosa; Juan Perez's Robby, a pug-nosed
tyke whose protruding tongue gives him the impish charm of a child being
throttled.

    Gallery of Dolls captures the essence of what is worst about our mass
culture in miniature: It's a dollhouse version of the queasy mix of senti-
mentality and sideshow grotesquerie that transformed the Hunchback of
Notre Dame into a cartoon face on a McDonald's Happy Meal. At the same
time, *Gallery of Dolls* neatly encapsulates what Umberto Eco called the
"America of furious hyperreality."[1] We are a nation obsessed with simulation and suspended animation, from the bronzed baby shoe to the open-
casketed loved one "revamped . . . to look like a living doll," as Jessica
Mitford put it in *The American Way of Death.*[2] Infancy, as every Hallmark card-
giver knows, is a time of heart-warming innocence, so it must be memori-
alized in the "remarkably realistic and anatomically correct" vinyl features
of HSN's Newborn Preemies. Likewise, Ms. Cleveland must impersonate
her high-school yearbook self through the judicious application of makeup
and hairspray, and the show's hard-sell spiel must be softened by the domestic glow of a set whose window looks out on artificial flowers and an
ersatz sky.

    The cumulative effect of all this sugary fakery is the nagging suspi-
cion that it protests too much; HSN's *Gallery of Dolls* hints at the gallery of
grotesques behind the relentless cuteness of mainstream America—the hair-
chewing monster lurking in every Cabbage Patch Snack Time Kid, so to
speak. It's impossible to look at the show's precocious coquettes without
mentally replaying news footage of the murdered six-year-old beauty queen
JonBenet Ramsey in her showgirl get-up, or pondering the Jekyll/Hyde
hypocrisy of a society that cries out for the castration of child molesters even
as it subsists on a steady diet of pop pedophilia: kiddie beauty pageants,
Calvin Klein ads, Jock Sturges photos, and virtually any movie featuring
Juliette Lewis.

    HSN's wide-eyed innocents also suggest a collective denial of the
death of childhood in a world where poverty, broken homes, and easy access to guns have triggered an upward spiral in violent crime by juveniles.
According to *The New York Times,* the arrest rate for 14-to-17-year-old kill-

ers has tripled in the past decade, and prepubescent sociopaths like the boys who hurled a five-year-old off a building because he refused to steal candy for them are routinely featured on the nightly news.

To Freud, the doll is a double, a magical attempt to ensure ourselves against death, sprung from the "narcissism which holds sway in the mind of the child as in that of the primitive man." But stumbling on cobwebbed childhood fantasies in the harsh light of adult reality can be a creepy experience, suggests Freud. "From having been an assurance of immortality," he writes, the doll becomes a "ghastly harbinger of death."[3] Welcome to the Dollhouse.

12 / EMPATHY BELLIES: CLONED SHEEP AND PREGNANT MEN

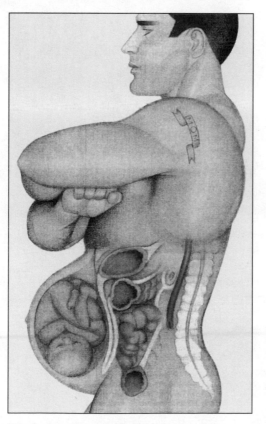

Womb envy. Copyright © Mel Odom.

Dolly, the cloned lamb, has given birth.

Her daughter Bonnie arrived on April 13, 1998, in a normal delivery, according to the Roslin Institute, where Dolly was cloned. It's proof, says the institute's director, Graham Bulfield, that "despite Dolly's unusual origins, she is able to breed normally."[1]

Of course, Dolly is already a mother many times over, in the metaphorical sense. She has given birth to a flock of Frankenstein references in media coverage of cloning, from researchers' fear, reported in *The New York Times,* that they'll "be looked upon as if they were Frankensteins" to the *New York Times* Op-Ed writer David Bromwich's prescription that "all scientists and their lawyers" should read *Frankenstein* once a year as an antidote to scientific hubris.[2]

To be sure, there was a whiff of gothic melodrama to Dolly's conception: A zap of electricity was used to fuse the DNA from one ewe's cell with another ewe's egg. A mad scientist straight from central casting brought the story's Frankensteinian subtext to the fore when he announced that he intended to clone babies for infertile couples. Seemingly overnight, an unemployed physicist allegorically named Dr. Richard (Dick?) Seed put a public face on scientific amorality and arrogance.

With Seed's unwitting help, cloning has become a lightning rod for popular anxieties about the reproductive technologies that, more and more, are enabling us to live outside the laws of nature: the in vitro fertilization that permits postmenopausal women to give birth, the custom-made embryos that allow infertile couples to choose their children's genetic qualities.

But in the rush to judge fertility researchers as clones of Dr. Frankenstein, other stories about the deeper meanings of Dolly's virgin birth have gone untold. Ironically, one of the many morals of this tabloid fable is hidden in plain sight, in Mary Shelley's novel. Whatever else it is, the story of Dolly is a story of womb envy in the age of reprogenetics (reproductive biology + genetics). Likewise, *Frankenstein,* which generations of English professors have taught as a morality play about scientific ambitions pursued in flagrant disregard of God's law or the public good, is equally about male dreams of usurping female procreative power.

Mary Shelley was the daughter of Mary Wollstonecraft, a founding feminist whose demand for women's rights, in *Vindication of the Rights of Woman,* was based on the social value of women's roles as mothers ("the grand duties annexed to the female character by nature").[3] At the same time, Mary Shelley traveled in intellectual circles where debates raged about experiments with "spontaneous generation," and whether or not "a creature might be manufactured . . . and endued with vital warmth" by galvanism, the electrical sorcery that made dead frogs jump.[4]

Feminist scholars have argued that *Frankenstein* is plagued by the author's anxiety over male scientists' dreams of creating life, and thereby ending the female monopoly on childbirth. "At every level, Victor Frankenstein is engaged upon a rape of nature, a violent penetration and usurpation of the female's 'hiding places,' of the womb," writes Anne K. Mellor, somewhat gothically, in *Mary Shelley: Her Life, Her Fiction, Her Monsters.* "Terrified of female sexuality and the power of human reproduction it enables, both he and the patriarchal society he represents use the technologies of science . . . to manipulate, control and repress women."[5]

Dr. Frankenstein's monster is the fruit of his high-tech womb (the creature refers to himself as an "abortion"), and the story's apocalyptic denouement is set in motion by the doctor's fear that his offspring will reproduce. When Frankenstein refuses to make a mate for the monster, fearful that a she-creature would be the mother of "a race of devils," the enraged brute vows that he'll be with the doctor on his wedding night, a date traditionally consecrated to creating life by more conventional means.[6]

The 1995 movie version of the novel, starring Robert De Niro, plays up the theme of male motherhood. The film begins with the blood-drenched death in childbirth of Victor Frankenstein's mother, a primal scene that rivals the prom night in *Carrie* for sheer gore. When the young doctor

attempts to build a better womb, he immerses his man-made baby in amniotic fluid—"the chief biogenic element," we're told, despite all the galvanic hocus-pocus. The movie ends with the monster agonizing over the
death of the man he calls his "father" (but who is, paradoxically, his mother
as well).

Of course, the fantasy of male motherhood and the womb envy
that inspired it didn't begin with Mary Shelley. In the Bible, a cosmic
paterfamilias, rather than the earth-mother of most pagan myths, gives
birth to the world, and Adam is the mother of Eve: in history's first C-
section, God removes one of Adam's ribs and fashions her from it. The
literary critic Northrop Frye interprets this "intolerably patriarchal" creation myth (his words) as a rationalization of the ethos that propped up
male-dominated Hebrew society. "We know only of a world in which
every human and animal form is born from a female body," he writes,
"but the Bible insists . . . [on] the first woman having been made out of
the body of the first man."[7]

Not that the authors of the Old Testament had any monopoly on
womb envy: In Greek myth, Athena is literally Zeus's brainchild, thought
into being by the father-god and delivered by means of a blow to his forehead from Hephaestus's ax. Here in full flower is the male desire to arrogate
the female dominion over birth, coupled, ironically, with the sour-grapes
tactic of devaluing childbirth in favor of intellectual labor: Athena, the
goddess of wisdom and the personification of mind, is a product of intellect, not intercourse. John Pinsent, a scholar of Greek mythology, reads
the story of Athena's birth as a reflection of "the resentment felt in a patriarchal society for woman's one indispensable function, actually bearing the
legitimate children of the father."[8]

To add insult to injury, the Greeks also concocted the theory of
preformation, the notion that each sperm contains the essence of a child,
reducing the womb to a glorified incubator. This belief survived well into
the seventeenth century, when the spermatozoa frolicking under van
Leeuwenhoek's microscope confirmed, beyond a doubt, that each male seed
is indeed a tiny, tadpolelike "animalcule" with a homunculus, or human embryo, curled up inside it. According to the medical historian F. Gonzalez-
Crussi, a savant of the day concluded as a result that "the ejaculation of semen
is 'male parturition,' since a preformed conceptus is thereby expelled. Bishop
Garden, learned man that he probably was, insisted that biologic theory illu-

minated with splendiferous meaning the Messianic prophecy 'that only Jesus is the true seed of Woman, and the rest of mankind is the seed of man.'"[9]

Fast-forward to our brave new world of asexual reproduction, where some feminists believe they've uncovered the buried dream of "male parturition" in the ever-increasing intervention of (mostly) male scientists, doctors, and medical technicians into the reproductive process, from the moment of conception to the act of giving birth.

In *Lying-In: A History of Childbirth in America,* Richard and Dorothy Wertz argue that the technologizing of childbirth, which has undeniably lowered maternal and infant mortality rates, also wrests control of the generative process away from women. They offer as an example the presumably male ultrasound technician who must interpret the blurry image that typically represents a woman's first contact with her unborn child, long before she can feel its stirrings. The social historian Hillel Schwartz would argue that this high-tech intercession is part of a long history of male attempts to mediate between women and their wombs. As Schwartz reminds us, it was a man, Saint Jerome, who begat the doctrine of the virgin birth; it was medieval churchmen who conceived of the male seed as the generative force in a passive womb; it was by and large male doctors who directed the hundreds of thousands of hysterectomies performed from the forties on; and it was mostly men who oversaw the 4,000 in vitro fertilization births that had taken place by 1989.[10]

To some feminists, cloning is the latest in a series of increasingly science-fictional attempts to usurp women's procreative power. In actual fact, however, cloning reaffirms the indispensable nature of the female, rendering the sperm superfluous and realizing the lesbian-separatist dream of being the only sex: genetic material is transplanted from one parent's cell into another parent's egg, which is then implanted in the mother's womb. A lesbian who became a mother through artificial insemination writes the gay magazine *The Advocate* to express her hope that cloning "may provide an opportunity, to lesbians at least, to create the families we have always desired, free from the encumbrances of individuals [i.e., men] who, no matter how fantastic, are now required to bring about life."[11]

Even so, some feminists are troubled by male meddling in the generative process at such a profound level, and by sci-fi prophecies of artificial wombs that would render the uterus (though not the egg) obsolete: "extra-uterine fetal incubators" have already been pioneered in a Tokyo laboratory, where goat fetuses have survived for as long as three weeks in vessels filled with artificial amniotic fluid heated to body temperature.[12] The scenario in a decidedly unauthorized story written by a *Star Trek* fan, in which Captain Kirk and Mr. Spock have a baby whose ovum is genetically engineered by Dr. McCoy and brought to term in an artificial womb designed by Scotty, doesn't seem quite so far-fetched.[13]

Seventeenth-century theories of "male parturition" may come true in ways their authors could never have imagined. In a 1994 article, the science writer Dick Teresi coolly asserted, "We have all the technology we need right now to make a man pregnant."[14] A womb doth not a mother make, he argues; engineers of the first male pregnancy might exploit the phenomenon of ectogenesis, or pregnancies that occur outside the womb, as in the case of the woman who gave birth to a healthy baby eight months after she had a hysterectomy (a stray fertilized egg had attached itself to her bowel and grown to term). In an undocumented account that some scientists question, researchers claim to have implanted a fertilized egg from a female baboon into the omentum (a fatty, blood-rich tissue that hangs over the intestines) of a male baboon, who allegedly carried the pregnancy for nearly five months before the researchers aborted it (for reasons unrelated to the success of the experiment).

On the basis of these developments, Teresi speculates that a human male pregnancy would begin with the in vitro fertilization of an egg and the insertion of the embryo into a male mom's abdominal cavity. With any luck, the embryo would implant in the omentum, a placenta would develop, and the rest would be business as usual—until birth, that is, when the baby would be delivered via laparotomy, which is somewhat like a caesarean section.

According to the Johns Hopkins professor John Money, who performed the first documented male-to-female sex change in the United States, "If male pregnancy ever became possible, the first applicants would be male-to-female transsexuals, because it's so terribly important to them to experience everything a woman can experience."[15]

Money's prediction is Janice Raymond's worst nightmare. In *The Transsexual Empire: The Making of the She-Male,* a shrill polemic understandably unpopular with male-to-female transsexuals, Raymond decries male-to-female gender reassignment, like cloning and test-tube fertilization, as a patriarchal "attempt to wrest from women the power inherent in female biology."[16] She writes, "Given the historical difficulties in molding both female flesh and energy to patriarchal standards, an alternative is to make the biological woman obsolete by the creation of man-made 'she-males.'"[17] For Raymond, the only thing worse than a "she-male," which she sees as the ultimate expression of womb envy—a "'he-mother' who rejects his mothered birth and gives birth to 'herself' (with the aid, of course, of the medical 'father-mothers')"—would be a "she-male" with the maternal urge.[18]

Ironically, Raymond's insistence on "the power that women have, by virtue of female biology" furthers the male chauvinist goal of defining women in terms of their reproductive functions.[19] Moreover, her argument ignores the established faction within feminism that rejects motherhood as a patriarchal plot to keep women barefoot, pregnant, and politically powerless. The surrealist painter Leonor Fini sneered at the "nearly inconceivable" humility, the "brutalized passivity" necessary, in her opinion, to have children. "I know that I belong with the idea of Lilith, the anti-Eve," she declared. "Physical maternity instinctively repulses me."[20]

Raymond's argument turns a blind eye on feminism's radical fringes, where a seething contempt for the maternal function has inspired women to espouse the very reproductive technologies she denounces. In her notorious *S.C.U.M. Manifesto* (1967), Valerie Solanas imagines a separatist utopia in which babies—only female, naturally—are produced in laboratories. Likewise, in *The Dialectic of Sex: The Case for Feminist Revolution,* Shulamith Firestone sings the praises of the artificial womb as a hypothetical means of "freeing women from the tyranny of their reproductive biology."[21]

Obviously, for now, at least, the Frankensteinian specter of male motherhood that lurches through feminist nightmares is science fiction. Although the technologization of childbirth is a fact of modern life, the use of human cloning, artificial wombs, or male pregnancy to commandeer women's control over the birth process, besides being ethically sticky, is legally unlikely. Furthermore, artificial wombs and male pregnancy are prey to technical bugs that may never be worked out.

Still, one can't help but wonder whether feminism wouldn't be better served by the sly tactic of *relinquishing* that control. Nine months of male morning sickness, mood swings, and mind-boggling mutations might just be the handicap women need to attain something like equality. Flo Kennedy, the feminist who popularized the one-liner "If men could get pregnant, abortion would be a sacrament," thinks so. When the authors of an *Omni* article on male pregnancy solicited her thoughts on the theoretical technology, she observed, "It's a possible step toward women gaining on men, at least in terms of cocktail-party jokes."[22]

We live at a moment when the popular imagination is fired by the womb-envy fantasies of Victor Frankenstein's heirs, from the researchers who cloned Dolly to artificial intelligence theorists like Daniel Hillis, who rhapsodizes about the silicon sentience he believes will one day "live free of bones and flesh, giving this child of mind an earthly immortality denied to us."[23]

It's also a time when the hairline cracks in traditional masculine roles are widening. *Penthouse* can't get it up, financially speaking, the way it could in its swinging youth, and *Playboy*'s last, best hope for cultural resurgence, a *New York Times* article implies, is a "small revival" fostered by the retro fad for lounge music, the martini, and other artifacts of what the recent book *Hi-Fi's & Hi Balls* calls "the Golden Age of the American Bachelor." Gag books like *Cad,* a "handbook for heels" that waxes nostalgic about "the forgotten lore of the red-blooded American male," make light of the nagging sense that none of the old definitions of manhood work anymore. A good part of the Rat Pack craze ratcheted up by Frank Sinatra's death has to do with nineties male nostalgia for a time before feminism and sexual-harassment suits, when men were men and broads were broads. Sinatra's "misogyny and promiscuity have been recast as healthy libido, his Mafia ties and thuggery as macho," writes the essayist David Plotz. The revisionist Sinatra is a nineties "tonic for political correctness," a "man's man" for nebbishy, Dockers-ad *guys* who've forgotten how to be *men*.[24]

Intuitively, many of us sensed that our national fixation with the castration of John Wayne Bobbitt was more than a tabloid morality play about a philandering man and the woman he'd wronged. Behind the nervous guffaws lurked the awareness that Bobbitt's bobbing was a goofy, ghastly symbol of American manhood (epitomized, after all, by John Wayne) cut down to size. The dizzily overeager reception American men have given the male potency drug Viagra amounts to a public confession of the fact that in the bedroom, where phallic power stands naked (or lies limply, as the case may be), Achilles' heel is the least of his worries. Viagra mania tacitly acknowledges the cruel, comic truth that even the King was haunted by the knowledge that his deepest sense of himself as a man was absurdly dependent on the unreliable hydraulics of the alter-ego he called Little Elvis.

The October 1996 issue of *Esquire* ("The Magazine for Men") announced that "after 30 years of Feminism," the "Alpha Male" was back— a coverline accompanied by a photo of a hot babe in a red dress straddling a panting Rottweiler in a spiked collar (her head is cut off by the top of the magazine, a design decision that speaks volumes about the ideal *Esquire* woman). But once we get past the cover story's hormonal bluster and the inevitable odes to phallic props (cigar, anyone?), the back-page ads for baldness cures, prostrate relief and foolproof ways to satisfy your partner in the sack reveal the alpha male's studly bulge for the rolled-up sock that it really is.

On a more serious note, the so-called crisis of masculinity is rooted in the rise of the two-income family and the growing presence of women in the workforce, a megatrend that has toppled the man of the house from his traditional position as sole breadwinner. Once, we lived in a world of iron-clad gender roles "built out of piled-on oppositions" such as "production versus reproduction, salaried versus unsalaried," writes the cultural anthropologist Richard A. Shweder. "But now those distinctions have been blurred. Women are in the workplace, where they are more productive, less reproductive and toiling harder than ever before. Men are being downsized and losing their jobs, and their part in reproduction was fleeting in the first place."[25]

Twenty-something males are rejecting the bite-the-bullet toughness of traditional masculinity for the androgyny of the electronic dance-music scene or the conflicted, diffident persona of alternative rockers like Pearl Jam's Eddie Vedder, who "express the doubts of young middle-class men about the power they inherit," according to the rock critic Ann Powers.[26]

Boomers, meanwhile, are adopting circle-the-wagons strategies like the Promise Keepers, the right-leaning Christian fundamentalist men's movement that encourages its members to "reclaim their manhood" by reasserting themselves as heads of their households, in accordance with the New Testament teaching that wives must "submit" to their husbands. Alternatively, middle-aged men are embracing go-with-the-flow adaptations like the nurturing "soft man" persona reviled by the men's movement guru Robert Bly.

The soft man is presumably the target demographic of the unintentionally hilarious "Empathy Belly" I saw advertised in a mail-order catalogue. A weighted canvas vest designed to simulate a pregnant stomach and swollen breasts, it's just the thing for the sensitive nineties male who wants to show his "appreciation, communication, and supportive behavior."[27] Dedicated empaths can even insert weights calculated to induce the urgent need to pee caused by bladder compression.

Any man who would wear this device is unquestionably in the terminal stage of *couvade,* or sympathetic pregnancy, and a likely candidate for history's first male pregnancy. They want it, girls; why not let them have it? It would be the perfect revenge on that cosmic chauvinist who decreed, in the book of Genesis, "I will greatly increase your pangs in childbirth; in pain you shall bring forth children." And it might have the added benefit of making American men a little more sympathetic to those tedious feminist arguments for paid maternity leave, mandated in more than 120 countries, but not the United States.[28] Or health insurance that permits longer hospital stays for recovering mothers. Or an equal division of labor when it comes to child care: According to a recent study, mothers spend four times as much time with their children as fathers do.[29]

But a less laughable future waits in the wings. A successful male pregnancy or the birth of a human cloned from a frozen egg and brought to term in an artificial womb might fan Gloria Steinem's "small, nagging fear that if we women lose our cartel on giving birth, we could be even more dispensable than we already are."[30] In *Junior,* the stillborn 1994 comedy about history's first male pregnancy, a female doctor discovers that one of her male colleagues has stolen one of her frozen eggs, fertilized it, and implanted it in himself in a demo-or-die attempt to prove that his fertility drug works. She becomes hysterical (from *hystera,* Greek for "womb"). "This is just so *male!*" she sputters. "Do you think men don't hold enough cards? You have to take this away from us as well?"

Amid the fears and fantasies stirred up by cloning, the male dream of creating life seems almost within reach. In the eeriest scenario, men born of men in a man's world of the future might look back on Frankenstein's monster and Dolly's virgin birth as the opening verses of a postmodern creation myth, the first pages in the book of Ectogenesis.

SECTION V
RIDING SHOTGUN WITH THE DOOM PATROL

13 / WILD NATURE, WIRED NATURE: THE UNABOMBER MEETS THE DIGERATI

The mailbomber's mailbox. Reuters/Parker/Archive Photos.

In his transformation from hooded cipher to Op-Ed essayist and explosive social critic, the Unabomber has undergone a mediamorphosis—a profusion of readings and rereadings that have turned him into a pop-culture palimpsest.

But the most obvious reading is conspicuous in its absence: the Unabomber as the Log Lady's dysfunctional cousin. For those not versed in TV trivia, the Log Lady was an eccentric minor character on the cult show *Twin Peaks*. In much the same way that *Twin Peaks*'s resident crackpot legitimated her cryptic revelations by invoking the higher power of her ever-present log, an oracular prop whose telepathic transmissions only she could hear, the Unabomber underpins his social critique with the incontrovertible authority of a mute, inscrutable Nature.

Like the Log Lady, the Unabomber (a.k.a. Ted Kaczynski) is filed, in the popular imagination, under "Wood." His infernal machines employed tiny homemade wooden levers rather than traceable electronic components; one even incorporated a twig from a cherry tree. They came packaged in lovingly (if somewhat inexpertly) handcrafted wooden boxes whose fake return addresses allegedly involved puns on wood, and one of his early victims, the president of United Airlines, received a bomb hidden in a book published by Arbor House, whose symbol is a leaf; the executive's name, too coincidentally, was Percy Wood.

Both Kaczynski and the Log Lady lived near small towns in the rural Northwest, the Unabomber in Lincoln, Montana, close by the largest expanse of uninterrupted wilderness in the continental United States, the continental divide. The symbolic conflict in *Twin Peaks,* which can be read as an environmentally unfriendly commentary on the confrontation between the logging industry and environmentalists, is literalized in Lincoln, which is the site of a power struggle between an open-pit gold-mining operation and local activists. Kaczynski knew and admired the head of Lincoln's activist group, and surely noticed the moribund state of the local economy, a casualty of the megatrend toward a postindustrial economy of knowledge workers and minimum-wage drones. "There aren't many good blue-collar jobs here anymore," notes the writer William Kittredge, writing in *Newsweek.* "There are just tourist jobs (which can also be thought of as the servant trade)."[2] Lincoln, like many of the state's former logging and mining towns, is broke.

Predictably, newsmagazine coverage of the Unabomber has neglected a socioeconomic analysis that would make sense of his individual pathologies in a larger cultural context. Instead, it has employed a psychobiographical approach more agreeable to our age of inner children and recovered memories. *Time* and *Newsweek* crossed Freud Lite with Old Testament allegory in pop psych parables that compared Kaczynski and his brother David, who turned him in to the FBI, to Cain and Abel.

The *Newsweek* article, "Blood Brothers," played up the story's Oedipal aspects, noting that Kaczynski excoriated his mother, Wanda, in "anti-Mom diatribes"—letters blaming her for his utter failure at forming romantic relationships with women.[3] Ever ready to seize the moral low ground, the *National Enquirer* reshot the Oedipal drama from a lurid angle halfway between Hitchcock and *Hard Copy,* casting Wanda Kaczynski (an atheist!) as the smotheringly protective Mrs. Bates who turned Ted into an unmanly little Norman by dandling him on her lap and reading *Scientific American* to him. "While other boys were playing rough-and-tumble games such as baseball," noted the *Enquirer,* with a delicious shudder, "Ted and his mother visited science museums, planetariums, and nature centers—and the little mama's boy loved every minute of it."[4] (For the record, Kaczynski's mother did, in fact, take her infant son to art museums in a behaviorist attempt to stimulate his intellect. As well, she reportedly demanded academic excellence of her boys. If only he'd played more "rough-and-tumble games," and stayed away from those *nature* centers . . .)

Oddly, the Unabomber echoes the *Enquirer*'s cold showers-and-saltpeter bluster about the sissifying effects of high culture and book learning. In his 35,000-word manifesto, "Industrial Society and Its Future," he writes, "It isn't natural for an adolescent human being to spend the bulk of his time sitting at a desk absorbed in study. . . . Among the American Indians, for example, boys were trained in active outdoor pursuits—just the sort of thing that boys like. But in our society children are pushed into studying technical subjects, which most do grudgingly."[5]

The moral of the *Enquirer*'s version of the Unabomber fable, memorably titled "From Mama's Boy to Murdering Madman," is straight out of Diane Eyer's *Motherguilt: How Our Culture Blames Mothers for What's Wrong with Society*. The Unabomber, we are given to understand, is a Skinnerian experiment gone horribly wrong, an object lesson in the dangers of too much "heir conditioning," to use Skinner's unforgettable phrase. With her hypodermic injections of cultural literacy and her "meticulous journal of [Ted's] development," Wanda Kaczynski created a nutty professor who would turn against the scientific America that made him.[6]

The Log Lady's dysfunctional cousin; Cain to brother David's Abel; Norman Batesian Mama's Boy turned Murdering Madman: These and other readings yield a composite portrait of the Unabomber as semiotic shape shifter. In fact, the shape-shifter trope is an illuminating one, spotlighting an unconsidered aspect of the eco-terrorist: the buried lines of connection between the Unabomber and the geek elite who style themselves the "digerati"—between wild nature (Kaczynski's utopian alternative to technological modernity) and *wired* nature.

The five head shots of Kaczynski in the *Time* cover story "Odyssey of a Mad Genius," spanning the fifties through the nineties, invite us to read that odyssey as the transformation scene from *An American Werewolf in London,* protracted over a lifetime. Kaczynski morphs from the high school and Harvard math nerd of the fifties and early sixties, neatly attired in regulation suit and tie, into the shaggy-haired, sallow-faced hermit of his 1996 mug shot. The story told, as in all werewolf tales, is of wild nature revenged upon culture—the nightmare, equal parts Darwin and Freud, of the return of what a *Cheers* episode hilariously called the "inner hairy man": the bestial self brought to heel by evolution and civilization. Here, however, the folktale's other elements are overshadowed by the image of a vengeful nature overmastering culture in the person of a skinny-tied math professor transformed into a furry, foul-smelling wild man, red in tooth and claw.

   If the Unabomber-wolfman analogy seems strained, consider the print media's tendency to collapse misanthrope and lycanthrope in their characterizations of Kaczynski. *Time, Newsweek,* and *U.S. News & World Report* had a field day (full moon?) with creep-show descriptions of the feral recluse: All three employed the phrase "lone wolf" in their sketches of the unwashed, unshaven mountain man, with *Time* reporting that FBI agents had gazed at long last on the "shaggy face" of the serial killer they had "tracked like a grizzly" for the past 18 years.[7]

   But, as in *American Werewolf,* where the transformation of human into animal is made possible, ironically, by technology (latex skin, inflatable bladders, and so forth), Wild Nature conceals wired nature: The Unabomber may be a wolfman, but he's a prosthetic one, a self-declared "techno-nerd" beneath his hairy neo-Luddite hide.

   Consider the Net's seemingly incongruous elevation of the poster boy for neo-Luddite resistance to the status of a Mansonesque anti-icon, a living symbol of chaos culture. Kaczynski's manifesto seems to be everywhere on the Net, and he is extolled in Usenet newsgroups like alt.fan.unabomber or the "Unabomber for President" Web site hosted by the Unabomber Political Action Committee, UNAPACK.

   Superficially, the Net's embrace of the neo-Luddite mad bomber has much to do with the black humor of the terminally ironic, but just beneath its brittle surface lies a gnawing anxiety over the superhuman speed of technological change and the deadening, disorienting white noise of the info-deluge. "The Unabomber is the only candidate really addressing the issues, which are the destruction of wild nature and the increasing poverty and destruction of our daily lives because of the onslaught of technology," says UNAPACK spokesman Chris Korda. "This is no joke."[8]

   The Unabomber gives vent to a simmering resentment toward the digerati who blithely advise the rest of us to sit back and enjoy the ride as they joystick our wired society into the coming millennium. Psycho-killer though he is, the Unabomber speaks at times for more reasonable minds, from lefties to liberals to the DOS-for-Dummies crowd that resented AT&T's imperious "You Will" ads, whose peremptory tone foreclosed any alternatives to a corporate-brand future ("Have you ever tucked your baby in from a phone booth? You will"). The Unabomber is the wild-eyed, lunatic-fringe tip of a demographic iceberg; while hardly neo-Luddite, the nondigerati who make up that iceberg resent the messianic self-righteousness and übernerd arrogance of cyberboosters like John Perry Barlow, MIT Media Lab director and *Being Digital* author Nicholas Negroponte, and, quintessentially, *Wired* magazine in its heady early days, when the founder Louis Rossetto's televangelistic exhortations resounded through its pages.

Debuting in 1993, *Wired* soon established itself as a bully pulpit for corporate futurists, laissez-faire evangelists, and prophets of privatization. In 1.5, the futurist Alvin Toffler bemoaned the fact that the shortsighted United States was air-dropping food rather than fax machines and camcorders in the former Yugoslavia, and that Washington was concerned with ho-hum Second Wave issues such as the decaying urban infrastructure when it should have been paving the information superhighway. In 1.4, George Gilder, an apostle of info-capitalism, rewove the threadbare myth that in the near future, when each of us commands the googlebytes of a supercomputer, economic and political power will be magically redistributed. (This cherished article of cybercratic faith buttressed Newt Gingrich's speculation that the government should provide "the poorest Americans" with laptops—after it has unburdened them of frivolous entitlements such as Aid to Families with Dependent Children, presumably.) And in issue 1.3, Peter Drucker, the Moses of management theory, reprised the corporate-friendly refrain that since our postindustrial culture runs on information, the blue-collar worker is obsolete—joyful noise to managerial ears in an age of outsourcing and downsizing, but bitter music to former laborers, now consigned to the subsistence-wage purgatory of the service industry. No matter, consoles the Drucker disciple and corporate futurologist Peter Schwartz: "Massive unemployment . . . became the fertile ground in which Silicon Valley bloomed."[9]

In the silicon social Darwinism ostensibly popular with the 33-year-old, 81k-earning male who is *Wired*'s typical reader, the evolutionary race goes to the wunderkind "small player" enshrined in computer industry myth (Bill Gates, the two Steves who founded Macintosh), while the unskilled and the deskilled masses are stampeded in the mad rush to the millennium. "Tofflerism-Gingrichism," Hendrik Hertzberg asserts in a *New Yorker* essay, is not unlike Marxism-Leninism in its "worship of technology," its "know-it-all certainty," its "scientism," its " 'revolutionary' rapture."[10] There is, he notes, a "similar exhilaration that comes from being among the select few to whom the mysteries and the meaning of history are vouchsafed . . . a similar patronizing contempt for those who don't 'get it' and are therefore fated to be swept into the dustbin of history."[11]

Wired's vision of a radically deregulated, privatized future is dangerously myopic, blind to environmental concerns, race relations, gender politics, and labor issues. It's a future so bright you've gotta wear shades, as the hit song put it; the digerati don't want to know about the downside of postindustrialization and global capitalism: the social dislocation and economic anxieties of the middle class, the hemorrhaging of domestic manufacturing jobs, the exploitation of nonunion, sometimes underage Third World labor.

As the critic Margie Wylie put it in her blisteringly funny essay "*Wired* Doesn't Speak for Me,"

> Everyone in *Wired*'s warped view of the world has either already become an instant millionaire through the infinite grace of the benevolent Free Market, or they yearn to be the ones standing on the backs of people just like themselves to get there. . . . It's a scramble to the increasingly small top of the heap: The last one up is a rotten egg—or worse, if you're on the bottom, an immigrant farm hand. For every million people on e-mail, another million have been killed by the 'obsolete' notions of war, poverty, and hunger. Of course, war, poverty, and hunger seem obsolete when your most pressing concern is the length of the line at Starbucks.[12]

The Unabomber's refusal to fall into lockstep with the digital revolution has struck a sympathetic chord with all who are weary of the ceaseless drumbeat of cyberhype. "I can't shake the 'Ultimate Truth' of those normal working stiffs in my straw poll," wrote *Wired* correspondent Brock Meeks in his electronic newsletter, *CyberWire Dispatch*. Sickened by people's seeming unconcern over the lives shattered by Unabombs, Meeks nonetheless concedes that there is something in the Unabomber's message that has "touched a nerve. And it may be a nerve that, beneath the warp and woof of all the current self-congratulatory cyber-masturbation, is very sensitive to the hundred-plus million people that *aren't* online."[13]

But at the same time that some among the off-line millions have come to see the Unabomber as the pathological embodiment of anxieties provoked by an ever more wired, increasingly denatured world, there are those in cyberculture who recognize him as one of their own—Yahoo Serious with an animus. (Clerks at a Sacramento bookstore where he used to browse the science books nicknamed the wild-haired Kaczynski Einstein.) He is a hardware hacker who began, in the best hacker tradition, as a teenage basement tinkerer and homemade-bomb freak. After reading "Industrial Society," *Wired*'s executive editor, Kevin Kelly, was lavish in his praise, pronouncing the Unabomber "pretty sophisticated" and "very broad," a "far more interesting critic than [Kirkpatrick] Sale or Jerry Mander or Langdon Winner" (well-known neo-Luddite, liberal, and left-wing critics of technoculture, respectively). Then Kelly dropped a bomb of his own: "Most important," he noted, "this guy is a nerd. He is a geek. He is one of us. The [manifesto] is structured like a doctoral thesis, or those computer science papers with numbered graphs. Very tidy. Like the bombs."[14]

Indeed, to fellow "techno-nerds," the Unabombs are unmistakably cyberpunk. Admittedly, Kaczynski invites interpretation as the psycho-killer reincarnation of William Morris, the late-nineteenth-century designer who called for a rejection of mass production and a return to medieval arts and crafts. Sprinkled with breathless references to "exquisite craft" and "painstaking care," journalistic descriptions of the Unabomb read like Pottery Barn blurbs for pricey reproductions of Shaker handicrafts. A *New York Times* feature lapsed into swooning prose worthy of *Martha Stewart Living,* calling the box that housed the first Unabomb "almost a work of art, carefully fashioned from four kinds of wood, meticulously sanded, polished and stained, like a piece of fine furniture from an old-world artisan."[15]

At the same time, Kaczynski can just as easily be read as a techno-bricoleur from the pages of William Gibson's science fiction, a close cousin to Rubin, the avant-garde tinkerer in "The Winter Market" who reanimates industrial rubbish in the form of cyberpunk robots, or as an alter-ego for Gibson himself, a "master of junk" trolling "the sea of cast-off goods our century floats on."[16] Before the FBI dubbed him the Unabomber, investigators called Kaczynski the "junkyard bomber" in reference to the fact that his engines of destruction were concocted from lamp cords, sink traps, furniture parts, old screws, match heads, and pieces of pipe. Considered as Outsider terror-art or exploding Joseph Cornell boxes, the Unabombs evince a decidedly hackerish love of the ad hoc and the DIY, of retrofitting and refunctioning; they cast an ominous light on Gibson's cyberpunk shibboleth "The street finds its own uses for things." They even suggest a mordant appropriation of the cyberhype that promises a future of exponentially bigger bytes in endlessly smaller boxes: "We expect we will be able to pack deadly bombs into ever smaller, lighter, and more harmless looking packages," the Unabomber bragged, in a letter to *The New York Times,* sounding for all the world like a nightmare parody of a trade-show salesman flakking the latest in palmtops.[17]

Even wild nature, the antitechnological ecotopia at the heart of the Unabomber's ideology, is consonant with the cyberpunk mythos. The manifesto offers a curiously Hobbesian vision of paradise regained, where humans rejoice in the fulfillment of what Kaczynski calls "a need (probably based in biology) for something that we will call the 'power process,'" by which he seems to mean the pursuit of the basic requirements of survival rather than the consumption of commodified images that characterizes consumer culture in the Digital Age. Untouched by Fordism, Taylorism, or any of the other command-and-control instrumentalities of industrial society, wild nature is the sole province of freedom, defined by the Unabomber as "being in control (either as an individual or as a member of a SMALL group) of the life-and-death issues of one's existence: food, clothing, shelter, and defense against whatever threats there may be in one's environment."

Reducing beings to bodies (i.e., their immediate physical needs) and redefining freedom as the struggle for survival, the social Darwinian ecopolitics of the Unafesto bear more than a passing resemblance to the postapocalyptic primitivism romanticized in cyberpunk movies like *Escape from New York* and *The Road Warrior.* A heady brew of masculinist power fantasies, frontier mythology, and the American cult of the anomic loner, SF films and fiction in this vein betray a nostalgia for a more embodied world, before the TV screen, the computer terminal, and the rest of the technological membrane grew between us and reality. "In such films as *Mad Max: Beyond Thunderdome,*" notes the cultural critic Scott Bukatman, "the bread-and-circuses barbarism of the future-archaic society masks a deeper utopianism: the 'perverse hope that someday conditions will indeed warrant a similar return to the body' as technology collapses into ruins."[18]

Survivalist and antistatist to the core, the Unabomber and cyber-punk make common cause in their libertarian leanings as well: The Una-bomber's statement, in a letter to the *New York Times,* that he "would like, ideally, to break down all society into very small, completely autonomous units" parallels cyberpunk's vision of society decentralized into self-sufficient autonomous zones like the Lo-Tek Nighttown in Gibson's "Johnny Mne-monic."[19] Libertarianism is the default politics of real-life cyberpunks like Japan's *otaku,* the hacker subculture that bends technology to its obsessive ends even as it embodies what *Wired* calls "the apotheosis of consumerism and an ideal work force for contemporary capitalism."[20] The libertarian philosophy of minimal government and maximal individual freedom appeals, as well, to the globe-trotting computer professionals who consider them-selves less citizens than "netizens," wired by cellphone, fax, and modem into the world space of ceaselessly circulating information and liquid capi-tal but increasingly disengaged from public space, civic life, and social responsibility.

Despite the Unabomber's obvious resonances with libertarian thought, however, neocon ideologues have typecast the self-declared "anti-communist, anti-socialist, anti-leftist" terrorist as a whipping boy for the creep-ing culture rot of the sixties, the lunatic excesses of the environmental movement, and the academic left's sullen refusal to ride capitalism's Carou-sel of Progress. Lance Morrow (*Time*'s answer to Ed Anger of *The Weekly World News*) laid the blame for the "fatal effects" of Wanda Kaczynski's "manic ide-alization" of little Ted on the "breezy California child-worship" of the sixties; *Newsweek*'s Joe Klein argued that the Unabomber is joined at the hip with "any number of left-pessimist academics" by the notion that "technological 'progress' will bring despair, unemployment and ecological ruin."[21]

There's no denying the cultural genes the Unabomber seems to have inherited, albeit in mutant form, from the sixties: his antitechnology bias, his back-to-nature philosophy, his romanticization of "primitive man" (spe-cifically, Native Americans), and his revolutionary faith in the power of a well-placed bomb to "strike at the heart of the state," as the Red Brigades put it.

In fact, though, Kaczynski was by all accounts a blurred face in the crowd scenes of the sixties, untouched by the emergence of S.D.S. during his time at Harvard and the University of Michigan or by the uprising at nearby San Francisco State College when he taught at Berkeley. The dogmas of the

New Left, as well as the communitarian ethos and Dionysian eros at the heart of the counterculture, are wholly absent from his worldview. In a journal entry dated somewhere between 1977 and '78, when he was just beginning his campaign of terror, Kaczynski wrote, "My ambition is to kill a scientist, big businessman, government official or the like. I would also like to kill a Communist."[22] The Unabomber's closest kin can be found, not among sixties radicals, but in the far-right militia movement of the nineties, whose antigovernment refrain harmonizes with the Unabomber's battle hymn of decentralization by any means necessary. The militias' tactic of "leaderless resistance" and their dream of the cellular society destined to follow the overthrow of the federal government parallels the manifesto's vision of atomized self-governance in "small, autonomous communities."

The Unabomber's radical libertarian vision of a "postnational" body politic, decomposed into scattered cells, is the missing link between wild nature and wired nature, the toggle switch that connects the Unabomber to cyberpunk on one hand and cybercapitalism on the other. In a crowning irony, the Unabomber's call for the atomization of the nation-state resonates sympathetically with the Tofflerist-Gingrichist rhetoric of decentralization dear to the hearts of *Wired* editors and the laissez-faire futurists they lionize (George Gilder, Peter Drucker, Peter Schwartz, and their ilk).

Although they prefer deregulation to demolition and obviously reject the antitechnology and anticorporate planks in his platform, the digerati share the Unabomber's libertarian contempt for politics with a capital *P,* by definition statist. "This is not to be a POLITICAL REVOLUTION," writes Kaczynski, in the Unafesto's opening section. "Its object will be to overthrow not governments but the economic and technological basis of the present society." He realizes, astutely, that political power's center of gravity is rapidly shifting from the nation-state to the multinational corporation, specifically to technology-dependent, postindustrial entities such as media conglomerates and financial-services firms.

Wired's editors were singing from the same page as Kaczynski when they wrote,

> We have basically ignored Clinton, Washington, and politics
> in general. The Revolution is definitely not happening in the

halls of the Capitol, and politics are becoming not only increasing obsolete, but irrelevant. . . . Everyone on the planet believes in the free market now, like they believe in gravity. . . .
There are other, better ways to affect [sic] change in society
today than pulling a lever in a voting booth. Politics isn't the
solution, it's become the problem—and the Digital Generation may be consciously rejecting politics . . . because they have
rationally decided that politics and government are fundamen-
tally discredited. . . . [Wired] reports on a Revolution without
violence that embraces a new, non-political way to improve the
future based on economics beyond macro control.[23]

(Clearly, the digerati for whom *Wired*'s editors speak also share the Unabomber's revolutionary fervor, the unshakable hubris of the true believer
confident that history has a telos, and it's going his way.)

Of course, as with their deregulatory soulmate, the "conservative
futurist" Newt Gingrich (to whose Progress and Freedom Foundation *Wired*
has contributed), the digerati's Tofflerist rhetoric of decentralization is a
blind for a massively parallel Reaganomics whose immediate business is the
dismantling of the rickety regulatory framework that (just barely) constrains
multinational corporate power. The digerati's ultimate goal is the elimination of the nation-state (and thus even an unreliable governor of utterly un-
fettered corporate power, answerable to no one).

In keeping with the social Darwinist undertones of their vision of a
cybercapitalist "revolution" masterminded by a technocratic elite, with the
Second Wave masses along for the ride (or part of the road, if they won't
hop aboard), the digerati lend their laissez-faire economics the force of
natural law by couching it in the language of chaos theory and artificial life
(a branch of computer science in which researchers create digital creatures
that feed, breed, struggle for survival, and pass on evolutionarily successful traits in imitation of their real world counterparts). The executive-
friendly jacket copy of Kevin Kelly's *Out of Control: The Rise of Neo-Biological
Civilization,* promises "'out-of-control' business strategies for an emerging
global economy built on networks." Inside, Kelly invokes both chaos and
AL to validate the notion that capitalism, unconstrained by Second Wave
assumptions (the necessity of governmental regulation presumably among
them), would evolve into something rich and strange—a "network

economy" of decentralized, outsourced "economic superorganisms," able to adapt to the nonlinear dynamics of the global economic ecosystem.

Visions of out-of-control cybercapitalism also dance in the heads of managerial gurus like Tom Peters (author of the business book *Thriving on Chaos*), whose corporate gospel of "crazy" nonlinear decision-making and perpetual reinvention echoes the chaos-theory thesis that turbulent natural systems, when sufficiently far from equilibrium, often give rise to startling new phenomena. Similarly, Peters's concept of the postindustrial "Atomized Corporation, with spirited, often pint-sized subunits with their own personalities and headed by disrespectful chiefs" recalls the chaos-theory notion of self-organizing natural phenomena such as hurricanes or amoeba colonies, in which previously disconnected elements suddenly reach a critical point where they begin to "cooperate" to form a more complex phenomenon.[24] "This is the age of biological models of organization, not mechanical models," says Peters. "I'm keen on companies such as CNN, which are creating something organic, something that recreates itself, invents itself each day."[25]

Management theorists like Peters are already living in William Gibson's cyberpunk future, where multinational corporations, highly evolved "life forms" whose DNA is "coded in silicon," are "the planet's dominant form of intelligence."[26] The notion of the corporate entity as a complex colonial organism is implicit in recent attempts to obtain a ruling conferring on corporations the legal status of individuals, thereby protecting corporate image advertising as free speech.

The global marketplace is increasingly conceived of in Darwinian terms, with the social and environmental depredations of multinationals rationalized as corporate life forms' struggle for survival in an economic ecosystem. "'Ecology' and 'economy' share more than linguistic roots," maintains the nanotechnologist K. Eric Drexler; corporations, he argues, are "evolved artificial systems" born of the marketplace's "Darwinian" competition.[27] In *Bionomics: The Inevitability of Capitalism,* the business consultant Michael Rothschild straightfacedly argues that "what we call capitalism (or free-market economics) is not an ism at all but a naturally occurring phenomenon" (and therefore presumably beyond reproach). In *Clockspeed: Winning Industry Control in the Age of Temporary Advantage,* Charles H. Fine offers sociobiological parables about "industrial fruit-flies" for anxious managers, whom he promises to turn into "'corporate geneticists' who do not react to the forces of change but master them to engineer their company's destiny."[28]

A 1996 issue of the business magazine *Fast Company* featured a profile of one such "geneticist": Eric Schmidt, Sun Microsystems's chief technology officer. Fraught with unintentionally hilarious examples of corporate biobabble, the article extols Schmidt's expertise at corporate crossbreeding—"organizational genetics," to those in the know, which means "combining organizational DNA in unique and inventive ways." What's organizational DNA, you ask? Why, "it's the stuff, mostly intangible, that determines the basic character of a business. It's bred from the founders, saturates the early employees, and often shapes behavior long after the pioneers have moved on."[29] Gene-splicing the latest in Darwinian metaphors with a sexual politics straight out of *The Flintstones,* the article's author analogizes venture capitalists and entrepreneurs to "the male urge to sow seed widely and without responsibilities and the female desire for a mate who'll settle down and help with the kids."[30]

We've heard this song before, and when the hundredth trend-hopping management consultant informs us, as James Martin does in *Cybercorp: The New Business Revolution,* that high-tech corporations are "creature[s] designed to prosper in the corporate jungle" and that "capitalist society is based on competition and survival of the fittest, as in Darwin's world," we realize where we've heard it. It's the theme song of Herbert Spencer's social Darwinism, as popular in its day with monopoly builders like John D. Rockefeller and Andrew Carnegie as Kelly's neobiological capitalism is with Tom Peters and his corporate flock. "'Social Darwinism,'" Stephen Jay Gould usefully reminds us, "has often been used as a general term for any evolutionary argument about the biological basis of human differences, but the initial 19th-century meaning referred to a specific theory of class stratification within industrial societies, and particularly to the idea that there was a permanently poor underclass consisting of genetically inferior people who had precipitated down into their inevitable fate."[31]

The genealogical links between the public musings of the self-anointed "digital elite" and the Spencerian rhetoric of the robber barons is apparent at a glance, though they're separated by a century or so. Nicholas Negroponte, a sharp-dressing pitchman who hawks visions of a brighter, broader-bandwidth tomorrow to Fortune 500 executives (and to the unwashed AOL millions in his book *Being Digital*), breezily redefines the "needy" and the "have-nots" as the technologically illiterate—the "digitally homeless," a phrase that wins the Newt Gingrich Let Them Eat Laptops Award for cloud-dwelling detachment from the lives of the little people.[32] Stewart Brand, a charter member of the digerati, blithely informs the *Los Angeles Times* that "elites basically drive civilization."[33] Rossetto rails against the technology critic Gary Chapman as someone who "attacks technologically advanced people," as if Web site design were an inherited trait, a marker of evolutionary superiority.[34]

If the analogy to social Darwinism seems overheated, consider *Wired* founder Rossetto's belief, earnestly confided to a *New York Times* writer, that *Homo cyber* is plugging himself into "exo-nervous systems, things that connect us up beyond—literally, physically—beyond our bodies. . . . We will discover that when enough of us get together this way, we will have created a new life form. It's evolutionary; it's what the human mind was destined to do."[35] As Rossetto readily acknowledges, his techno-Darwinian epiphany is borrowed from Pierre Teilhard de Chardin, the Jesuit philosopher and Lamarckian evolutionist who predicted the coming of an "ultra-humanity" destined to converge in a transcendental "Omega Point" that would be "the consummation of the evolutionary process."[36]

De Chardin's ideas are well known in theological and New Age circles and, increasingly, among the digerati. Less known is his passionate advocacy of eugenics as a means of preparing the way for ultra-humanity. "What fundamental attitude . . . should the advancing wing of humanity take to fixed or definitely unprogressive ethnical groups?" he wrote in *Human Energy*. "The earth is a closed and limited surface. To what extent should it tolerate, racially or nationally, areas of lesser activity? More generally still, how should we judge the efforts we lavish in all kinds of hospitals on saving what is so often no more than one of life's rejects? . . . Should not the strong (to the extent that we can define this quality) take precedence over the preservation of the weak?"[37] Happily, the answer is readily at hand: "In the course of the coming centuries it is indispensable that a nobly human form of eugenics, on a standard worthy of our personalities, should be discovered and developed," he writes in *The Phenomenon of Man*.[38]

Since there is an implied guilt by association here, it's important to note that Rossetto and the other digital de Chardinians may well be unfamiliar with the philosopher's thoughts on eugenics. But given our increasingly "genocentric" mind-set and the creepy popularity of books like Richard

Herrnstein and Charles Murray's *The Bell Curve: Intelligence and Class Structure in American Life,* as well as the potential misuses of vanguard technologies like gene therapy and genetic screening, the digerati would do well to consider the ugly underside of their techno-Darwinian vision of the ultra-human apotheosis of the "technologically advanced"—"de Chardin's advancing wing of humanity," by any other name.

Obviously, the *Wired* ideology is far less pervasive, and not quite as nasty and brutish, as social Darwinism in its heyday; none of the digerati has embraced eugenics, at least publicly. But nineteenth-century capitalists like Carnegie and Rockefeller, who in the words of Andrew Ross "seized for themselves the mantle of the fittest survivors as if it were indeed biologically ordained," would undoubtedly note a family resemblance in the digerati, way cool white guys secure in the knowledge that they are Stewart Brand's fabled "elite," guiding civilization from their rightful place atop the Great Chain of Being (Digital).

The digerati, with their Darwinian marketplace ruled by corporate life-forms and their societal ecology presided over by a "technologically advanced" elite, and the Unabomber, with his inviolate wilderness peopled by neo-Luddites gone native, have built contrary worldviews on a common cornerstone: the notion of nature as a legitimator of theories about culture.

On the surface, the back-to-nature rhetoric of the digerati and the Unabomber is only the most recent example of a technodeterministic tendency in Western history to map the mechanical metaphor of the moment onto human affairs and the natural world. The world of the mechanical clock gave us Julien Offray de la Mettrie's theory of the clockwork human, in *Man a Machine* (1748); the nineteenth century, dubbed the Railway Age by C. S. Peirce, begat the concept of the living organism as a steam engine; and the Information Age has seen Norbert Wiener's redefinition of humans and animals as cybernetic systems gain currency, with the metaphor undergoing periodic upgrades as computers themselves have evolved. The current proliferation of biological and evolutionary metaphors signals the emergence of biotechnology and genetic engineering as *the* flagship technologies of the next millennium.

But metaphors don't come cheap: The costs of turning culture into nature, transforming it from social construction into elemental force, are

merely hidden, buried in Western history. A little spadework reveals that
the indisputable authority of natural "law" has been invoked, throughout
European history, to legitimate the subjugation of women and the en-
slavement or extermination of nonwhites, as well the exploitation of
nature itself.[39] Andrew Ross notes, "Nature is the ultimate people-pleaser,
whose name can even be lent to and honored by causes associated with its
destruction."[40]

A single example speaks volumes: In *Nature's Body: Gender in the
Making of Modern Science,* Londa Schiebinger describes how eighteenth-
century anatomists, anthropologists, and natural historians, "working under
the banner of scientific neutrality," cited the supposedly simian anatomy of
Africans to account for the lowly status Europeans assigned them on the
evolutionary and, consequently, social ladder. Similarly, the childlike "com-
pressed crania" of women of all races were adduced as evidence of impulsive, emotional, and generally inferior intellectual qualities.[41]

The Unabomber's feral ecotopia and the digerati's free-market
ecology are only the latest examples of nature used as a ventriloquist's
dummy in the service of social agendas, few (if any) of which are pretty to
look at. In the last hundred years or so we've seen the social Darwinism of
the Gilded Age; the eugenics movement of the twenties, which resulted in
the Immigration Restriction Act of 1924, designed to limit immigration to
"superior" Northern European stock, and the forced sterilization in more
than two dozen states of the "socially defective"; and, most recently, the
voodoo sociology of *The Bell Curve.*[42]

The Unabomber and the digerati aren't alone in ventriloquizing
nature. Ross contends that we are witnessing "a wholesale revival of appeals to the authority of nature and biology. . . . Nature's laws are invoked
once again as the ground of judgement and the basis of policy. . . . Biolo-
gism and social Darwinism have returned with a vengeance, and are a driving force behind the sweeping new world view engineered by biotechnology
and genetic medicine."[43] He worries that "the authority of nature, and hence
of the status quo," will ultimately become "a despotic vehicle for curtailing
rights and liberties."[44]

Already, *The Bell Curve*'s Herrnstein and Murray have argued that
immigration should be restricted and birth control aggressively promoted
among the lower classes to prevent "dysgenesis," or the dissipation of intelligence through the muddying of the gene pool. The psychologist Jean

Phillippe Rushton believes that blacks have evolved to develop smaller brains and display more sexual and aggressive characteristics than, say, "Orientals," who have larger brains, tamer sex drives, and are more easily socialized. Christopher Brand, a psychologist and self-declared "scientific racist" who stresses the supposed genetic link between race and intelligence, has suggested that women should be encouraged to mate with high-I.Q. males to improve their descendants' inherited traits.[45] Can a kinder, gentler eugenics be far away?

Nearly 40 years ago, Roland Barthes argued, in *Mythologies,* that one of ideology's most insidious aspects was that it converts constructed social reality, and the power relations embedded in it, into innocent, immutable "nature." Ideology, he noted, "has the task of giving an historical intention a natural justification, and making contingency appear eternal."[46] Wild nature and wired nature are pernicious because they do just that, foreclosing debate by camouflaging the manmade as the god-given.

In the Unabomber's case, the deceit is writ small in the life he led in his crude, one-room cabin at the edge of the Scapegoat Wilderness. Beneath his shaggy exterior, Kaczynski was a prosthetic wolfman, more scientific American than American Werewolf. The public image of obdurate technophobia remained at heart a techno-nerd, striking at the heart of the state in the name of wild nature while living in what *Newsweek* described as a "do-it-yourself bomb lab." At night, surrounded by books on electrical circuitry and chemistry, he read *Scientific American* and *Omni* by candlelight, a live bomb under his bed. Though he lived in God's country, his life was far from being a *Walden*esque idyll: "It's no fun having to spend all your evenings and weekends preparing dangerous mixtures, filing trigger mechanisms out of scraps of metal or searching the Sierras for a place isolated enough to test a bomb," he lamented, in a letter to *The New York Times.*[47]

Like the rest of us, the Unabomber was entangled in the web of cultural complicity, hopelessly implicated in technological modernity. The question is: Where does technology begin? Clearly, bombs are infernal machines, although he may have symbolically inoculated himself against the technological virus by nestling his contraptions in wooden boxes and fashioning many of their working parts out of wood. Did he make a distinction between the postindustrial, cybernetic technologies favored by the techno-nerds he reviled and Machine Age artifacts such as his bicycle or the antique typewriter on which he wrote the Unafesto? Did he reflect on the irony of communicating his opposition to technology and his dream of wild nature via language, the ur-technology whose invention cast us out of nature, into culture?

Perhaps he suspected, all along, the futility of his project. The Unabomber's symbolic return to culture was acted out in a National Public Radio segment on his haircut.[48] Unwittingly conjuring the image of a werewolf the morning after, NPR's Howard Berkes reported that Kaczynski's "wild and matted hair" was gone, that his hair was "close-cropped" and his beard "neatly trimmed." According to Berkes, the local woman who works as the jailhouse barber described him as a "courteous man" who "did not have the demeanor of a monster."

While having his mustache trimmed, the woman recalled, Kaczynski told her a story about "an ancient tribe in Japan that used to grow their hair as long as possible. He said that he had heard that they even had a special tool designed to lift the hairs of their mustaches off their lips so they could eat. And he said, 'I'd love to see that tool.'" In this droll fable, we hear the first, shy overture toward a détente with technology.

Of course, the machine was always there, lurking in the garden, be it a broken-down typewriter, a bicycle cobbled together from spare parts, or the bombs themselves. Ironically, even the Unafesto's imagined return to wild nature would inevitably have given rise to *Road Warrior*–esque techno-bricolage, setting in motion the historical dynamic that begins with *Robinson Crusoe* and ends with *Robinson Crusoe on Mars*. The Unabomber realized this: In the manifesto, he warns that the "greatest danger is that industrial society may begin to reconstitute itself within the first few years after the breakdown. . . . If and when industrial society breaks down, its remnants [must] be smashed beyond repair, so that the system cannot be reconstituted. The factories should be destroyed, technical books burned, etc."

For humans after the Fall, symbol-manipulating animals that we are, nature—in the sense of an absolute authority, the Transcendental Signified that anchors all of culture's free-floating signifiers—has always been an epistemic mirage, seen through the haze of language. Now, in a historical moment when technologies such as genetic engineering and theoretical ones such as nanotechnology hold forth the promise of hacking the operating systems of the physical world and organic life, nature and culture—the wild and the wired—are more maddeningly (and literally) intertangled than ever. "I'm always a little amazed when I run into people who feel that technology is something that's *outside* of the individual, that one can either accept or reject," says William Gibson. "At this stage of the game, we *are* technology."[49] Even the Unabomber's most ardent fans seem to have embraced this paradox: A poster displayed on the UNAPACK Web site asks, "If the Unabomber prevails and we return to wild nature, can I still have my car phone?"

Postscript

On May 5, 1998, Theodore J. Kaczynski, the Unabomber, was sentenced
to four life terms plus 30 years in prison for 13 of his 16 acknowledged
Unabombings, three of which were fatal. Kaczynski's bombs killed Thomas
J. Mosser, a public relations executive; Hugh Scrutton, the owner of a
computer rental store; and Gilbert P. Murray, an official of the California
Forestry Association, a trade group.

Throughout this essay, I have set aside the obvious fact that the
Unabomber was a serial-bombing murderer, focusing instead on his tangled
relationship to the digerati and the philosophical debt these unlikely bed-
fellows owe nature. Obviously, there's more than a little irony in airbrushing
the bloodstains out of an essay that takes the digerati to task for their Laputan
disengagement from the human realities of everyday life.

In truth, there's blood all over the Unabomber's story. When one
of his bombs blew away the 38-year-old Scrutton, whose apparent crime
against humanity was renting computers, Kaczynski wrote in his journal,
"Excellent. Humane way to eliminate somebody. He probably never felt a
thing."[50] The bomb that killed Murray mutilated him so horribly, according
to Kaczynski's prosecutors, "that his family was allowed only to see and touch
his feet and legs, below the knees, as a final farewell." Kaczynski, who had
actually intended the deadly package for another official, wrote that he had
"no regret" that the wrong man—46, married, and a father of two—was his
accidental victim.[51] When Mosser opened his bomb, he was torn apart by a
blast of nails and razor blades. In court, his wife told of rushing into the room
where her husband lay, "his stomach slashed open," his "heart perforated."
One of the couple's three children approached. Ms. Mosser recalled the "un-
bearable pain" she felt when she told her daughter, "Daddy's dead. It was a
bomb."[52] In his diary, Kaczynski wrote, "A totally satisfactory result."[53]

Without wanting to exploit the unimaginable agony wrought by what
Kelly called Kaczynski's "tidy" little bombs, I feel compelled to remind my
readers—and myself—that the Unabomber is more than a repressed "techno-
nerd" and/or a sociopathic symbol of the resentment many feel at being stampeded into a future they've had little hand in building, by a hubristic elite that
routinely dismisses them as "clueless." He is also a conscienceless sociopath
who killed and maimed in the name of an imaginary army, the one-man Freedom Club, whose lost cause hasn't even merited a Movie of the Week.

14 / SPACE ODDITIES: HEAVEN'S GATE AND *HOMO CYBER*—STRANGE ALLEGIANCES ON THE LEVEL ABOVE HUMAN

"How a Member of the Kingdom of Heaven Might Appear," from the Heaven's Gate website.

They came from cyberspace.

Sporting *My Favorite Martian* haircuts and *Star Trek*-inspired arm patches that read HEAVEN'S GATE AWAY TEAM, some of them willingly castrated and (perhaps even more horrifically) all of them unrepentant Trekkers, the 39 saucer-worshipping "cybergeeks" found neatly laid out in a luxurious estate in the wealthy Southern California suburb of Rancho Santa Fe were "never of this earth" in the eyes of the *New York Post* columnist Andrea Peyser.[1]

To many in the "old media," as those in the digital vanguard call them, the Heaven's Gate cultists who committed suicide in an attempt to rendezvous with the UFO they believed was lurking behind the Hale-Bopp comet were an object lesson in the evils of spending too much time on-line. As the number of newspapers shrinks and the gradual exodus of young viewers from one-way, "monologic" media like TV to two-way, "dialogic" media such as electronic bulletin boards and MUDs proceeds apace, the old guard casts an anxious eye on the Internet, the upstart medium supposedly destined to supersede traditional media. On-line conferencing, where anyone can initiate a discussion topic and where the stump, like Speaker's Corner in Hyde Park, is open to all, offers a glimpse of public discourse unmediated by the celebrity anchors, expert commentators, and pundits of broadcast news. Moreover, in a society where freedom of the press is guaranteed only to those who own one, as A. J. Liebling memorably observed, electronic conferencing, Internet mailing lists, and personal Web sites nibble away at the cultural hegemony of corporate media, countering its bland, self-censored monovocality with the fractious cacophony of irreverent, dissenting voices.

At such a historic juncture, those with a stake in the status quo are well served by horror stories about the Internet as a black lagoon of conspiracy theories and mind-control cults where the masses are left to their own critical devices, without Cokie Roberts to explain it all for them or the editors of *The New York Times* to shield them from all the news that's unfit to print. The *New York Post*'s coverage of the Heaven's Gate suicides is a case in point, setting the Victorian penny-dreadful flourishes the *Post* is famous for to a steady backbeat of cyberphobia. In the issue that kicked off the *Post*'s coverage of the cult, the Heaven's Gaters, who supported themselves as cut-rate Web site designers, were described as "computer-geek cultists," a "cult of computer wizards," a "cybercult."[2] A mastery of computers, an obsession with the Net, and the sort of terminal dorkiness that stamps the individual in question as a prime candidate for Klingon language camps (or suicidal saucer cults) are implicitly linked in a pop psych Devil's Triangle. Hilariously, the opening page of the same issue features a grainy photo of a PC, emblazoned with the I.D. POLICE VIDEO and accompanied by the caption, "Logged off: Computer rests on a tidy desk in the suicide house of horrors." At a stroke, an innocuous, ubiquitous machine is transformed into a portentous clue at the scene of the crime, a *Poltergeist*-like gateway to the millennial id.

Undeniably, there are cults on the Net, as elsewhere, in search of naïve young brains in need of a thorough washing. The *Time* columnist Joshua Quittner quoted a creepy on-line exchange between a Heaven's Gater and a young techie identifying himself as an 18-year-old boy. The cultist's come-on begins: "Are you looking for work? We are always looking for associates."[3] And there's more than a grain of truth in the concern, raised by cult experts, that sensitive seekers in search of community or spiritual solace in cyberspace are especially susceptible to the blandishments of cults. Among the 39 victims in the Rancho Santa Fe estate was Yvonne McCurdy-Hill, a 38-year-old postal worker and avid Net surfer who learned of the cult through its Web site. Shortly after discovering Heaven's Gate, she left her Cincinnati home for California, forsaking her newborn twins and three other children for the promise of an extraterrestrial apotheosis. "This thing came from the Internet," her mother-in-law lamented.[4]

Still, while highlighting the computer connection adds millennial frisson, and a ready-made moral, to news coverage of the cult suicides, the notion that the Internet is the root of all evil is belied by the facts, in this case. The cult's leader, Marshall Applewhite (a.k.a. "Do," as in do-re-mi), only discovered the Net in 1995, after two decades of trolling for converts off-line, lecturing in places like the Bayshore Inn in Waldport, Oregon, and the public library in Littleton, Colorado. Despite Do's assertion that a message mass-mailed to Internet newsgroups "doubled" the size of the cult (a less-than-awe-inspiring claim, considering the final body count of 39), a document on the Heaven's Gate Web site makes it clear that the group's on-line proselytizing wasn't exactly a thumping success. In fact, the barrage of "ridicule, or hostility, or both" that the cult said greeted its communiqué was sufficiently withering for the group to take it as a wakeup call to begin its preparations "to return 'home,'" a space odyssey undertaken with the aid of lethal doses of phenobarbital.[5]

Rather than being a "folly amplifier," as one expert characterized it, the Net proved (at least in this case) not to suffer fools gladly. "Obviously there *are* people online who by virtue of their dissatisfaction with the real world are susceptible to cults or other, more benign forms of groupmind phenomenon" such as virtual communities, wrote Patrizia DiLucchio, in a discussion topic on the WELL. Even so, she noted, "the Net works *against* cults in one very real way: people online generally feel empowered to speak up for themselves and to express their opinions in a way that they frequently *won't* face-to-face. This makes it hard for demagogues to establish real beachheads. Charisma is generally an audio-visual phenomenon. Hitler might have had a hard time on Usenet. And someone surely would have pointed out to Charlie Manson that he couldn't spell."[6]

In essence, much of the commentary on Heaven's Gate amounts to cultural border patrol, the policing of the dividing line between new and old media, between cyberspace addicts and the millions of Americans who don't even own computers, let alone modems (roughly 60 percent of U.S. households as of 1997, according to the Electronic Industries Association). More generally, gatekeepers of official reality have used the cult to spotlight the putative differences between the mainstream and the fringe, the sanctioned and the stigmatized. To religious conservatives, for instance, the cultists were evidence of the spiritual vacuum left by the suppression of traditional religion by church-and-state separatists.[7] Their belief in a flying saucer that would transport them to a "Level Beyond Human" once they abandoned their bodily "vehicles" and beamed up from a doomed world dominated by a conspiracy of "Luciferian" E.T.s wasn't a bona fide religion, but "a delusional cocktail" (*Newsweek*), "New Age gibberish" (*Time*), "ad hoc mumbo-jumbo" (*New York Times*)—in short, a cult. To be sure, Applewhite's teachings were a theological crazy quilt, loosely stitched together from the born-again belief in an apocalyptic rapture, New Age millennialism, the paranoid zeitgeist mythologized in *The X-Files,* and a faith in alien saviors familiar from *Close Encounters of the Third Kind* and Whitley Strieber's *Communion.*

Still, to atheists and agnostics, the distinction between mainstream religion and marginalized cult is a theological nicety in a country where the religious "mainstream" presumably includes the 72 percent of us who believe in angels, the 56 percent of us who believe in the devil, and the 42 percent of us who believe in demonic possession.[8] "I'm still having trouble with the religion-cult distinction," wrote the *Nation* columnist Katha Pollitt, who answered the charge that "only cults, not real religions, practice suicide" by noting that in her irreligious opinion, "Jehovah's Witnesses who refuse blood transfusions, or Christian Scientists who refuse life-saving medical attention" adequately earn the adjective "suicidal."[9] But a mainstream believer might counter that Jehovah's Witnesses and Christian Scientists are themselves considered cults by mainline Protestants. Nonetheless, as a conscientious objector in a country that reeks to heaven of religion, I can't resist noting that the "mainstream" faith embraced by a reported 86 percent of Americans is surely the limit case for human credulity: a bizarre, archaic death cult revolving around sublimated cannibalism, vampirism, and human sacrifice whose most extreme adherents believe in the literal transformation, with the proper incantations, of a hunk of bread into the undead flesh of a 2,000-year-old revenant.[10]

Ironically, while neocons bemoaned the supposed crisis of faith, secular humanists and hardheaded rationalists in the Carl Sagan mold contended that the Heaven's Gaters were casualties of *too much* faith, grim testimony to mounting scientific illiteracy and "the hazards of living a life innocent of empirical rigor," as Timothy Ferris put it in *The New Yorker.*[11]

Meanwhile, to the unwired masses, the cultists were lightning rods for the anxiety many feel in the face of the runaway technological and social change symbolized by inscrutable, unpredictable computers that crash without warning, voice-mail hells whose endless options never include a live human, VCR clocks insistently blinking "12:00." There was a revenge-on-the-nerds subtext to much of the coverage of the ritual suicides, a mixture of old-fashioned anti-intellectualism and a newfound resentment toward the software barons, corporate consultants, and way cool young entrepreneurs surfing Alvin Toffler's Third Wave. This same wave, the digital revolution that *Wired* magazine claims is "whipping through our lives like a Bengali typhoon," is sweeping many of us into the ranks of the permanent temps or the working poor.

We live at a moment when it seems as if the geek will inherit the earth: Cyberpunk SF pulled off the improbable feat of making techno-weenies cool, transforming the pencil-necked geek into the mirror-shaded outlaw hacker, and software mogul Bill Gates is richer than God, his iconic status unaffected by his terrible sweaters. An ad for Rockport shoes in a recent *Wired* was a study in nerd hubris. "I'm comfortable being a geek," declares Clint Rosemund, an archetypically dweeby Web-site builder for the Web design firm Razorfish. "Be comfortable," the tagline urges. "Uncompromise. Start with your feet"—advice unwittingly followed by the Heaven's Gaters, who died wearing fashionable black Nikes with cometlike white swooshes ("Just do it?").

But there's an element of cultural denial in the overemphatic assurances that the Heaven's Gaters were nerds, techies, geeks—in short, not like the rest of us, who presumably know the difference between a ball of dirty ice hurtling through space and an alien mothership traveling incognito. The truth, in this case, is less out there, as *The X-Files* would have it, than right here, reflected in our computer monitors: the Heaven's Gate cult is a fun house-mirror exaggeration of ourselves as a wired society.

For example, Applewhite's contempt for the flesh and the mundane world is pervasive among computer scientists, hackers, and others in the advance guard of digital culture. Of course, the late twentieth century holds no patent on body loathing; stripped of its *Star Trek* jargon, Applewhite's credo sounds a lot like gnosticism, a philosophical sect that flourished in the second century A.D. Fiercely dualistic, it denigrated the body and taught that freedom from the shackles of matter lay not in faith, but in self-denial and esoteric knowledge (*gnosis,* in Greek).[12] Despite zealous efforts to suppress it, gnosticism left its stamp on Judaeo-Christian thought.

But there's no need to look to the second century for parallels to the cultists' article of faith that the glitch-ridden "vehicle" we call the body is just so much hardware, piloted by a mind whose destiny lies on what the Heaven's Gaters called the "Evolutionary Level Above Human," free from the limits of matter. In *The Enchanted Loom: Mind in the Universe,* Robert Jastrow speculates that, one day soon, a scientist will manage to "tap into the contents of his mind and transfer them into the metallic lattices of a computer," emancipating our minds from "the weakness of the mortal flesh" and transforming us into a race of disembodied intellects, as evolutionarily suited for life in the future "as man is designed for life on the African savanna."[13]

Jastrow, the director of the Mount Wilson Observatory, is no flake. Nor is he alone: Hans Moravec, who heads the Mobile Robot Laboratory at Carnegie-Mellon University, goes further, imagining the fusion of Jastrow's "downloaded" consciousnesses into a "community mind."[14] Omniscient and omnivorous, it would spread throughout the cosmos, transforming matter into mind through some form of data conversion. In Nerdvana, all is cerebration; the "mind" half of the mind/body dualism would vanquish its detested opposite forever.

Like Applewhite's vision of "shedding the vehicle" and beaming up to that great *Enterprise* in the sky, the science-fiction dream of "downloading" our minds is essentially a religious one, sheathed in techno-babble— gnosticism with rocket fins. As if to underscore that point, scientists often slip into the language of religious transcendence when they envision the triumph of sublime mind over base matter. The computer scientist Charles Lecht asserts that "when we do *become mind* . . . we will be given a boost, 'out of the physical, and from there into—where else?—the spiritual.'"[15]

Of course, Lecht, Moravec, and Jastrow are hardly household names. But the neognosticism that they share with Applewhite and his followers—the belief that the body and the material world are so much dead weight, impeding our long-awaited lift-off from gravity, mortality, and limited disk space—is creeping into our cultural conversation about who we are and where we're going as a high-tech society. In a 1990 speech, Sprint chairman William Esrey predicted that the interconnectedness of the planet, through telecommunications, would give rise to a "global mind," possessed of a "capacity for miracles that would give even the Dalai Lama pause for thought."[16] Similarly, the New Age futurist John Perry Barlow believes that cyberspace is "the new home of Mind," a separate reality fashioned from "thought itself." In his "Declaration of the Independence of Cyberspace," written in heated response to Congress's passage of the Communications Decency Act, Barlow straightfacedly suggests that cyberspace secede from the physical world, like the bridge of the *Enterprise* uncoupling from the rest of the ship in *Star Trek: The Next Generation*. "We will create a civilization of the Mind in Cyberspace," he proclaims.[17] Similarly, George Gilder, a breathless rhapsodist of technological progress, celebrates the "overthrow of matter" and the "exaltation of mind" by information technologies. He ends *Microcosm: The Quantum Revolution in Economics and Technology* with a homily that reconciles our national faith in technological progress with our puritanical distrust of the flesh. "Overthrowing matter," writes Gilder, "humanity also escapes from the traps and compulsions of pleasure into a higher morality of spirit"—a thought that would have gladdened the heart of Marshall Applewhite.[18]

Thus, the Heaven's Gate cultists are merely a cyberspace-cadet caricature of the growing alienation of our minds from our bodies in an information society where we spend ever greater amounts of our lives sitting in chairs, staring at screens. Of course, the mind/body split—the curious fact that we both *have* bodies and *are* bodies, that our flesh is both "it" and "I"—has always bedeviled us, from Descartes to philosophers of consciousness like Daniel Dennett. But the sense that our bodies are dead meat, mere "vehicles" for the mind, is especially acute at a time when voice-mail and e-mail are gradually supplanting face-to-face or even voice-to-voice interaction and embodied experience is giving way to electronic immersion in virtual worlds. "We live now, more than ever, in an America where a great many people are gnostics without knowing it," writes Harold Bloom, in *Omens of Millennium* Bloom sees connections between gnosticism, which "denied both matter and energy, and opted instead for information above all else," and the "future-shock cyberspace apocalypticism" of technophiles like Newt Gingrich, who "tells us that our future depends completely upon information."[19]

Obviously, most of us aren't going to be packing our carry-on luggage for a one-way flight to the Evolutionary Level Above Human anytime soon. But as increasing numbers of us spend more and more of our working lives and leisure time on the other side of the screen, a neognostic alienation from our own fleshly "vehicles" and the world around us is beginning to haunt mainstream America. The relocation, in technology, of many of our mental and muscular skills, what McLuhan called the "self-amputation of our physical bodies," has made the supposedly obsolete body a source of creeping anxiety, if not outright fear and loathing. Tales of the Body Awful are all the rage, from the body-bag fiction of Patricia Cornwell to the designer splatter of the movie *Seven* to the emerging genre of biohazard horror, typified by, books like *The Hot Zone,* a real-life thriller about a deadly virus in which the subtext is the notion that the body and nature are hotbeds of disease. Ironically, our mass-media images of the Body Beautiful also bear witness to the Information Age belief that mind has triumphed over matter: With the aid of Nautilus machines, plastic surgery, and photographic retouching, celebrities remake the faces and physiques nature gave them in the image of a machine-tooled, posthuman beauty.

Not surprisingly, our collective dream life is filled with images of a better world than this, where the mind leaves the body behind like the booster stage of a rocket. Ours is a brave new age of alien saviors and guardian angels, near-death experiences and signs of the rapture—visions of incorporeal beings and immaterial realities that are eerily in tune with the digital zeitgeist. The philosopher Mortimer Adler has suggested that our fascination with angels is essentially a fantasy about the lofty intellect freed from the lowly flesh. It's an insight that harmonizes nicely with the futurist Stewart Brand's belief that "when you communicate through a computer, you communicate like an angel," by which he means that users who conference or "chat" on-line communicate as "disembodied intelligences of great intimacy."[20] Not coincidentally, the interactive program that guides Michael Douglas through cyberspace in the movie *Disclosure* appears in the guise of an angel. It's no coincidence that the out-of-body experiences recounted in the New Age confessional, *Saved by the Light,* sound a lot like the bodiless flights through virtual reality in William Gibson's cyberpunk novel, *Neuromancer.* The disembodied narrator of *Saved by the Light* banks and swoops over a dazzling city of crystal cathedrals; the plugged-in consciousness of Gibson's hacker streaks across "an endless neon cityscape, complexity that cut the eye, jewel bright . . ."[21]

Clearly, the Heaven's Gaters aren't alone; the information society as a whole seems to be dreaming of out-of-body experiences these days. But our daydreams don't come cheap: Escapist visions of a cyberrapture in which the mind scraps its broken-down "vehicle" and beams up from a trashed planet "about to be recycled," as Applewhite put it, are a fatal seduction, a weird mix of conspicuous consumption and divine assumption that distracts us from political action in the face of ecological crises, the unraveling of the social fabric, and the widening chasm between the high-tech elite and the downsized masses. Barlowian talk of seceding from the physical world into cyberspace takes place amid a worrisome flight from civic life, into the electronic cottages of self-employed knowledge workers or the gated communities of an increasingly fearful upper class.

Our neognostic exaltation of mind over body, of cyberspace over "meatspace," dovetails a little too neatly with mounting anxieties about global warming, environmental pollutants, and pesticides and growth hormones in our factory-farmed food. The technology critic Yaakov Garb traces the roots of our "enthusiasm for self-sufficient space colonies, disembodied intellects, and cyborg futures" to the growing recognition that our unshakable faith in progress and the profit margin has been rewarded by an increasingly lethal environment where "toxins and radiation trickle into the most fundamental recesses of our cells and ecosystems."[22]

Ironically, if Applewhite's followers had taken a closer look in the media mirror, they might have realized that the creatures they were seeking—megabrained beings who disdain the messy reality of the material world and wander, disembodied, through the playgrounds of the mind—were staring back at them. From the economic elite of software moguls and others who juggle information for a living to the data-entry cyberproles in the low-wage service sector, our information economy requires brains, eyeballs, and keyboard-hammering hands; the rest of the body is increasingly vestigial.

Some believe that evolution will gradually adapt to the demands of a high-tech world that increasingly values brain over brawn. Richard Dawkins, whose evolutionary theories stress the synergy of biology and technology, has a software program that morphs a human skull into the giant cranium of some far-future *Homo cyber*. "This is what our skulls might look like in thousands of years, should we be around that long," he told *Wired* magazine.[23] Metaphorically, we *already* look like the brainiac on Dawkins's screen—or, more immediately, the Whitley Strieberesque E.T. on the Heaven's Gate Web site, with its bulging brain, overgrown eyes, and undersized, irrelevant body. We have met the alien, and he is us.

CONCLUSION:
LAST THINGS

Tabloid eschatology. Photo courtesy *Weekly World News*.

We live in "end times," if not *the* end time. The air is thick these days with talk of ends: *The End of Nature* (Bill McKibben), *The End of Work* (Jeremy Rifkin), *The End of Science* (John Horgan), *The End of Education* (Neil Postman), *The End of the Nation State* (Kenichi Ohmae and Jean-Marie Guehenno), *The End of Affluence* (Jeffrey Madrick), *The End of Equality* (Mickey Kaus), and, most portentously, *The End of History and the Last Man* (Francis Fukuyama).

As I've argued throughout this book, the information revolution and globalization have greatly amplified the historical tensions in postwar American society—between capitalism and democracy, private and public, the elite and the masses, national and global, suburban and urban, the mainstream and the margins, "normal" and "deviant," mind and matter, culture and nature, unreal and real. America on the brink of the millennium is less a coherent society than a fault zone, a network of interconnected societal fractures.

The major rupture is the income gap between the postindustrial elite and the downsized masses, a socio-economic San Andreas fault that is dividing America into a two-tiered society. Moreover, the existence of tough-love philanthropists like George Soros notwithstanding, those well rewarded by our current economic boom are for the most part blissfully unburdened by the sense of social responsibility that prompted the flamboyant philanthropy of the turn-of-the-century railroad and oil barons. According to the *New York Times* writer Carey Goldberg, members of the nouveau-riche geek elite, many of whom have retired in their mid-thirties, thanks to skyrocketing stock portfolios, are especially self-centered. "The upstart geekocracy of high technology is not known for sharing," writes Goldberg. "In general, techno-millionaires, who make up one of the biggest pools of new wealth in the country, have been regarded as one of the stingiest."[1] When they do give, they often have more than altruism in mind: Bill Gates's $200 million donation toward hooking up libraries around the nation to the Internet or his virtual donation of a ton of old software to the Philippines are obvious sources of tax relief as well as a stealthy means of ensuring future markets for his company's software.

Simultaneously, some in the cellphone, frequent-flyer class are retreating from civic life and public space to the privatized commons of the gated communities that an estimated 8.4 million Americans now call home. Others are hunkering down in homes that the corporate futurist Faith Popcorn calls "armored cocoons," the most heavily bunkered of which feature the hidden, hardened inner sanctums known as "safe rooms." Fortified with steel-plated doors and fiberglass "wall armor" of the sort used in federal building lobbies, they are often outfitted with emergency power generators, separately buried phone lines, fully stocked refrigerators, and weapons. Some feature what Kurt Alizade, the president of City Safe, Inc., calls "high-voltage cattle-prod technology" concealed in the carpet on the attack side of the door. In Aspen, Greenwich, Malibu, and especially Manhattan (which enjoys the unenviable distinction of having the widest income gap in the United States between rich and poor), the upper-class fear of a gathering storm of underclass discontent manifests itself in the vogue for what one member of the anxious elite calls her "God-forbid" room.[2]

Communism may have been consigned to the desktop recycle bin of history, as free-market cheerleaders never tire of reminding us, and Marx may be an ironic icon of nineties retro chic, but the old bearded devil may have the last laugh: As we round the bend to the new millennium, class war and the percolating rage of the "workers of the world" are emerging as *the* lightning-rod social issues of the coming century. Growing income inequality, accompanied by the hemorrhaging of U.S. manufacturing jobs because of automation or their relocation in the low-wage, nonunion "developing world," is sowing dragon's teeth. The disappearance of even unskilled factory work at a time when economic growth is insufficient to absorb dislocated workers is dire enough; that it is happening at a moment when traditional safety valves no longer function—owing to the wasting away of the labor movement, the conservative dismantling of social services in favor of "market solutions" to social ills, and the ongoing buyout of representa-

tive government by corporate power—has created fertile soil for the apocalyptic politics of the disaffected.

"A huge proportion of the American public, maybe a majority, has
been quite skeptical of the system for years," notes William Greider, author of *One World, Ready or Not: The Manic Logic of Global Capitalism.* "They
don't have any political power in this country, because they're mostly lower
middle-class, working-class, or poor." He contends that "it's one of the great
delusions of our leaders that all Americans are sharing in the wealth. I've
talked to lots of groups around the country, and they don't even want to
hear about it, because it's so irrelevant to their lives. . . . So if our leaders
don't respond to these realities, this [income] split will get wider and harder
and turn into some pretty nasty stuff. . . . If you downsize people year after
year, you are sowing the seeds of some real irrational politics."[3]

Chicken Little liberal alarmism? Consider Russia. As this is written,
it's in economic convulsions induced by the laissez-faire "shock therapy" of
radical free-market economists like Jeffrey Sachs. Writing in a 1994
issue of the *Journal of Democracy,* John H. Fairbanks, Jr., argued that "many of
the preconditions of fascism are now or will soon be present in Russia: hyper-
inflation, mass unemployment, seething status resentments, disillusion with
democracy, a society that is 'De-Christianized' but still craves 'spirituality,'
bitter border conflicts, constant fighting waged not by state armies but by
Freikorps-like volunteer groups, and residual socialist and nationalist feelings."[4]

The New World Order of transnational capitalism is profoundly
imperiling democracy on a global scale. Noam Chomsky argues, in *The
Prosperous Few and the Restless Many,* that we're witnessing the emergence of
a "de facto world government" whose institutions answer, first and foremost, to transnational corporations and international banks, not individual
nations.[5] These institutions include the International Monetary Fund, the
World Bank, executive bodies like the World Trade Organization (founded
"to achieve greater coherence in global economic policy-making"), the
G-7 (an economic policy association of the seven richest nations), and trading
structures like NAFTA (the North American Free Trade Agreement) and
GATT (the General Agreement on Tariffs and Trade).[6]

The I.M.F., for example, is a secretive organization staffed by
unelected bureaucrats, largely unaccountable to the American taxpayers
whose $36 billion in annual funding helps underwrite its operations. "Fund

board meetings are closed, annual reviews of countries are sealed, and only an inner circle knows how much is available for loans," writes Jonathan Tasini in *They Get Cake, We Eat Crumbs: The Real Story Behind Today's Unfair Economy*.[7] Quietly funneling billions into the "underdeveloped" world, the I.M.F. claims to foster local growth; not incidentally, it also brings Third World nations to heel, taking the whip hand to anticapitalist, welfare-state tendencies and mustering new conscripts for the low-wage workforce required by the global economy.

"In return for loans, countries must undergo 'structural adjustment,'" notes Tasini. "This means government spending must be severely cut (leading to cuts in jobs and higher prices on basic necessities like milk and corn as government price supports decline); imports must be replaced with an export-oriented economy; wages are frozen; and many public enterprises are privatized. Obviously, this hurts hundreds of millions of citizens around the world. These severe austerity measures have caused massive unrest such as the 1987 bread riots in Zambia." Walden Bello, an economist critical of the I.M.F., notes that during recent I.M.F. negotiations with Thailand, Korea, and Indonesia, "All the deals were arranged behind closed doors with the bureaucrats. . . . There was no consultation with the public. And how can they say this is promoting prosperity? In Thailand, 800,000 people will be out of work. In Korea, they have what they call 'I.M.F. suicides,' when a laid-off worker kills himself and his family."[8]

If such developments, ominous as they are, seem reassuringly faraway, bear in mind that the global economy is frequently subject to a grim version of the Butterfly Effect, the parable used by chaos theoreticians to illustrate the notion that small disturbances can have grand-scale consequences: The beat of a butterfly's wings in Brazil could set off a tornado in Texas. The I.M.F.'s imposition of the "American model"—the laissez-faire macroeconomic theology of uncontrolled trade, deregulation of finance, and privatization of social services—is wreaking social and economic havoc on developing nations in both the third and first worlds. I.M.F. loan conditions mandate that countries establish export-processing zones; on the ground these often take the form of the infamous clusters of American-owned Mexican factories known as *maquiladoras*. In return for its infusions of cash, the I.M.F. stipulates that workers' wages be slowed or frozen. Low labor costs and lax or nonexistent workplace and environmental regulations attract multinational corporations, who shut down U.S. plants and ship jobs to these zones. Meanwhile, in the underdeveloped nation in question, starvation wages ensure a dwindling demand for U.S. imports. According to a 1994 report by the Institute for Policy Studies, U.S. exports declined in 33 of 54 countries funded by I.M.F. and World Bank loans, and 20,000 U.S. jobs have been lost *annually* as a result of I.M.F. and World Bank policies that encourage the relocation of American manufacturing to low-wage nations.[9] Your tax dollars at work.

What do all these number-crunching, balance-sheet calculations have to do with the system of government that Lincoln called our last, best hope? The answer is brutally simple: the murder of the democratic dream. Its obituary is written in the hot, dirt-streaked face of Honorina Ruiz, a six-year-old Mexican girl who rubber-bands onions into bunches from 5:30 A.M. until 4:00 P.M. for around three dollars a day. Her onions might end up on your dinner table, brought to you by Honorina's employer, the U.S. vegetable producer Muranaka Farms. The human cost of the "American model" is legible, too, in the faces of the teenage Mexican girls who work in the *maquiladoras* of Juarez from dawn till dusk, six days a week. They make about five dollars a day, and some of them go downtown after work to sell their bodies for money or food. Increasingly, they're ending up dead—kidnapped, raped, and murdered.

"Juarez is an example of the fabled New World Order in which capital moves easily and labor is trapped by borders," writes Charles Bowden in *Harper's*. "Real wages have been falling since the 1970s. And since wages are just a hair above starvation level, [*maquiladoras*] contribute practically nothing toward forging a consumer society. . . . [But] industry is thriving. . . . Labor is virtually limitless. . . . There are few environmental controls. . . . El Paso/Juarez is one of the most polluted spots in North America. And yet it is a success story. In Juarez, the economic growth in 1994 was 6 percent, and last year it registered 12 percent. . . . This is as good as it gets. With the passage of NAFTA, *narcotraficantes* began buying maquiladoras in Juarez. They didn't want to miss out on the advantages of free trade."[10] The New World Order of borderless, postnational capitalism is profoundly oligarchic and virulently antidemocratic, militating at home and abroad against progressive social policies and the health, welfare, and fundamental human rights of working people everywhere.

Yet another example: Although child labor is as illegal in Mexico as it is in the States, it is increasingly widespread there as a direct result of

NAFTA. "NAFTA helped create the economic crisis that brought on the peso's devaluation in December 1994," writes David Bacon, the associate editor of Pacific News Service. "The incomes of poor Mexicans have dropped by almost half, and the ensuing economic desperation brought new waves of children into the fields to supplement their parents' shrinking earnings."[11] According to one investigator, "the practice is growing under the impact of the country's successive economic crises and the rise in export-oriented agriculture. Joint ventures between Mexican and U.S. growers producing for the U.S., European and Japanese markets 'are achieving greater competitiveness at the cost of children working in the fields.'"[12] NAFTA and GATT have had a similar effect at a global level as well: The number of working children worldwide has spiraled to more than 200 million, the result of both trade agreements' regulatory, rather than prohibitive, approach to child labor.

Meanwhile, U.S. employers vociferously oppose ratification of international worker-protection accords advocated by the International Labor Organization. They do so in part, says Mark Anderson of the A.F.L.-C.I.O. task force on trade, because such accords might require changes in U.S. law that "would afford a more permanent protection for American workers than our own legislation."[13] In the global economy, the butterflies of chaos always come home to roost.

This is only one of numberless illustrations of what Noam Chomsky means when he says that the New World Order of global capitalism is "an effective blow against democracy." Its organizational structures "raise decision making to the executive level, leaving what's called a 'democratic deficit'—parliaments and populations with less influence."[14] The Stanford University economist Paul Krugman, hardly one to rally 'round the red flag for a hearty chorus of "The Internationale," has observed that "governments have consented to a regime that allows markets to boss them around."[15] Perhaps Walter Wriston, the former Citicorp chairman and the author of a gleeful obituary for the nation-state called The Twilight of Sovereignty, put it best when he remarked that "200,000 monitors in trading rooms all over the world" now conduct "a kind of global plebiscite on the monetary and fiscal policies of the governments issuing currency"—a plebiscite, he neglected to mention, of a tiny power elite. "There is no way for a nation to opt out," he observed, with unconcealed relish.[16]

In a supreme irony, the unchecked depredations of what Aleksandr Solzhenitsyn has called "savage capitalism" are sweeping aside the democratic nation-state itself, the very entity whose interventions—tax incentives, government subsidies, export credits, state-supported research, state-funded occupational training, legal protection from monopolistic practices—ensure healthy economies. Eric Hobsbawm invokes the article of Marxist faith that capitalism is a "permanent and revolutionizing force," radically transforming even those societal values and social relationships that nurtured it. The global capitalism whose Hobbesian logic leaves what Marx, in less feminist times, called "no other nexus between man and man than naked self-interest" will end, Hobsbawm prophesies, "by sawing off at least one of the branches on which it [sits]."[17] But there's little comfort in placing our hopes for democracy in Hobsbawm's apocalypse. For even if global capitalism does saw through the branch on which it sits, the elite may well be left unbruised and unbowed, while those without a financial safety net plummet into mass immiseration.

Hobsbawm also takes note of the "sociological puzzle" of the bourgeois society ushered in by capitalism, a society that sanctifies radical individualism in economic theory even as it demonizes radical individualism in personal behavior or morality. The seeming conundrum is easily solved, he contends, when one realizes that the "most effective way to build an industrial economy based on private enterprise was to combine it with motivations which had nothing to do with the logic of the free market—for instance, with the Protestant ethic; with abstention from immediate gratification; with the ethic of hard work; with family duty and trust; but certainly not the antinomian rebellion of individuals."[18]

As Coney's infernal carnival amply evidences, however, the Protestant work ethic and Puritan abstemiousness that ensure a tractable, reliable workforce are at odds with the consumer economy, whose wheels are greased by instant gratification and the seductive promise of a return to carefree adolescent, even infantile pleasures.

Nonetheless, the cultural chaos churned up by the titanic forces of postindustrialization and globalization is surrounded by vortices and eddies of social change. As I've argued throughout this book, some of these riptides are profoundly destructive, spinning off the large-scale turbulence of the information revolution and transnational capitalism to uproot the notions of the self, civic life, public space, social responsibility, and even reality that undergird our sense of the common good.

But others, as I've also pointed out, are cathartically deconstructive. Swirled into being by the "antinomian rebellion of individuals," subcultural rituals of resistance, and postwar social movements like feminism, multiculturalism, gay rights, and transgender activism, these social countercurrents are washing away the foundations of monolithic orthodoxies of gender, race, class, and sexual preference, one grain at a time. In countless small ways, they're challenging status-quo notions of who commands the media spotlight and who stands in the wings, whose explanations of the Way Things Are should be taken as holy writ and whose seen as satanic verses, what's normal and what's freakish, what's nature and what's culture, what we think about self and Other, individual and community, childhood and adulthood, sex and death, the here and the hereafter. Obviously, their culture-quakes are mere tremors compared to the earth-shaking shock waves of the New World Disorder of postindustrial, post-national capitalism, but they're heartening, even so.

On the cusp of the millennium, the only certainty seems to be that the Uncertainty Principle will be an ever-present fact of everyday life, metaphorically speaking, for the foreseeable future. In a final, ironic twist to the absurdist plot of the twentieth century, it seems clear, as the year 2000 looms, that the end times will never arrive. The literal fin-de-millennium will come and go in a calendric sense, but we'll never reach the apocalyptic exclamation point at the end of all this century's utopian daydreams and dystopian nightmares. Postmodernism means never having to say, "The End."

In the late eighties, the postmodern philosopher Jean Baudrillard moved that we vote to skip immediately to the year 2000 in order to put an end to the interminable waiting and move directly into postmillennial consciousness. But Steven Shaviro's argument that the millennium will never arrive because it has already arrived, or rather is always arriving, is more precisely tuned to the spirit of our age. "Postmodern" also means "post-apocalyptic," he contends. "The modernists proclaimed the millennium, finalities and absolutes of all sorts," he writes.

But today, as the literal millennium approaches, we are more likely to conceive the end of life as we know it as an everyday

and almost casual process, without a 'final conflict' or an impressive, stirring narrative climax. All through the Cold War,
we were waiting for an ultimate cataclysm, some all-consuming
event. But nothing is ever *really* over. There are more wars and
insecurities than ever before. . . . Now we must learn that history is always ending, so that in fact there is no end to history. . . . And so, we may say that the Apocalypse has already
happened; or better, that it is happening right now, continu-
ally and inconclusively, even as we speak.[19]

As that millennial visionary Sun Ra so memorably put it: "It's after
the end of the world! Don't you know that yet?"[20]

NOTES

A COMMENT ON SOURCES

All unattributed sources in this book are taken from interviews conducted by the author.

Introduction

1. Quoted without attribution in *Coney Island: A Documentary Film,* directed by Ric Burns.
2. Rem Koolhaas, *Delirious New York* (New York: Oxford University Press, 1978), p. 22.
3. Judith A. Adams, *The American Amusement Park Industry: A History of Technology and Thrills* (Boston: Twayne Publishers, 1991), p. 41.
4. Ibid., p. 53.
5. Senator John Kerry on *The MacNeil/Lehrer NewsHour,* April 27, 1995; Bill Moyers interviewed by Terry Gross on the NPR program *Fresh Air,* October 9, 1996; the Unabomber, "Industrial Society and Its Future," archived in "Topic 230: The Unabomber's Screed" in the "Weird" conference on the WELL, a Sausalito-based on-line service.
6. Christopher John Farley, "America's Bomb Culture," *Time,* May 8, 1995, p. 56.
7. James Gardner, *The Age of Extremism: The Enemies of Compromise in American Politics, Culture, and Race Relations* (New York: Birch Lane Press, 1997), pp. 13, 12.
8. Don DeLillo, *Underworld* (New York: Scribner, 1997), p. 76.
9. Michael R. Gordon, "A Whole New World of Arms Races to Contain," *The New York Times,* May 3, 1998, "Week in Review" section, p. 1.
10. Quoted in Mike Davis, *Beyond Blade Runner: Urban Control/The Ecology of Fear* (Westfield, N.J.: Open Media, 1992), p. 21.

272   Notes

11. William J. Broad and Judith Miller, "Germ Defense Plan in Peril As Its Flaws Are Revealed," *The New York Times,* August 7, 1998, "National" section, p. A16.

12. See Wendy Marston, "The Fungus Among Us," *The New York Times Magazine,* February 11, 1996, p. 43.

13. *Panic Encyclopedia,* ed. David Cook, Arthur Kroker, and Marilouise Kroker (New York: St. Martin's Press, 1989), p. 15.

14. Quoted in David Bennahum, "Mr. Big Idea," *New York,* November 13, 1995, p. 75.

15. Quoted in Jeff Zaleski, *The Soul of Cyberspace* (New York: HarperEdge, 1997), pp. 46, 48.

16. Quoted in Edwin Diamond and Stephen Bates, "VR, MUD, ROM, BOMFOG!" *The Nation,* February 5, 1996, p. 31.

17. *Popular Science Monthly* 61, no. 1 (1899), p. 72.

18. John F. Kasson, *Amusing the Million* (New York: Hill and Wang, 1978), p. 98.

19. Those who have read my earlier book, *Escape Velocity: Cyberculture at the End of the Century,* will recognize the roots of this argument—and indeed, this book—in the *Escape Velocity* chapter section "The Magic Kingdom and the Pyrotechnic Insanitarium."

20. Kasson, *Amusing the Million,* p. 42.

21. Ibid., p. 50.

22. Ibid., p. 59.

23. Koolhaas, *Delirious New York,* p. 55.

24. Kasson, *Amusing the Million,* p. 96.

25. Ibid., pp. 96–97; see also "Social Psychology and the Quest for the Public Mind," in Stuart Ewen, *PR!: A Social History of Spin* (New York: Basic Books, 1996).

26. Ewen, *PR!: A Social History of Spin,* p. 141.

27. Kasson, *Amusing the Million,* p. 96.

28. Quoted in Stuart Ewen, *All Consuming Images: The Politics of Style in Contemporary Culture* (New York: Basic Books, 1988), p. 25.

29. John Perry Barlow, "A Declaration of the Independence of Cyberspace," February 8, 1996, archived at www.eff.org/Publications/John_Perry_Barlow/barlow_0296.declaration.

30. Quoted in Burns, *Coney Island.*

31. Kasson, *Amusing the Million,* p. 112.

32. Carl Sagan, *The Demon-Haunted World: Science as a Candle in the Dark* (New York: Random House, 1995), p. 26.

33. "Fund for the Future" advertisement, *The Skeptical Inquirer,* July–August 1997, p. 10.

34. John A. McClure, "Postmodern Romance" in Frank Lentricchia, ed., *The Fiction of Don DeLillo*, vol. 89, no. 2 of *The South Atlantic Quarterly* (Durham, N.C.: Duke University Press, 1990), p. 341.

35. Umberto Eco, *Foucault's Pendulum* (New York: Harcourt Brace Jovanovich, 1989), p. 620.

36. Quotes from photocopied handout, "J.R. 'Bob' Dobbs: Big Brother-A-Go-Go."

37. Bill Barker, quoted in *The Happy Mutant Handbook*, ed. Mark Frauenfelder, Carla Sinclair, Gareth Branwyn, Will Kreth (New York: Riverhead Books, 1995), p. 150.

38. Schwa, *Schwa World Operations Manual* (San Francisco: Chronicle Books, 1997), unnumbered page.

39. David Cox, "Media Meltdown," *21.C,* issue no. 25, p. 56.

40. Charles McGrath, "It Just Looks Paranoid," *The New York Times Magazine,* June 14, 1998, p. 58.

41. James Sterngold, "'X-Files' Looks for the Room to Stretch Out," *The New York Times,* September 21, 1997, "Arts & Leisure" section, p. 9.

42. Ibid.

43. Herman Melville, *Moby-Dick, or The Whale* (New York: Vintage Books, 1991), p. 197.

44. Don DeLillo, *Running Dog* (New York: Alfred A. Knopf, 1978), p. 111.

45. Eco, *Foucault's Pendulum,* pp. 381, 467.

46. Richard Hofstadter, *The Paranoid Style in American Politics* (New York: Alfred A. Knopf, 1965), pp. 36–37.

47. Ron Rosenbaum, *Travels with Dr. Death and Other Unusual Investigations* (New York: Viking, 1991), pp. xiv.

48. Ibid., pp. 57–58.

49. Anthony DeCurtis, "'An Outsider in This Society': An Interview with Don DeLillo," in Lentricchia, *Fiction of Don DeLillo,* pp. 286, 291–92.

50. James Shelby Downard, "King-Kill/33: Masonic Symbolism in the Assassination of John F. Kennedy," in *Apocalypse Culture,* ed. Adam Parfrey (New York: Amok Press, 1987), pp. 239–40.

51. Ibid., p. 243. See also Jonathan Vankin and John Whalen, *The 60 Greatest Conspiracies of All Time* (Secaucus, N.J.: Citadel Press, 1996), pp. 206–210.

52. DeLillo, *Running Dog,* pp. 149–50.

53. See *The Daily Telegraph,* December 16, 1997, issue 936, at *www.telegraph. co.uk:80/.*

54. Robert Ellis Smith, "The True Terror Is in the Card," *The New York Times Magazine,* September 8, 1996, p. 59.

55. For more on the FBI's genetic databank, see Jeffrey Rothfeder, *Privacy for Sale: How Computerization Has Made Everyone's Private Life an Open Secret* (New York: Simon & Schuster, 1992), pp. 133–36.

56. For more on MK-ULTRA and remote viewing, see Vankin and Whalen, *The 60 Greatest Conspiracies of All Time,* pp. 3–10, 401–6.

57. Ibid., pp. 35–42, for more on germ warfare experiments.

58. Sven Birkerts, *American Energies: Essays on Fiction* (New York: William Morrow, 1992), p. 128.

59. Ibid.

60. Ibid., p. 136.

61. David Burnham, "The FBI," *The Nation,* August 11–18, 1997, pp. 11, 23.

62. Edward S. Herman and Noam Chomsky, *Manufacturing Consent: The Political Economy of the Mass Media* (New York: Pantheon Books, 1988), p. 2.

63. Ibid., p. 298.

64. See ibid., p. 17.

65. See Martin A. Lee and Norman Solomon, *Unreliable Sources: A Guide to Detecting Bias in News Media* (New York: Lyle Stuart, 1991), pp. 77–78.

66. See Stuart Ewen, *PR!: A Social History of Spin* (New York: Basic Books, 1996), pp. 28–29.

67. Herman and Chomsky, *Manufacturing Consent,* p. xii.

68. David Darlington, *Area 51: The Dreamland Chronicles—The Legend of America's Most Secret Military Base* (New York: Henry Holt, 1997), p. 32.

69. Kenneth S. Stern, *A Force Upon the Plain: The American Militia Movement and the Politics of Hate* (New York: Simon & Schuster, 1996), p. 13. The estimated numbers of militia members are also taken from Stern.

70. Robin Littleton, quoted in Elizabeth Gleick, "Something Big Is Going to Happen," *Time,* May 8, 1995, p. 52.

71. For details on militia beliefs, see Jill Smolowe, "Enemies of the State," *Time,* May 8, 1995, p. 62, and Gardner, *The Age of Extremism,* pp. 31–66.

72. For details on McVeigh's beliefs, see John Kifner, "Oklahoma Bombing Suspect: Unraveling of a Frayed Life," *The New York Times,* December 31, 1995, p. 1.

73. Ibid., p. 24.

74. James Ridgeway, "The Sting?" *The Village Voice,* April 23, 1996, p. 19.

75. James Ridgeway, "A Conspiratorial Gathering," *The Village Voice,* April 8, 1997, p. 33.

76. Joan Didion, *Slouching Towards Bethlehem* (New York: Dell, 1968), p. 161.

77. Hillel Schwartz, *Century's End: A Cultural History of the Fin-de-Siecle from the 990s Through the 1990s* (New York: Doubleday, 1990), pp. 12–13.

78. Ibid., p. 9.

79. Ibid., p. 12.

80. Hayes B. Jacobs, "Warning: New Century Ahead," *The New Yorker,* April 27, 1963, p. 142.

81. Schwartz, *Century's End,* p. 12.

82. Ibid., pp. 11, 239.

83. Eric Hobsbawm, *The Age of Extremes: A History of the World, 1914–1991* (New York: Vintage Books, 1996), p. 13.

84. Ibid., p. 6.

85. Ibid., p. 403.

86. Ibid., p. 8.

87. Ibid., p. 10.

88. Ibid., p. 11.

89. David Corn, "Tribes and Tariffs," *The Nation,* May 25, 1998, p. 25.

90. See Louis Uchitelle, "More Downsized Workers Are Returning as Rentals," *The New York Times,* December 8, 1996, pp. 1, 34.

91. *McJob,* issue no. 4, p. 11.

92. "Approximately 50 million Americans," unbylined editorial, "Underground Economy," *The Nation,* January 12–19, 1998, p. 3.

93. For statistics on executive pay, see Adam Bryant, "Flying High on the Option Express," *The New York Times,* "Business" section, p. 1; income concentration and investment income, see Robert L. Borosage, "Suckering the Poor," *The Nation,* December 30, 1996, p. 24.

94. See Louis Uchitelle, "As Taste for Comfort Rises, So Do Corporations' Profits," *The New York Times,* September 14, 1997, p. 34.

95. Jonathan Tasini, *They Get Cake, We Eat Crumbs: The Real Story Behind Today's Unfair Economy* (Washington, D.C.: Preamble Center, 1998), p. 15.

96. Carl Jensen and Project Censored, *Censored: The News That Didn't Make the News—and Why* (New York: Seven Stories Press, 1996), p. 141.

97. Robert Reich, "Secession of the Successful," *The New York Times,* January 20, 1991, p. 16.

98. Hobsbawm, *The Age of Extremes,* p. 581.

99. James (Bo) Gritz, quoted in Carey Goldberg, "The Freemen Sought Refuge in an Ideology That Kept the Law, and Reality, at Bay," *The New York Times,* "National" section, June 16, 1996, p. 14.

100. Richard Lacayo, "A Moment of Silence," *Time,* May 8, 1995, p. 46.

101. Hobsbawm, *The Age of Extremes,* p. 584.

102. J. G. Ballard, "Introduction to the French Edition," *Crash* (New York: Vintage Books, 1985), pp. 4–5.

103. Ibid., p. 1.

104. Quoted in John Leonard, "Culture Watch: Alien Nation," *The Nation,* June 15–22, 1998, pp. 25–26.

105. Constance Jones, *1001 Things Everyone Should Know About Women's History* (New York: Doubleday, 1998), p. 265.

106. Mark Jurkowitz, "Scared Witless," *Media Culture Review* 3, no. 3 (Summer 1994), p. 15.
107. Quoted in Jurkowitz, "Scared Witless," p. 16.
108. Excerpt from unpublished 1989 interview with the author.
109. Kasson, *Amusing the Million,* p. 95.
110. Patricia Leigh Brown, "Techno-Dwellings for the Cyber-Egos of the Mega-Rich," *The New York Times,* August 4, 1996, p. 39.
111. Ralph Rugoff, *Circus Americanus* (New York: Verso, 1995), p. 6.

A User's Guide to *The Pyrotechnic Insanitarium*

1. Quoted in McKenzie Wark, *The Virtual Republic: Australia's Culture Wars of the 1990s* (St. Leonards, Australia: Allen & Unwin, 1997), p. 3.
2. Gilles Deleuze and Felix Guattari, *A Thousand Plateaus* (Minneapolis: University of Minnesota Press, 1987), p. 7.
3. Sadie Plant, *Zeros + Ones: Digital Women + the New Technoculture* (New York: Doubleday, 1997), p. 10.
4. Gregory Bateson, *Mind and Nature: A Necessary Unity* (New York: Bantam Books, 1988), p. 105.
5. Marshall McLuhan and Quentin Fiore, *The Medium Is the Message: An Inventory of Effects* (New York: Bantam Books, 1967), unnumbered page.
6. Michel Foucault, *The Archeology of Knowledge* (London: Tavistock Publications, 1978), p. 23.

Have an Angst Day: The *Scream* Meme

1. Quoted in John Leonard, "Culture Watch: Alien Nation," *The Nation,* June 15–22, 1998, p. 23.
2. Simon Reynolds, *Generation Ecstasy: Into the World of Techno and Rave Culture* (New York: Little, Brown, 1998), p. 86.
3. Richard Dawkins, *The Selfish Gene* (Oxford: Oxford University Press, 1989), p. 192.
4. Robert Reich, "The Fracturing of the Middle Class," *The New York Times,* August 31, 1994, section A, p. 19.
5. Stanley B. Greenberg, *Middle Class Dreams: The Politics and Power of the New American Majority* (New York: Times Books, 1995), p. 165.

6. D. Keith Mano, "Thy Neighbor's Job," *The New York Times Book Review,* June 29, 1997, p. 17.

7. Marshall McLuhan and Quentin Fiore, *The Medium is the Massage: An Inventory of Effects* (New York: Bantam Books, 1967), unnumbered page.

8. Fredric Jameson, *Postmodernism, or The Cultural Logic of Late Capitalism* (Durham, N.C.: Duke University Press, 1991), p. 14.

9. Quoted in Bertrand Russell, *A History of Western Philosophy* (New York: Touchstone, 1945), p. 662.

10. Sherry Turkle, "Who Am We?" *Wired,* January, 1996, pp. 194–95.

11. Ibid., p. 198.

12. Mary S. Glucksman, "The Dark Side of the Boom," *Omni,* April 1991, p. 78.

13. Statistics from William A. Council, "Introduction to Telecommuting," archived at www.networx.com/au/mall/secrets/articles/telearts.htm Intro.

14. Ibid.

15. Mark Kingwell, *Dreams of Millennium: Report from a Culture on the Brink* (Boston: Faber and Faber, 1996), pp. 161–62.

16. David Denby, "The Moviegoers," *The New Yorker,* April 6, 1998, p. 97.

17. Ibid., p. 98.

18. Quoted in Stuart Ewen, *All Consuming Images: The Politics of Style in Contemporary Culture* (New York: Basic Books, 1988), p. 25.

19. Denby, "The Moviegoers," p. 97.

20. Jameson, *Postmodernism,* pp. 15–16.

21. J. G. Ballard, "Introduction to the French Edition," *Crash* (New York: Vintage Books, 1985), p. 5.

22. Quoted in Steven Shaviro, *Doom Patrols: A Theoretical Fiction About Postmodernism* (New York: Serpent's Tail, 1997), p. 34.

23. Jameson, *Postmodernism,* p. 34.

24. Quoted in Reinhold Heller, *Munch: His Life and Work* (Chicago: University of Chicago Press, 1984), p. 105.

25. Walter Benjamin, *Illuminations* (New York: Schocken Books, 1968), p. 242.

26. Kingwell, *Dreams of Millennium,* p. 161.

27. Mark Crispin Miller, *Boxed In: The Culture of TV* (Evanston, Ill.: Northwestern University Press: 1989), p. 14.

28. Shaviro, *Doom Patrols,* p. 2.

29. *Panic Encyclopedia,* ed. David Cook, Arthur Kroker, and Marilouise Kroker (New York: St. Martin's Press, 1989), p. 14.

30. *The Postmodern Scene: Excremental Culture and Hyper-Aesthetics,* ed. Arthur Kroker and David Cook (New York: St. Martin's Press, 1991), p. i.

Cotton Candy Autopsy: Deconstructing
Psycho-Killer Clowns

1. Ruth G. Davis, "Bring Me the Head of Ronald McDonald," *New York*, January 5, 1994, p. 22.
2. Bruce Feiler, "Bedtime for Bozo," *The New York Times*, October 27, 1996, section 6, p. 80.
3. Chris O'Flaherty, "Clown! Killer," *Film Threat Video Guide*, no. 8, p. 75.
4. All quotes from "Stories from You," archived on "Clowns Are Evil Incarnate: The Anti-Clown Website," at www.geocities.com/Colosseum/2430/clown.html.
5. "Topic 557: Clowns Suck," in the WELL's "GenX" conference, June 19, 1994, busy or unstable (mykej) and mark (mark).
6. Ibid., June 18, 1994, Holly GoDensely (marybeth).
7. Ibid., Julia Davy (punque).
8. Kaz, *Sidetrack City and Other Tales* (Seattle: Fantagraphics, 1996), p. 14.
9. Stephen King, *It* (New York: Viking Penguin, 1986), p. 13.
10. John Kifner, "Gacy, Killer of 33, Is Put to Death as Appeals Fail," *The New York Times*, May 11, 1994, p. A19.
11. Clifford L. Linedecker, *The Man Who Killed Boys* (New York: St. Martin's, 1980), p. 173.
12. Tim Cahill, *Buried Dreams: Inside the Mind of a Serial Killer* (New York: Bantam Books, 1986), p. 300.
13. Quoted by Robert Ressler, profiler of serial killers, in "Mind Hunters," an episode of the Discovery Channel program *The New Detectives: Case Studies in Forensic Science*, April 22, 1997.
14. Jim Knipfel, "Twilight of the Clowns: Big Shoes and a Black Heart," *New York Press*, May 11–17, 1994, p. 18.
15. "Clowns Suck," June 16, 1994, Ken Knutson (kdk); Knipfel, "Twilight of the Clowns," p. 18.
16. Ibid., June 18, 1994, Je Suis Un . . . Un . . . Un . . . CLOWN! (kafclown).
17. Phil Snyder, "Exorcising Shameful Visions," *Eyewash* magazine, issue no. 5, 1993, unnumbered page. *Eyewash* is available from Cyclone Publications, P.O.B. 20013, Dayton, OH 45420-0013.
18. Knipfel, "Twilight of the Clowns," p. 18.
19. Cahill, *Buried Dreams*, p. 159.
20. William Willeford, *The Fool and His Scepter: A Study in Clowns and Jesters and Their Audience* (Evanston, Ill.: Northwestern University Press, 1969), p. 89.
21. Phil Snyder, "Exorcising Shameful Visions."

22. Knipfel, "Twilight of the Clowns," p. 20.

23. Willeford, *The Fool and His Scepter,* pp. 13–14.

24. Randy Newman, *Randy Newman* (Reprise, 1968).

25. J. E. Cirlot, *A Dictionary of Symbols* (New York: Dorset Press, 1971), pp. 111, 162.

26. Frank Rich, "Send in the Clowns," *The New York Times,* January 22, 1995, section 4, p. 15.

27. Jennifer Steinhauer, "'I Want a Movie After I Kill Everyone,'" *The New York Times,* March 5, 1995, "National Report" section, p. 12.

28. Quoted in Marshall Blonsky, *American Mythologies* (New York: Oxford University Press, 1992), p. 348.

29. James B. Twitchell, *Carnival Culture: The Trashing of Taste in America* (New York: Columbia University Press, 1992), p. 6.

30. Graham Fuller, "Quentin Tarantino: Answers First, Questions Later," introduction to Quentin Tarantino, *Reservoir Dogs and True Romance: Screenplays by Quentin Tarantino* (New York: Grove Press, 1994), pp. xiv–xv.

31. Anthony Lane, "Trick and Treat: Can We Still Be Scared of 'Halloween'?" *The New Yorker,* August 10, 1998, p. 79.

32. Ralph Rugoff, *Circus Americanus* (New York: Verso, 1995), p. 147.

33. Jane Kuenz, "It's a Small World After All: Disney and the Pleasures of Identification," in Susan Willis, ed., *The World According to Disney*, vol. 92, no. 1, of *The South Atlantic Quarterly* (Durham, N.C.: Duke University Press, 1993), p. 71.

34. John F. Kasson, *Amusing the Million* (New York: Hill and Wang, 1978), p. 57.

35. Asswipe the Clown, "Bad Clowns," *Twisted Times,* Winter 1994, pp. 13–17.

36. Jac Zinder, "The Cacophony Society's Carnival of the Absurd," *The L.A. Weekly,* July 29–August 4, 1994, p. 17.

37. Fredric Jameson, *Postmodernism, or The Cultural Logic of Late Capitalism* (Durham, N.C.: Duke University Press, 1991), p. 413.

38. Gilles Deleuze and Felix Guattari, *Anti Oedipus: Capitalism and Schizophrenia* (New York: Viking Press, 1977), p. 15.

39. Alan Moore and Brian Bolland, *Batman: The Killing Joke* (New York: DC Comics, 1988), unpaginated.

40. Camille Bacon-Smith with Tyrone Yarbrough, "Batman: The Ethnography" in Roberta E. Pearson and William Uricchio, eds., *The Many Lives of the Batman: Critical Approaches to a Superhero and His Media* (New York: Routledge, 1991), p. 106.

41. Christopher Sharrett, "Batman and the Twilight of the Idols: An Interview with Frank Miller," in Pearson and Ulricchio, *The Many Lives of the Batman,* p. 44.

42. Cirlot, *A Dictionary of Symbols,* p. 51.

43. Grant Morrison and Dave McKean, *Arkham Asylum* (New York: DC Comics, 1989), unnumbered page.

Return to Abnormalcy: Freaks, Gaffes, and Geeks at the Fin-de-Millennium

1. Letter-writer quoted in Rachel Adams, "An American Tail: Freaks, Gender, and the Incorporation of History in Katherine Dunn's *Geek Love,*" in Rosemarie Garland Thompson, ed., *Freakery: Cultural Spectacles of the Extraordinary Body* (New York: New York University Press, 1996), p. 283; Donna J. Haraway, *Simians, Cyborgs, and Women: The Reinvention of Nature* (New York: Routledge, 1991), p. 150.

2. Leslie Fiedler, *Freaks: Myths and Images of the Secret Self* (New York: Simon and Schuster, 1978), p. 14.

3. George L. Hersey, *The Evolution of Allure: Sexual Selection from the Medici Venus to the Incredible Hulk* (Cambridge, Mass.: MIT Press, 1996), p. 169.

4. Ibid., pp. 174–75.

5. *Star,* September 19, 1988.

6. David D. Yuan, "The Celebrity Freak: Michael Jackson's 'Grotesque Glory,'" in Thompson, *Freakery,* p. 372.

7. Ibid., p. 370.

8. Ibid., p. 372.

9. Hersey, *The Evolution of Allure,* p. 166.

10. Dan Barry, "The Hidden Aspects of Showy Muscles," *The New York Times,* "Metro" section, December 21, 1996, p. 28.

11. Elizabeth Haiken, *Venus Envy: A History of Cosmetic Surgery* (Baltimore: Johns Hopkins University Press, 1997), p. 274.

12. Wendy Whoppers, "All About Me," archived at www.wendy-whoppers.com.

13. Ian Grey, *Sex, Stupidity, and Greed: Inside the American Movie Industry* (New York: Juno Books, 1997), p. 148.

14. James B. Twitchell, *Carnival Culture: The Trashing of Taste in America* (New York: Columbia University Press, 1992), pp. 2–3.

15. Ibid., p. 238.

16. Ibid., p. 240.

17. Joshua Gamson, *Freaks Talk Back: Tabloid Talk Shows and Sexual Nonconformity* (Chicago: University of Chicago Press, 1998), p. 3.

18. Maureen Dowd, "Talk Is Cheap," *The New York Times,* October 26, 1995, "Op-Ed" section, p. A25.

19. William Neuman, "Secret Sharers: Talk-Show Guests Reveal All," *Elle,* June 1993, p. 60.

20. David Skal, *The Monster Show: A Cultural History of Horror* (New York: Penguin Books, 1993), p. 384.

21. Figure cited in Richard Goldstein, "The Devil in Ms. Jones: Trash TV and the Discourse of Desire," *Village Voice,* November 21, 1995, p. 45. See also Jane M. Shattuc, *The Talking Cure* (New York: Routledge, 1997), pp. 11–12.

22. Ellen Willis, "Bring in the Noise," *The Nation,* April 1, 1996, pp. 22–23.

23. Donna Gaines, "How Jenny Jones Saved My Life," *Village Voice,* November 21, 1995, p. 43.

24. Gamson, *Freaks Talk Back,* pp. 59–60, 65.

25. Howard Kurtz, *Hot Air: All Talk, All the Time* (New York: Times Books, 1996), p. 201.

26. Ibid., p. 50.

27. Vito Russo, *The Celluloid Closet: Homosexuality in the Movies* (New York: Harper and Row, 1987), p. 78.

28. Gamson, *Freaks Talk Back,* p. 21.

29. All quotes from Goldstein, "The Devil in Ms. Jones," pp. 44–45.

30. Deb Schwartz, "Who Really Killed Scott Amedure, and Why Are Journalists Protecting Him?" *Village Voice,* March 28, 1995, p. 21.

31. Kurtz, *Hot Air,* p. 263.

32. Ibid., p. 266.

33. Demographic statistics from Goldstein, "The Devil in Ms. Jones," p. 45.

34. Gamson, *Freaks Talk Back,* p. 6.

35. Andrea Stulman Dennett, "The Dime Museum Freak Show Reconfigured as Talk Show," in Thompson, *Freakery,* p. 315.

36. Gamson, *Freaks Talk Back,* p. 4.

37. Jerry Springer viewer statistics from Erik Hedegaard, "This Show Is Good for America," *Rolling Stone,* May 14, 1998, p. 43.

38. Eric Alterman, *Sound and Fury: The Washington Punditocracy and the Collapse of American Politics* (New York: HarperCollins, 1992), p. 107.

39. Sadie Plant, *Zeros + Ones: Digital Women + The New Technoculture* (New York: Doubleday, 1997), p. 43.

40. See Michel Marriott, "Multiracial Americans Ready to Claim Their Own Identity," *The New York Times,* July 20, 1996, p. 7.

41. Robert Bogdan, "The Social Construction of Freaks," in Thompson, *Freakery*, p. 24.
42. Pamela Ditchoff, *The Mirror of Monsters and Prodigies* (Minneapolis: Coffee House Press, 1995), unnumbered page.

Anus Horribilis

1. Georges Bataille, "The Notion of Expenditure," in George Bataille, *Visions of Excess: Selected Writings, 1927–1939,* ed. Allan Stoekl (Minneapolis: University of Minnesota Press, 1985), p. 125.
2. Georges Bataille, *The Absence of Myth: Writings on Surrealism,* ed. Michael Richardson (New York: Verso, 1994), p. 142.
3. Julia Kristeva, *Powers of Horror: An Essay on Abjection* (New York: Columbia University Press, 1982), p. 71.
4. Bataille, *The Absence of Myth,* p. 97.
5. Georges Bataille, "The Jesuve," in Bataille, *Visions of Excess,* p. 78.
6. Ibid., p. 74.
7. Allan Stoekl, "Introduction" to Bataille, *Visions of Excess,* p. xii.
8. Bataille, "The Jesuve," p. 77.
9. William S. Burroughs, *Naked Lunch* (New York: Grove Press, 1966), p. 132.
10. Ibid., p. xxv.
11. Mikhail Bakhtin, *Rabelais and His World* (Bloomington, Ind.: Indiana University Press, 1984), p. 18.
12. David Hochman, "Gross Encounters," *Entertainment Weekly,* July 31, 1998, p. 25.
13. Lawrie Mifflin, "TV Stretches Limits of Taste, to Little Outcry," *The New York Times,* April 6, 1998, p. 1.
14. Hal Foster, *The Return of the Real* (Cambridge, Mass.: MIT Press, 1996), p. 160.
15. Patti Smith, *Babel* (New York: G. P. Putnam's Sons, 1978), p. 140.
16. Dave Stewart, "We're Just Lonely, Miserable, Terrified People," *GQ,* September 1995, p. 27.
17. Cited in David Humphrey, "The Abject Romance of Low Resolution," *The Abject, America* 1, no. 4, p. 156.
18. James Gardner, *Culture or Trash?: A Provocative View of Contemporary Painting, Sculpture, and Other Costly Commodieies* (New York: Birch Lane Press, 1993), p. 195.
19. Kurt Andersen, "Blunt Trauma," *The New Yorker,* March 30, 1998, p. 14.
20. Dana Kennedy, "King of the Jungle," *Entertainment Weekly,* November 10, 1995, p. 22.

21. Bakhtin, *Rabelais and His World,* p. 10.

22. Ibid., p. 373.

23. Benjamin Svetkey, "Jenny on the Spot," *Entertainment Weekly,* October 10, 1997, p. 30.

24. Statistics on the teenage buying public taken from Michiko Kakutani, "Adolescence Rules!" *The New York Times Magazine,* May 11, 1997, p. 22.

25. Quoted in Paul Spinrad, ed., *The Re/Search Guide to Bodily Fluids* (San Francisco: Re/Search Publications, 1994), p. 7.

26. Quoted in Stuart Ewen, *All Consuming Images: The Politics of Style in Contemporary Culture* (New York: Basic Books, 1988), pp. 244–45.

27. Ralph Rugoff, *Circus Americanus* (New York: Verso, 1995), p. 53.

28. Hochman, "Gross Encounters," p. 30.

29. Bakhtin, *Rabelais and His World,* p. 370.

30. Quoted in Humphrey, "The Abject Romance of Low Resolution," p. 156.

31. Stoekl, "Introduction" to Bataille, *Visions of Excess,* p. xiii.

Mad Cows and Englishmen:
Reading Damien Hirst's Entrails

1. Stuart Morgan, "An Interview with Damien Hirst," *No Sense of Absolute Corruption* (New York: Gagosian Gallery, 1996), p. 27.

2. Susan Willis, "Disney World: Public Use/Private State," in Susan Willis, ed., *The World According to Disney,* vol. 92, no. 1 of *The South Atlantic Quarterly* (Durham, N.C.: Duke University Press, 1993), p. 123.

3. See *Re/Search #11: Pranks!,* ed. Andrea Juno and V. Vale (San Francisco: Re/Search Publications, 1987), pp. 144–49.

4. Allan Ludwig, "4 × 6 Drug Store Prints in Glorious Color: 1993–1998," March 1998 press release.

5. Statistics on salmonella deaths and illness from Marian Burros, "Sweeping Changes Set for System of Meat and Poultry Inspection," *The New York Times,* March 14, 1996, "National Desk" section, p. 21; for more on red meat as most frequent cause of deadly epidemics, see Gina Kolata, "Irradiating Red Meat Approved as Means to Kill Deadly Germs," *The New York Times,* December 3, 1997, p. 1.

6. Richard Preston, *The Hot Zone* (New York: Anchor Books, 1995), p. 16.

7. Richard Dawkins, *The Selfish Gene* (Oxford: Oxford University Press, 1989), p. 192.

8. Colin Harrison, "A Hotter Zone," *The New York Times Book Review,* November 2, 1997, p. 11.

9. See "Herd Journalism," unbylined item in *The New York Times,* April 7, 1996, "Week in Review" section, p. 2.

10. C. J. Peters, *Virus Hunter: Thirty Years of Battling Hot Viruses Around the World* (New York: Anchor Books, 1997), pp. 114, 15.

11. Ibid., p. 23.

12. Preston, *The Hot Zone,* p. 85.

13. Joanne Reynolds, "Beef, Beef, Everywhere, but Hardly a Nibble to Eat," *The New York Times,* April 24, 1996, "Living Desk" section, p. 8.

14. Richard Rhodes, "Pathological Science," *The New Yorker,* December 1, 1997, p. 55.

15. Oliver Sacks, "Eat, Drink, and Be Wary," *The New Yorker,* April 14, 1997, p. 83.

16. Quoted in John Darnton, "The Logic of the 'Mad Cow' Scare," *The New York Times,* March 31, 1996, "Week in Review" section, March 31, 1996, p. 1.

17. Quoted in Marshall McLuhan, *The Mechanical Bride: Folklore of Industrial Man* (Boston: Beacon Press, 1951), p. 130.

18. Lance Morrow, "Parental Guidance Suggested," *Time,* April 22, 1996, p. 41.

19. Donna Haraway, *Simians, Cyborgs, and Women: The Reinvention of Nature* (New York: Routledge, 1991), p. 154.

20. Ibid., p. 151.

21. Preston, *The Hot Zone,* p. 411.

Mysteries of the Organism: *The Operation*

1. Quoted in *Re/Search #8–9: J. G. Ballard,* ed. V. Vale and Andrea Juno (San Francisco: Re/Search Publishing, 1984), p. 157.

Nature Morte: Formaldehyde Photography and the New Grotesque

1. Lawrence Weschler, *Mr. Wilson's Cabinet of Wonder* (New York: Pantheon Books, 1995). See pp. 90, 126.

2. Rosemarie Garland Thompson, "From Wonder to Error: A Genealogy of Freak Discourse in Modernity," introduction to Rosemarie Garland

Thompson, ed., *Freakery: Cultural Spectacles of the Extraordinary Body* (New York: New York University Press, 1996), p. 3.

3. Brooks Adams, "Grotesque Photography," *The Print Collector's Newsletter* 21, no. 6 (January–February 1991), p. 206.

4. Quoted in Rosamond Wolff Purcell and Stephen Jay Gould, *Finders, Keepers: Eight Collectors* (New York: W. W. Norton, 1992), p. 30.

5. Ibid., p. 25.

6. Umberto Eco, *Travels in Hyperreality* (New York: Harcourt Brace Jovanovich, 1986), p. 5.

7. Londa Schiebinger, *Nature's Body: Gender in the Making of Modern Science* (Boston: Beacon Press, 1993), p. 3.

8. Rosamond Purcell, essay for the catalogue of the exhibition "Special Cases: Natural Anomalies and Historical Monsters," September 24–January 6, 1994, Getty Center for the History of Art and the Humanities,.

9. Purcell and Gould, *Finders, Keepers,* p. 145.

10. Emily Dickinson, *Final Harvest* (Boston: Little, Brown and Company, 1961), p. 43.

11. Gwen Akin and Allan Ludwig, untitled catalogue essay, *Un Regard Autre* (New York: Farideh Cadot Gallery, 1987).

12. Quoted in *Grotesque: Natural Historical and Formaldehyde Photography* (Amsterdam: Fragment Uitgeverij, 1989), p. 15.

13. Ibid., p. 11.

14. Quoted in Weschler, *Mr. Wilson's Cabinet of Wonder* (New York: Pantheon Books, 1995), pp. 136–38.

15. Julia Kristeva, *Powers of Horror: An Essay on Abjection* (New York: Columbia University Press, 1982), pp. 3–4.

16. Wolfgang Kayser, *The Grotesque in Art and Literature* (New York: McGraw-Hill, 1966), p. 11.

17. Ibid., p. 185.

18. Ibid.

19. Ibid., p. 33.

20. Ibid., p. 183.

21. Geoffrey Galt Harpham, *On the Grotesque: Strategies of Contradiction in Art and Literature* (Princeton, N.J.: Princeton University Press, 1982), p. xix.

22. Kayser, *The Grotesque in Art and Literature,* p. 188.

23. Rosamond Purcell, *Special Cases: Natural Anomalies and Historical Monsters* (San Francisco: Chronicle Books, 1997), p. 94.

24. Jessica Mitford, *The American Way of Death* (New York: Fawcett Crest, 1978), p. 75.

25. *Morning Edition,* NPR, December 16, 1996.
26. C. J. Peters, *Virus Hunter: Thirty Years of Battling Hot Viruses Around the World* (New York: Anchor Books, 1997), p. 52.

Past Perfect: Disney Celebrates Us Home

1. Amy Wallace, "Like It's So L.A.! Not Really," *The Los Angeles Times,* February 29, 1992, p. A22.
2. Ibid., p. A23.
3. Eric Hobsbawm, *The Age of Extremes: A History of the World, 1914–1991* (New York: Vintage Books, 1996), p. 11.
4. Since I'm paraphrasing, not quoting, I haven't asked Kelly for permission to quote, as on-line etiquette dictates. The original post is #5 in Topic 79, "Is Disneyland a place to live?" in the WELL's "Futures" conference.
5. Quoted in Thomas Frank, "Twentieth Century Lite," *The Baffler,* no. 7, p. 6.
6. Esther Dyson, *Release 2.0* (New York: Broadway Books, 1997), p. 32.
7. Quoted in Guy Trebay, "Dirty Boulevard," *Village Voice,* July 18, 1995, p. 18.
8. Stephen Jay Gould, "Curveball" in Steven Fraser, ed., *The Bell Curve Wars: Race, Intelligence, and the Future of America* (New York: Basic Books, 1995), p. 21.
9. Greil Marcus, *Lipstick Traces: A Secret History of the Twentieth Century* (Cambridge, Mass.: Harvard University Press, 1989), p. 173.
10. Trebay, "Dirty Boulevard."
11. Ibid.
12. Quoted in Eric Nee, "(It's) Get Real-Time," *Upside,* October 1997, p. 148.
13. Lynette Lamb, "Show Biz Shopping," *Utne Reader,* March–April 1995, p. 32.
14. Ralph Rugoff, *Circus Americanus* (New York: Verso, 1995), p. xi.
15. *Utne Reader,* July–August, 1997, p. 49.
16. All "promotional brochure" quotes are from the guidebook *Downtown Celebration: Architectural Walking Tour,* text by Beth Dunlop, © Disney, 1996.
17. Neal Stephenson, *Snow Crash* (New York: Bantam, 1992), p. 29.
18. Russ Rymer, "Back to the Future: Disney Reinvents the Company Town," *Harper's Magazine,* October 1996, p. 71.
19. Ibid.
20. Quoted in Alan Bryman, *Walt Disney and His Worlds* (London and New York: Routledge, 1995), p. 14.
21. Ibid., p. 146.

22. Quoted in Rymer, "Back to the Future," p. 68.
23. Rhoda Koenig, "Happy All the Time," *New York,* April 15, 1991, p. 70.
24. Rymer, "Back to the Future," p. 76.
25. Quoted in ibid., p. 76.
26. Quoted in ibid., p. 65.
27. Ibid., p. 75.
28. Bryman, *Walt Disney and His Worlds,* p. 14.
29. Richard Schickel, *The Disney Version* (New York: Avon Books, 1969), p. 131.
30. Jamie Malanowski, "When Disney Ran America: A Speculative History of the Near Future," *Spy,* June 1991, p. 43.

Trendspotting: I Shop, Therefore I Am

1. Noah Adams, "Tattooed Ears Cause Teen Craze," *All Things Considered,* NPR, April 1, 1994.
2. "Nike's Tattooed Ekins," unbylined item in *The New York Times Magazine,* May 22, 1994, p. 15.
3. Leslie Savan, *The Sponsored Life: Ads, TV, and American Culture* (Philadelphia: Temple University Press, 1994), pp. 9, 177.
4. Randall Lane, "You Are What You Wear," *Forbes 400,* October 14, 1996, p. 45.
5. Bob Herbert, "In America, Trampled Dreams," *The New York Times,* July 12, 1996, "Editorial Desk" section, p. 27.
6. Eyal Press, "Moore vs. Nike," *The Nation,* May 25, 1998, p. 5.
7. "Nothing to Lose, Except Your Job," unbylined item in *Solidarity,* November, 1996, p. 27.
8. Donald Katz, "Triumph of the Swoosh," *Sports Illustrated,* August 16, 1993, pp. 58, 63. "Power brand survey" statistics from same article, p. 57.
9. Ibid., p. 63.
10. Donald Katz, *Just Do It: The Nike Spirit in the Corporate World* (New York: Random House, 1994), p. 88.
11. Quoted in the video documentary *Cyberpunk,* by Peter von Brandenburg and Marianne Schaefer-Trench.
12. See Steven Kotler, "The Kingdom of José Cuervo," *Wired,* January 1997, archived at www.wired.com/archive/5.01/scans.html.
13. Evan McKenzie, "Trouble in Privatopia," *The Progressive,* October 1993, p. 30.
14. Neal Stephenson, *Snow Crash* (New York: Bantam, 1992), p. 6.

Grim Fairy Tales: Renée French's Kinderculture

1. Shirley R. Steinberg and Joe L. Kincheloe, "Kinderculture, Information Saturation, and Postmodern Childhood" in Steinberg and Kincheloe, eds., *Kinderculture: The Corporate Construction of Childhood* (Boulder: Westview Press, 1997), p. 6.
2. David Edelstein, "Kitsch and Tell," *Village Voice Film Supplement,* June 30, 1987, p. 20.
3. Pauline Kael, *For Keeps: 30 Years at the Movies* (New York: Dutton, 1994), p. 1114.
4. William Golding, *Lord of the Flies* (New York: Perigree, 1954), p. 143.
5. Ralph Rugoff, "Dirty Toys," *XX Century*, Winter 1991–92, p. 86.
6. Quoted in Lawrence Sutin, *Divine Invasions: A Life of Philip K. Dick* (New York: Harmony Books, 1989), p. 24.
7. The Gallery of Dolls catalogue, vol. 2, p. 6.
8. Tom Engelhardt, "The Shortcake Strategy" in Todd Gitlin, ed., *Watching Television* (New York: Pantheon Books, 1986), p. 110.

The *Unheimlich* Maneuver: *The Doll Hour*

1. Umberto Eco, *Travels in Hyperreality* (New York: Harcourt Brace Jovanovich, 1986), p. 7.
2. Jessica Mitford, *The American Way of Death* (New York: Fawcett Crest, 1979), p. 75.
3. Sigmund Freud, "The Uncanny," *On Creativity and the Unconscious* (New York: Harper & Row, 1958) p. 141.

Empathy Bellies

1. Quoted in an Associated Press story archived at www.abcnews.com/sections/science/DailyNews/dolly 980423.html.
2. Gina Kolata, "Proposal for Human Cloning Draws Dismay and Disbelief," *The New York Times,* January 8, 1998, "National" section, p. A22; David Bromwich, "Experience Can't Be Cloned," *The New York Times,* January 11, 1998, "Op-Ed" section, p. 19.

3. Gerda Lerner, *The Creation of Feminist Consciousness: From the Middle Ages to Eighteen-Seventy* (New York: Oxford University Press, 1993), p. 212.

4. Mary Shelley, "Introduction" to *Frankenstein* (New York: Oxford, 1990), p. 9.

5. Anne K. Mellor, *Mary Shelley: Her Life, Her Fiction, Her Monsters* (New York: Routledge, 1989), p. 122.

6. Shelley, "Introduction," p. 165.

7. Northrop Frye, *The Great Code: The Bible and Literature* (New York: Harcourt Brace Jovanovich, 1982), p. 107.

8. John Pinsent, *Greek Mythology* (New York: Peter Bedrick Books, 1991), p. 25.

9. F. Gonzalez-Crussi, *Suspended Animation: Six Essays on the Preservation of Bodily Parts* (New York: Harcourt Brace, 1995), p. 100.

10. Hillel Schwartz, *The Culture of the Copy: Striking Likenesses, Unreasonable Facsimiles* (New York: Zone Books, 1996), pp. 341 42.

11. Simone Ryals, letter to the editor, *The Advocate,* May 13, 1997, p. 6.

12. See Perri Klass, "The Artificial Womb Is Born," *The New York Times Magazine,* September 29, 1996, p. 117.

13. See Constance Penley, "Brownian Motion: Women, Tactics, and Technology" in Constance Penley and Andrew Ross, eds., *Technoculture* (Minneapolis: University of Minneapolis Press, 1991), p. 158.

14. Dick Teresi, "How to Get a Man Pregnant," *The New York Times Magazine,* November 27, 1994, p. 54.

15. Quoted in Dick Teresi and Kathleen McAuliffe, "Male Pregnancy," *Omni,* December 1985, p. 56.

16. Janice G. Raymond, *The Transsexual Empire: The Making of the She-Male* (Boston: Beacon Press, 1979), p. xvi.

17. Ibid., p. xvii.

18. Ibid., p. xvi.

19. Ibid.

20. Quoted in *Re/Search #13: Angry Women,* ed. Andrea Juno and V. Vale (San Francisco: Re/Search Publications, 1991), p. 224.

21. Shulamith Firestone, *The Dialectic of Sex: The Case for Feminist Revolution* (New York: Morrow, 1970), p. 233.

22. Teresi and McAuliffe, "Male Pregnancy," p. 118.

23. Quoted in *Re/Search #13,* p. 228.

24. David Plotz, "Frank Sinatra: Can Even Death Stop Ol' Blue Eyes?" *Slate,* October 4, 1997.

25. Richard A. Shweder, "A Few Good Men? Don't Look in the Movies," *The New York Times,* January 25, 1998, "Arts & Leisure" section, p. 25.

26. Ann Powers, "The Male Rock Anthem: Going All to Pieces," *The New York Times,* February 1, 1998, "Arts & Leisure" section, p. 46.
27. *Childhood Graphics,* a division of WRS Group Inc., 1994 catalogue, p. 10.
28. Statistic on maternity leave from unbylined item, "Maternity at Work," *Solidarity,* May 1998, p. 27.
29. See Carin Rubenstein, "Superdad Needs a Reality Check," *The New York Times,* "Op-Ed" section, April 16, 1998, p. A23.
30. Teresi and McAuliffe, "Male Pregnancy," p. 118.

Wild Nature, Wired Nature:
The Unabomber Meets the Digerati

1. Kevin Kelly, *Out of Control: The Rise of Neo-Biological Civilization* (Reading, Mass.: Addison-Wesley, 1994), p. 200.
2. William Kittredge, "The War for Montana's Soul," *Newsweek,* April 15, 1996, p. 43.
3. Evan Thomas, "Blood Brothers," *Newsweek,* April 22, 1996, p. 28.
4. Jim Nelson and Denny Johnson, "Unabomber: From Mama's Boy to Murdering Madman," *National Enquirer,* April 23, 1996, p. 29.
5. All quotes from the Unabomber's manifesto are taken from "Topic 230: The Unabomber's Screed" in the "Weird" conference on the WELL, a Sausalito-based on-line service. Posted on August 10, 1995, before the entire text began cropping up all over the Internet, the version in question was conflated from excerpts that appeared in *The New York Times* on August 2 of that year and an article that was posted anonymously to the *alt.fan.unabomber* Usenet newsgroup on August 4. "Careful examination of the latter leads us to conclude that it is authentic, and that the combination of the two is more readable and effective than either text by itself," notes Jerod Pore, who posted the document. "Though we have made every effort to weave the two texts together seamlessly, the 4,870 word result is obviously no substitute for the original 35,000 words." It is, however, an infinitely breezier read that preserves the manifesto's essential points.
6. Thomas, "Blood Brothers," p. 30.
7. Nancy Gibbs, "Tracking Down the Unabomber," *Time* (Australian edition), April 15, 1996, pp. 24–25.
8. Joshua Quittner, "The Web's Unlikely Hero," *Time,* April 22, 1996, p. 47.
9. Peter Schwartz, "Post-Capitalist," *Wired,* July–August 1993, p. 82.

10. Hendrik Hertzberg, "Marxism: The Sequel," *The New Yorker,* February 13, 1995, p. 7.

11. Ibid.

12. Margie Wylie, "*Wired* Doesn't Speak for Me," *C | Net,* December 17, 1997, *www.news.com/Perspectives/perspectives.html?ntb.pers.*

13. Brock Meeks, "Unabomber as Folk Hero," *CyberWire Dispatch,* September 19, 1995, HTTP://Cyberworks.com:70/0/Cyberwire/CWD/CWD. 95.09.19.

14. "Topic 283: The UNABOM Manuscript in Cyberspace" in the WELL's *Fringeware* conference, September 21, 1995, Kevin Kelly (kk).

15. Robert D. McFadden, "From a Child of Promise to the Unabom Suspect," *The New York Times,* May 26, 1966, p. 24.

16. William Gibson, "The Winter Market" in *Burning Chrome* (New York: Ace, 1987), p. 118.

17. Michael D. Lemonick, "The Bomb Is in the Mail," *Time,* May 8, 1995, p. 72.

18. Scott Bukatman, *Terminal Identity: The Virtual Subject in Postmodern Science Fiction* (Durham, N.C.: Duke University Press, 1993), p. 302.

19. Quoted in Tom Morganthau, "Who Is He?" *Newsweek,* May 8, p. 40.

20. Karl Taro Greenfeld, "The Incredibly Strange Mutant Creatures Who Rule the Universe of Alienated Japanese Zombie Computer Nerds," *Wired,* 1993 premiere issue (no month given), p. 69.

21. "strictly anti-communist, anti-socialist, anti-leftist": Ted Kaczynski, in a letter to the *San Francisco Examiner,* quoted in Evan Thomas, "The End of the Road," *Newsweek,* April 15, 1996, p. 39; "fatal effects": Lance Morrow, "Parental Guidance Suggested," *Time,* April 22, 1996, p. 41; "any number of left-pessimist academics": Joe Klein, "The Unabomber and the Left," *Newsweek,* April 22, 1996, p. 39.

22. David Johnston, "In Unabomber's Own Words, a Chilling Account of Murder," *The New York Times,* April 29, 1998, "National" section, p. A18.

23. From an on-line statement "crafted, at its core, by [founder and publisher] Louis Rossetto" and posted by then managing editor John Battelle (jbat) in "Topic 129: New Republic Slams Wired!" in the WELL's *Wired* conference, January 14, 1995.

24. Vintage Books, "The Nine 'Beyonds,'" press release for Tom Peters's *Crazy Times Call for Crazy Organizations,* 1994.

25. Thomas Kiely, "Unconventional Wisdom," *CIO,* December 15, 1993–January 1, 1994, p. 26.

26. William Gibson, *Neuromancer* (New York: Ace, 1984), p. 203; William Gibson, "New Rose Hotel," in *Burning Chrome* (New York: Ace, 1987), p. 107.

27. K. Eric Drexler, *Engines of Creation: The Coming Era of Nanotechnology* (New York: Anchor Books, 1986), pp. 32, 182.

28. Both quotes from Perseus Books 1998 catalogue, p. 5.

29. James F. Moore, "How Companies Have Sex," *Fast Company,* October—November, 1996, p. 66.

30. Ibid., p. 68.

31. Stephen Jay Gould, "Curveball" in Steven Fraser, ed., *The Bell Curve Wars* (New York: Basic Books, 1995), p. 12.

32. Nicholas Negroponte, "Homeless@info.hwy.net," *The New York Times,* February 11, 1995, "Op-Ed" section, p. 19.

33. Paul Keegan, "The Digerati," *The New York Times Magazine,* May 21, 1995, p. 42.

34. Paul Keegan, "Reality Distortion Field," *Upside.com,* February 1, 1997, *www.upside.com/texis/mvm/story?id=34712c1778.*

35. Keegan, "The Digerati," p. 88.

36. See Mark Dery, *Escape Velocity: Cyberculture at the End of the Century* (New York: Grove Press, 1996), pp. 45–48.

37. Pierre Teilhard de Chardin, *Human Energy* (New York: Harcourt Brace Jovanovich, 1962), pp. 132–33.

38. Pierre Teilhard de Chardin, *The Phenomenon of Man* (New York: Harper & Brothers, 1959), p. 282.

39. This is not to say that the Second Law of Thermodynamics and other natural laws have been wished out of existence, by an act of postmodern will; only that "nature," for naked apes, is first and foremost an object of knowledge, mediated by language. Given the historical abuses perpetrated in nature's name, it behooves us to be wary of those who presume to speak on its behalf.

40. Andrew Ross, *The Chicago Gangster Theory of Life: Nature's Debt to Society* (New York: Verso, 1994), p. 4.

41. Londa Schiebinger, *Nature's Body: Gender in the Making of Modern Science* (Boston: Beacon Press, 1993), pp. 5, 7.

42. For more on the Immigration Restriction Act and the American eugenics movement, see Ross, *The Chicago Gangster Theory of Life,* pp. 246–50, 260.

43. Ibid., pp. 5, 15.

44. Ibid.

45. For more on Rushton and Brand, see Evette Porter, "The Race Myth: Dividing the Melting Pot," *Village Voice,* February 11, 1997, pp. 40–41.

46. Roland Barthes, *Mythologies* (New York: Noonday Press, 1972), p. 142.

47. Quoted in Morganthau, "Who Is He?" p. 40.
48. This story in Howard Berkes, "Grand Jury Could Get Unabomber Evidence Next Week," *Weekend Edition,* NPR, April 20, 1996.
49. Quoted in the video documentary *Cyberpunk,* by Peter von Brandenburg and Marianne Schaefer-Trench.
50. Johnston, "In Unabomber's Own Words," p. A18.
51. Ibid.
52. David Johnston, "Judge Sentences Confessed Bomber to Four Life Terms," *The New York Times,* May 5, 1998, p. 1.
53. William Finnegan, "Defending the Unabomber," *The New Yorker,* March 16, 1998, p. 62.

Space Oddities: Heaven's Gate and *Homo Cyber*— Strange Alliances on the Level Above Human

1. Andrea Peyser, "Cybergeeks Were Never of This Earth," *New York Post,* March 28, 1997, p. 6.
2. *New York Post,* March 28, 1997, passim.
3. Joshua Quittner, "Life and Death on the Web," *Time,* April 7, 1997, p. 47.
4. Barry Bearak, "Time of Puzzled Heartbreak Binds Relatives," *The New York Times,* March 29, 1997, p. 8.
5. Jwnody, "Overview of Present Mission," April 1996, archived at www.heavensgatetoo.com/misc/ovrview/htm.
6. "Topic 1354: Internet Linked to Cult Suicides—Film at 11," in the WELL's "Media" conference, March 29, 1997, Patrizia DiLucchio (PDIL).
7. See David Gelernter, "A Religion of Special Effects," *The New York Times,* March 30, 1997, "Op-Ed" section, p. E11.
8. Statistics from Katha Pollitt, "Mea Culpa," *The Nation,* December 8, 1997, p. 11.
9. Ibid.
10. "A reported 86 percent of Americans": Ed Doerr, executive director of Americans for Religious Liberty, in a letter to the editor, *The New York Times,* April 1, 1997, Section A, p. 22.
11. Timothy Ferris, "The Wrong Stuff," *The New Yorker,* April 14, 1997, p. 31.
12. See Uta Ranke-Heinemann, *Eunuchs for the Kingdom of Heaven: Women, Sexuality, and the Catholic Church* (New York: Penguin, 1999), p. 15.

13. Robert Jastrow, *The Enchanted Loom: Mind in the Universe* (New York: Simon & Schuster, 1981), pp. 166–67.

14. Pamela McCorduck, *Machines Who Think* (San Francisco: W. H. Freeman, 1979), pp. 354–55.

15. Grant Fjermedal, *The Tomorrow Makers: A Brave New World of Living-Brain Machines* (Redmond, Wash.: Tempus Books, 1986), p. 202.

16. William T. Esrey, "Infonics: Toward a Global Mind," speech delivered at the National Association of State Telecommunications Directors 1990 Annual Conference, San Francisco, California, September 3, 1990.

17. John Perry Barlow, "Declaration of the Independence of Cyberspace," disseminated on the Internet, February 8, 1996, archived at www.wired.com/archives/if/declaration.

18. George Gilder, *Microcosm: The Quantum Revolution in Economics and Technology* (New York: Simon & Schuster, 1989), p. 381.

19. Harold Bloom, *Omens of Millennium: The Gnosis of Angels, Dreams, and Resurrection* (New York: Riverhead Books, 1996), pp. 27, 220.

20. Ken Kelley, "The Interview: Whole Earthling and Software Savant Stewart Brand," *SF Focus,* February 1985, p. 78.

21. William Gibson, *Neuromancer* (New York: Ace, 1984), p. 256.

22. Yaakov Garb, "Is the Body Obsolete?" *Whole Earth Review,* no. 63 (Summer 1989), p. 53.

23. Michael Schrage, "Revolutionary Evolutionist," *Wired,* July 1995, p. 120.

Conclusion: Last Things

1. Carey Goldberg, "Computer Age Millionaires Redefine Philanthropy," *The New York Times,* July 6, 1997, "National" section, p. 9.

2. All quotes and details about "safe rooms" from Patricia Leigh Brown, "The New 'God Forbid' Room," *The New York Times,* September 25, 1997, "House & Home" section, pp. F1, F13.

3. "Global Roulette: In a Volatile World Economy, Can Everyone Lose?" "Colloquy," *Harper's Magazine,* June 1998, pp. 43, 46, 50.

4. John H. Fairbanks, Jr., "The Politics of Resentment," *Journal of Democracy* 5, no. 2 (April 1994), p. 16.

5. Noam Chomsky, *The Prosperous Few and the Restless Many* (Berkeley: Odonian Press, 1993), p. 7.

6. Quote on the World Trade Organization's prime directive from Kristin Dawkins, *NAFTA, GATT, & The World Trade Organization—The Emerging New World Order* (Westfield, N.J.: Open Magazine Pamphlet Series, 1994), p. 1.

7. Jonathan Tasini, *They Get Cake, We Eat Crumbs: The Real Story Behind Today's Unfair Economy* (Washington, D.C.: Preamble Center, 1998), p. 60.

8. David Corn, "Auditing the I.M.F.," *The Nation,* May 11, 1998, p. 6.

9. Cited in Tasini, *They Get Cake,* pp. 61–62.

10. Charles Bowden, "While You Were Sleeping: In Juarez, Mexico, photographers expose the violent realities of free trade," *Harper's Magazine,* December 1996, pp. 48–49.

11. David Bacon, "Mexico's New Braceros," *The Nation,* January 27, 1997, p. 19.

12. Ibid.

13. Ibid.

14. Chomsky, *The Prosperous Few and the Restless Many,* p. 7.

15. Thomas L. Friedman, "When Money Talks," *The New York Times,* July 24, 1994, p. E3.

16. Quoted in Jeremy Brecher, "Global Village or Global Pillage?" in Dawkins, *NAFTA, GATT, & The World Trade Organization*, pp. 17–18.

17. Eric Hobsbawm, *The Age of Extremes: A History of the World, 1914–1991* (New York: Vintage Books, 1996), p. 16.

18. Ibid.

19. Steven Shaviro, *Doom Patrols: A Theoretical Fiction about Postmodernism* (New York: High Risk Books, 1997), pp. 95–96.

20. Sun Ra and His Intergalactic Research Arkestra, *It's After the End of the World: Live at the Donaueschingen and Berlin Festivals* (BASF, 1972).